Debugging with Fiddler

The complete reference from the creator of the Fiddler Web Debugger

Second Edition

Eric Lawrence

ACKNOWLEDGEMENTS

This book, and Fiddler itself, would not have been possible without myriad contributions from hundreds of people around the world.

First, I'd like to thank my wife and son for their inspiration and encouragement as I spent innumerable nights and weekends working on Fiddler and authoring this book. Next, thanks to my parents and grand-mother, who instilled in me a voracious appetite for books and the idea that one day I should try my hand at writing one.

I'm grateful for the many contributions of colleagues too numerous to mention (they know who they are!), and to the broader Fiddler community for providing a steady stream of encouragement, suggestions and bug reports. I'd like to thank my employer, Telerik, who acquired Fiddler in 2012 and generously continues to fund my work on the platform.

Finally, I thank you, dear reader, for caring enough about Fiddler to pick up this book!

TABLE OF CONTENTS

Acknowledgements iii

Table of Contents iv

INTRODUCTION 1

Origins 1

About this book 3

A Quick Primer 5

Basic Concepts 5

Usage Scenarios 6

An Incomplete List of Things Fiddler Can Do 6

An Incomplete List of Things Fiddler Cannot Do 7

EXPLORE FIDDLER 9

Get Started 11

System Requirements – Windows 11

System Requirements - Mono 11

Install Fiddler on Windows 12

Permissions and XCOPY Deployment 12

Update Fiddler 12

Uninstall Fiddler 13

The Fiddler User-Interface 14

Web Sessions List 15

Drag and Drop Support 15

Icons and Colors 16

Keyboard Reference 17

Web Sessions Context Menu 18

Customize Columns 22

Fiddler's Main Menu 25

File Menu 25

Edit Menu 25

Rules Menu 27

Performance Submenu 28

Tools Menu 28

View Menu 29

Help Menu 30

Fiddler's About Box 31

Fiddler's Toolbar 32

Fiddler's Status Bar 33

QuickExec 35

QuickExec Selection Commands 35

Default FiddlerScript Commands 38

Application Hotkeys 40

Statistics Tab 41

Filters tab 43

Hosts 43

Client Process 44

Request Headers 45

Breakpoints 45

Response Status Code 46

Response Type and Size 46

Response Headers 47

Timeline tab 48

Mode: Timeline 48

Mode: Client Pipe Map 50

Mode: Server Pipe Map 50

Using the Timeline for Performance Analysis 50

AutoResponder tab 52

Specify the Match Condition 53

Match Request Method 54

Match Session Flags 54

Match Request Headers 55

Match Request Bodies 55

"Dice Roll" Matches 56

Specify the Action Text 56

Use RegEx Replacements in Action Text 57

Drag-and-Drop support 59

Work with the Rules List 59

FARX Files 60

Playback Mode 60

TextWizard 61

Composer tab 63

Request Options 63

Scratchpad Requests 63

Raw Requests 64

Parsed Requests 64

    The Composer History List...64

    Send Sequential Requests 65

    File Upload Requests..66

    Edit with an Automatic Request Breakpoint..68

    Send Binary Body Data 68

    Override the Host Header 68

Log tab...69

Find Sessions Window 70

Session Clipboards..72

SAZ AutoSave 73

Host Remapping Tool 74

TECHNIQUES AND CONCEPTS...75

Retarget Traffic with Fiddler 77

    Method #1 - Rewrite 77

    Method #2 - Reroute 77

    Method #3 - Redirect...78

Features to Retarget Requests...79

Compare Sessions 80

    UltraDiff 81

Compare Multiple Sessions at Once 81

Debug with Breakpoints 82

    Set Breakpoints...82

    Tamper Using Inspectors 83

    The Breakpoint Bar 84

    Resuming Multiple Sessions..84

CONFIGURE FIDDLER AND CLIENTS 85

Fiddler Options 87

General Tab 87

HTTPS Tab 88

Connections Tab 90

Gateway Tab 91

Appearance Tab 92

Extensions Tab 93

Tools Tab 93

HeaderEncoding Setting 94

Preferences 95

Configure Clients 96

Capture Traffic from Browsers 96

Chrome 96

Firefox 96

Opera 97

Other Browsers 98

Capture Traffic from Other Applications 98

WinHTTP 98

.NET Framework 99

Java 100

PHP / cURL 100

Capture Traffic from Services 100

Capture Traffic to Loopback 100

Loopback Bypasses 101

Loopback Authentication 102

Loopback Blocked from Metro-style Windows 8 Apps 102

Run Fiddler in a Virtual Machine on Mac OS X 103

Capture Traffic from Other Computers 105

Capture Traffic from Devices 106

Apple iOS Proxy Settings 107

Windows Phone Proxy Settings 107

Windows RT Proxy Settings 107

Other Devices 108

Use Fiddler as a Reverse Proxy 108

Acting as a Reverse Proxy for HTTPS 109

Chain to Upstream Proxy Servers 109

Chain to SOCKS / TOR 110

VPNs, Modems, and Tethering.. 111

DirectAccess 112

Windows Phone Tethering.. 112

Memory Usage and Fiddler's Bitness 113

Buffering vs. Streaming Traffic 115
   Request Buffering 115
   Response Buffering 115
   COMET 116
HTML5 WebSockets 117
   WebSocketMessage Objects 119
     Payload Masking 119
Fiddler and HTTPS 120
   Trust the Fiddler Root Certificate 121
     Machine-wide Trust on Windows 8+ 122
     Manually Trust the Fiddler Root 123
     Additional HTTPS Options 123
Configure Clients for HTTPS Decryption 125
   Browsers 125
     Firefox 125
     Opera 125
   Cross-machine scenarios 125
   HTTPS and Devices 126
     Windows Phone 126
     Android and iOS 126
   Buggy HTTPS Servers 128
   Certificate Validation 128
   Certificate Pinning 129
   Use an Existing Certificate 129
Fiddler and FTP 131
Fiddler and Web Authentication 132
   HTTP Authentication 132
   Automatic Authentication in Fiddler 133
   Authentication Problems 134
     Channel-Binding 134
     WinHTTP Credential Release Policy 134
     Loopback Protection 135
   HTTPS Client Certificates 135

INSPECTORS 137
   Overview 139

Auth 141

Caching 143

Cookies 144

Headers 145

   Context Menu 146

   Keyboard Shortcuts 146

   Editing 146

HexView 148

ImageView 150

   Metadata Display 151

   ImageView Tools 151

      PNGDistill Image Tool 152

JSON... 153

Raw... 154

PDFView 155

SyntaxView 156

TextView 158

Transformer 159

   Background on HTTP Encodings 159

   Add and Remove Encodings using the Transformer 160

   Other Ways to Remove Encodings... 161

WebForms 162

WebView 163

XML.. 164

EXTENSIONS 165

Overview 167

   Popular 3rd Party Extensions 167

      Performance Add-ons 167

      Security Add-ons.. 167

   Extensions I've Built 168

JavaScript Formatter 169

Gallery.. 170

   Full-Screen View 170

Show Image Bloat.. 172

Content Blocker 174

Traffic Differ 175

FiddlerScript Editors 176

    FiddlerScript Tab 176

    ClassView Sidebar 177

    Fiddler ScriptEditor 177

AnyWHERE 179

STORE, IMPORT, AND EXPORT TRAFFIC 181

Session Archive Zip (SAZ) Files 183

    Protecting SAZ Files 184

FiddlerCap 185

    Capture Box 185

    Capture Options Box 186

    Tools Box 187

Fiddler's Viewer Mode 189

Import and Export Sessions 190

    Import Formats 190

        Build Your Own 191

    Export Formats 191

        cURL Script 191

        HTML5 AppCache Manifest 191

        HTTPArchive v1.1 and v1.2 193

        MeddlerScript 194

        Raw Files 194

        Visual Studio WebTest 195

        WCAT Script 195

        Build Your Own 195

FIDDLERSCRIPT 197

Extend Fiddler with FiddlerScript 199

    About FiddlerScript 199

    Edit FiddlerScript 201

        Update FiddlerScript at Runtime 201

        Reset to the Default FiddlerScript 201

FiddlerScript Functions 202

    Session Handling Functions 202

        OnPeekAtRequestHeaders 202

OnBeforeRequest 202

OnPeekAtResponseHeaders 202

OnWebSocketMessage 203

OnBeforeResponse 203

OnReturningError 203

OnDone 203

General Functions... 203

Main 203

OnRetire 203

OnBoot 204

OnShutdown 204

OnAttach.. 204

OnDetach 204

OnExecAction(sParams: string[]) 204

FiddlerScript and Automation Tools.. 205

Quiet Mode.. 205

Driving Fiddler from Batch Scripts 205

Driving Fiddler from Native or .NET Code.. 206

Extend Fiddler's UI - Menus.. 208

Extend the Tools Menu 208

Extend the Web Sessions Context Menu 209

Extend the Rules Menu 209

Boolean-bound Rules 209

String-bound Rules 211

Binding Script variables to Preferences 212

Creating New Top-Level Menus 213

Extend Fiddler's UI - Adding Tabs 215

Extend Fiddler's UI - Adding Columns to the Web Sessions List.................................... 216

Binding Columns using Attributes 216

Binding Columns using AddBoundColumn 218

FiddlerObject Functions 220

FiddlerObject.ReloadScript() 220

FiddlerObject.StatusText 220

FiddlerObject.log(sTextToLog).. 220

FiddlerObject.playSound(sSoundFilename) 221

FiddlerObject.flashWindow() 221

FiddlerObject.alert(sMessage) 221

FiddlerObject.prompt(sMessage) 221

FiddlerObject.createDictionary() 221

FiddlerObject.WatchPreference(sPrefBranch, oFunc) 222

Import Assemblies 223

Example Scripts 224

Request Scripts 224

Add (or Overwrite) a Request Header 224

Remove Request Headers 224

Flag Requests that Send Cookies 224

Rewrite a Request from HTTP to HTTPS 224

Swap the Host Header 225

Drop a Connection 225

Prevent Response Streaming 225

Response Scripts 226

Hide Sessions that Returned Images 226

Flag Redirections 226

Replace Text in Script, CSS, and HTML 226

Remove All DIV Elements 226

Other Scripts 227

Add a Systemwide Hotkey 227

Certificate Info Custom Column 227

Generate Mock Sessions 228

Show Response Hash 228

Combine Partial Responses 229

Remove Many Headers at Once 230

Override MIME Types 230

Hide Traffic based on Process Name 231

Add a Color Picker to the Tools Menu 231

More Examples 231

EXTEND FIDDLER WITH .NET CODE...233

Extend Fiddler with .NET 235

Project Requirements and Settings 235

Debugging Extensions 235

Best Practices for Extensions 236

Best Practice: Use an Enable Switch 236

Best Practice: Use Delay Load 236

Best Practice: Beware "Big Data" 238

Best Practice: Use the Reporter Pattern for Extensions 238

Interact with Fiddler's Objects 240

The Web Sessions List 240

Session[] GetAllSessions() 240

Session GetFirstSelectedSession() 240

Session[] GetSelectedSessions() 240

Session[] GetSelectedSessions(int iMax) 240

void actSelectAll() 240

void actSelectSessionsMatchingCriteria(doesSessionMatchCriteriaDelegate oDel) 240

void actRemoveSelectedSessions() 241

void actRemoveUnselectedSessions() 241

bool actLoadSessionArchive(string sFilename) 241

void actSaveSessionsToZip() 241

void actSaveSessionsToZip(string sFilename, string sPwd) 241

void actSessionCopyURL() 241

void actSessionCopySummary() 241

void actSessionCopyHeadlines() 241

int FiddlerApplication.UI.lvSessions.SelectedCount 242

SimpleEventHandler FiddlerApplication.UI.lvSessions.OnSessionsAdded 242

Session Objects 242

oRequest 242

RequestHeaders 242

requestBodyBytes 242

oResponse 243

RequestHeaders 243

responseBodyBytes 243

oFlags 243

void Abort() 243

void Ignore() 244

bBufferResponse 244

bHasResponse 244

bypassGateway 244

clientIP 244

clientPort 244

bool COMETPeek() 244

fullUrl 244

PathAndQuery 244

port 244

host 244

hostname 244

bool HostnameIs(string) 244

bool HTTPMethodIs(string) 245

bool uriContains(string) 245

id 245

isFTP 245

isHTTPS 245

isTunnel 245

LocalProcessID 245

string LocalProcess 245

bool utilDecodeRequest() 245

bool utilDecodeResponse() 245

bool RefreshUI() 245

RequestMethod 245

responseCode 245

state 246

BitFlags 246

Timers 248

HostList Objects 249

Sending Strings to the TextWizard 250

Logging 251

Interacting with the FiddlerScript Engine 252

Program with Preferences 253

Preference Naming..253

The IFiddlerPreferences Interface 253

Store and Remove Preferences 254

Retrieve Preferences..254

Watch for Preference Changes 255

Notifications in Extensions 255

Notifications in FiddlerScript 255

Build Extension Installers...256
Build Inspectors...259
    Inspect Session Objects 263
Deal with HTTP Compression and Chunking 265
    Decode a Copy of the Body 265
    Use the GetRe*BodyAsString Methods 266
    Use the utilDecode* Methods...266
    Inspector Assemblies..267
Build Extensions...268
    Understand Threading...269
    Integrate with QuickExec 269
    Example Extension 270
    Extension Assemblies..275
Build Import and Export Transcoders..276
        Direct Fiddler to load your Transcoder assemblies 276
        The ProfferFormat Attribute 276
        The ISessionImporter Interface 277
        The ISessionExporter Interface 278
    Handle Options...278
        Provide Progress Notifications 279
        Notes on Threading and Transcoders in FiddlerCore.....................................280
    Beyond Files 280
    Example Transcoder..280
FIDDLERCORE 285
Overview 287
    Legalities and Licenses..288
    Get Started with FiddlerCore 288
    Compile the Sample Application..288
    FiddlerCoreStartupFlags 291
The FiddlerApplication Class 292
    FiddlerApplication Events 292
        OnReadRequestBuffer Event 292
        RequestHeadersAvailable Event 292
        BeforeRequest Event 292
        OnValidateServerCertificate Event 292

OnReadResponseBuffer Event 293

ResponseHeadersAvailable Event 294

BeforeResponse Event 294

BeforeReturningError Event..294

AfterSessionComplete Event 295

OnWebSocketMessage 295

FiddlerAttach Event..295

FiddlerDetach Event...295

OnClearCache Event 295

OnNotification Event..295

FiddlerApplication Methods 295

Startup()...295

Shutdown() 296

IsStarted()...296

IsSystemProxy()...296

CreateProxyEndpoint() 296

DoImport() 296

DoExport() 297

GetVersionString()..297

GetDetailedInfo()..297

ResetSessionCounter()..297

FiddlerApplication Properties and Fields..297

isClosing..297

Log 297

oDefaultClientCertificate 297

oProxy..297

oTranscoders..297

Prefs 298

The Rest of the Fiddler API...298

Common Tasks with FiddlerCore 299

Keep Track of Sessions 299

Get Traffic to FiddlerCore...299

Trust the FiddlerCore Certificate 300

Generate Responses 301

Other Resources 301

APPENDICES 303

  Appendix A: Troubleshooting..305

    Missing Traffic 305

    Interference from Security Software 306

      Problems Downloading Fiddler 306

      Problems Installing Fiddler..306

      Problems Running Fiddler 306

    Corrupted Proxy Settings 307

    Resetting Fiddler..307

    Troubleshoot Certificate Problems..308

    Wipe all traces of Fiddler 309

    Fiddler complains about the "Configuration System" 309

    Fiddler randomly stops capturing traffic 310

    Fiddler may stall when streaming RPC-over-HTTPS traffic 310

  Appendix B: Command Line Syntax 312

    Option Flags 312

      Examples...312

  Appendix C: Session Flags 313

    Session Display Flags 313

    Breakpoint and Editing Flags...315

    Networking Flags 315

    Authentication Flags 317

    Client Information Flags 317

    Performance Simulation Flags 318

    HTTPS Flags 318

    Request Composer Flags...320

    Other Flags...321

  Appendix D: Preferences...324

    Network Preferences 324

    HTTPS Preferences 329

    Fiddler UI Preferences 331

    FiddlerScript Preferences..336

    TextWizard Preferences 336

    Request Composer Preferences...337

    Path Configuration 337

    Miscellaneous..338

    Extension Preferences 339

        Raw Inspector...339

        JavaScript Formatter 340

        Certificate Maker Add-on..340

Index 343

Introduction

ORIGINS

First, a confession—the Fiddler Web Debugger is not the result of a grand vision or the ambition to develop the world's most popular debugging proxy. A tool born of necessity, I never set out to build a platform so flexible, powerful, and complicated that I'd be forced to spend a year writing a book to explain how to fully take advantage of it. But here we are.

Before diving into the technical chapters, I will begin by sharing the story behind how Fiddler came to be.

As a student at the University of Maryland in the spring of 1999, I had the chance to interview for a Program Management internship on a new team at Microsoft. One of my final interviewer's first questions was *"How does HTTP work?"* Knowing only the basics, I gave an incomplete and somewhat inaccurate answer, but didn't embarrass myself too badly. That summer and the following, I worked on features for the first version of SharePoint. On rare occasions, I found myself looking at web traffic in Microsoft Network Monitor (NetMon), a powerful but then primitive and difficult-to-use packet sniffer. In the early summer of 2001, I joined Microsoft full-time as the Program Manager for the Office Clip Art client and website.

At that time, most of the developers and testers working on my team were new to web development, having previously been responsible for writing native code applications in C and C++. It was quickly apparent that the debugging process was overly cumbersome—many of my colleagues were loath to use NetMon. I even watched some developers debugging HTTP requests by hovering over variables in Visual Studio, examining the raw traffic in hex:

Having developed several small Windows utilities, I was confident that I could code *something* to make web debugging simpler. My first simplistic effort was based on taking an existing C++ proxy server and making minor modifications to it so that it would spew HTTP traffic to the system console:

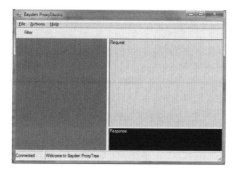

It's generous to call this effort primitive—the proxy couldn't handle secure traffic or authentication protocols. Non-text content was another problem—comically, the utility would try to render binary content as ASCII. Old-school console users may recall that the octet 0x07 represents the "bell" character, and when it's displayed in the console, a system beep is played. Soon after its release, the hallways of the Office Online team sounded like a Las Vegas casino, as binary content flowed through the debug proxies running in each tester's office.

Despite the very annoying limitations, this tool was still popular, and I was inspired to get started on the next version. I mocked up a quick little demo in Borland Delphi, a native code language used for most of my development work at the time. The colorful UI foreshadowed Fiddler's eventual appearance:

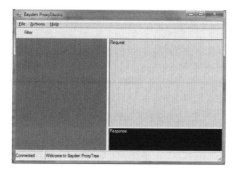

However, as I pondered the security and memory-management implications of writing a proxy server in native code, I soon decided that my next effort would be developed in C#, a new language being developed by the Visual Studio team that my best friend had just joined. The notion of writing a HTTP proxy server from scratch in .NET posed just two significant challenges: I didn't *really* know how HTTP worked, and I didn't know how to code in C#.

Fortunately, given a few trips to the bookstore and a lot of spare weekends, both shortcomings would be remedied. Two books were my constant companions: HTTP: The Definitive Guide and the C# Cookbook. Chapter by chapter, I learned about HTTP and C#, and week-by-week Fiddler came to life. About six months after I started, I had a basic version of Fiddler ready:

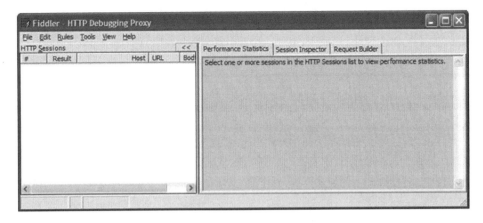

Like its predecessors, it too had a large number of limitations (and thousands of bugs) but it was eagerly adopted by colleagues whose PC speakers were in danger of burning out from the incessant beeps of my first proxy utility.

Over the subsequent years, Fiddler was progressively enhanced with two extensibility models, a mechanism to automatically generate and modify responses, and support for secure (HTTPS) traffic, FTP, and HTML5 WebSockets. In 2012, Fiddler was ported to the Mono Framework, enabling it to run directly on Mac and Linux PCs and virtual machines.

About this book

Over twelve years and through more than a hundred version releases, Fiddler has evolved into a powerful utility and platform that can perform a wide variety of tasks. It has a rich extensibility model and a community of add-on developers who have broadened its usefulness as a performance, security, and load-testing tool. Questions in email, online discussion groups, and numerous conferences over the years made it overwhelmingly apparent that most users only exploit a tiny fraction of Fiddler's power. I came to realize that thousands of users would get a lot more out of Fiddler if there were a complete reference for the tool. The first version of this book, released in 2012, was the product of that realization. This Second Edition, released in early 2015, builds upon the first and adds new content covering major enhancements to Fiddler since the book was originally published.

As Fiddler's developer, I've found it both easy and challenging to write this book. It's easy, because I understand Fiddler deeply, down to its very foundation, and can consult the source code to research obscure details. On the other hand, it's been very challenging, as every time I choose an interesting scenario or feature to write about, I'm forced to think deeply about that scenario or feature. Commonly, I've found myself developing improvements to revise Fiddler and minimize or eliminate the need to write about the topic in the first place. As a result, I've rewritten large portions of both this book and Fiddler itself. It's been a slow process, but both projects have benefitted.

Publication of this edition roughly coincided with the release of Fiddler version 4.5 in the spring of 2015. If you're using a later version of Fiddler, you will find some minor differences, but the core concepts will remain the same.

This book is deliberately limited in scope—it covers nearly every aspect of Fiddler and FiddlerCore, but it is not a tutorial on HTTP, SSL/TLS, HTML, Web Services, or the myriad other topics you may want to understand to fully exploit Fiddler's feature set. If you want a deeper understanding of web protocols, I can recommend the references that I consulted during the development of Fiddler:

- Hypertext Transfer Protocol -- HTTP/1.1 from http://www.ietf.org/rfc/rfc2616.txt, later obsoleted by the HTTPbis Working Group's release of RFC7230 through RFC7235.

- HTTP: The Definitive Guide by David Gourley

- Web Protocols and Practice: HTTP/1.1, Networking Protocols, Caching, and Traffic Measurement by Balachander Krishnamurthy and Jennifer Rexford

- SSL & TLS Essentials: Securing the Web by Stephen A. Thomas

- Bulletproof SSL and TLS by Ivan Ristić

This book can be read either "straight through" or you can use the Table of Contents and Index to find the topics most interesting to you. Please consider skimming all of the chapters, even those that don't seem relevant to your needs, because each chapter often contains tips and tricks you might not find elsewhere.

I encourage you to begin by reading the primer in the next section, which lays out some terminology and the basic concepts that you'll need to understand to get the most out of Fiddler and this book.

Happy Fiddling!

A QUICK PRIMER

In this section, I'll provide some basic information about Fiddler that will help you get started and build a foundation for the rest of the book.

Basic Concepts

Fiddler is a special-purpose **proxy server** that runs on your Windows, Linux, or Mac computer. Locally-running programs like web browsers, Office applications, and other clients send their HTTP and HTTPS **requests** to Fiddler, which then (typically) forwards the traffic to a web server. The server's **responses** are then returned to Fiddler, which passes the traffic back to the client.

Virtually all programs that use web protocols support proxy servers, and therefore Fiddler can be used with almost any app. When it starts **capturing**, Fiddler registers itself with the Windows Internet (WinINET) networking component (or the environment variables on Linux/Mac) and asks that all applications begin directing their requests through Fiddler.

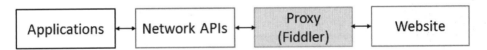

Some applications do not automatically respect the system's networking configuration and may require manual configuration in order for Fiddler to capture their traffic. Fiddler can be configured to work in more exotic scenarios, including server-to-server (e.g. Web Services) and device-to-server traffic (e.g. iPad or Windows Phone clients). By default, Fiddler is designed to automatically **chain** to any **upstream proxy** server that was configured before it began capturing—this allows Fiddler to work in network environments where a proxy server is already in use.

Filters enable hiding of traffic which is not of interest to you, as well as highlighting of traffic deemed interesting. Filters can be applied based on the source of the traffic (e.g. the specific client process) or based on some characteristic of the traffic itself (e.g. what hostname the traffic is targeted to, or what type of content the server returned).

Fiddler supports a rich extensibility model which ranges from simple **FiddlerScript** to powerful **Extensions** that can be developed using any .NET language. Fiddler also supports several special-purpose extension types, the most popular of which is called an **Inspector**, so named because it enables you to inspect a single request or response. Inspectors can be built to display all response types (e.g. the HexView Inspector) or tailored to support a type-specific format (e.g. the JSON Inspector). If you're a developer, you can build Fiddler's core proxy engine into your applications using a .NET class library named **FiddlerCore**.

Fiddler can use a **man-in-the-middle** decryption technique to display and modify HTTPS requests and responses that would otherwise be inscrutable to network observers. To permit seamless debugging without security warnings, Fiddler's **root certificate** may be installed in the Trusted Certificates store of the system or web browser.

A **Web Session**, sometimes known as a *request/response pair*, represents a single transaction between a client and a server. Each Session appears as a single entry in the **Web Sessions List** shown at the left side of the Fiddler interface. Each Session object has a **Request** and a **Response**, representing what the client sent to the server and what the server returned to the client. The Session object also maintains a set of **Flags** that record metadata about the Session, and a **Timers** object that stores timestamps logged in the course of processing the Session.

Proxy servers are not limited to simply viewing network traffic—Fiddler got its name from its ability to "fiddle" with outbound requests and inbound responses. Manual tampering of traffic may be performed by setting a request or response **breakpoint**. When a breakpoint is set, Fiddler will pause the processing of the Session and permit manual alteration of the request and the response. Traffic rewriting may also be performed automatically by script or extensions running inside of Fiddler. By default, Fiddler operates in **buffering mode**, whereby the server's response is completely collected before any part of it is sent to the client. If the **streaming mode** is instead enabled, the server's response will be immediately returned to the client as it is downloaded. In streaming mode, response body tampering is not possible.

Captured Sessions can be saved in a **Session Archive Zip (SAZ)** file for later viewing. This compressed file format contains the full request and response, as well as flags, timers, and other metadata. A lightweight capture-only tool known as **FiddlerCap** may be used by non-technical users to collect a SAZ file for analysis by experts. Fiddler supports **Exporter** extensions that allow storing captured traffic in myriad other formats for interoperability with other tools. Similarly, Fiddler supports **Importer** extensions that enable Fiddler to load traffic stored in other formats, including the **HTTP Archive (HAR)** format exported by many browsers' developer tools, and the **Packet Capture (PCAP)** format used by many networking products.

Usage Scenarios

Some of the most common questions I get are of the form: *"Can I use Fiddler to accomplish <x>?"* While there are a huge number of scenarios for which Fiddler is useful, and a number of scenarios for which Fiddler isn't suitable, the most common tasks fall into a few buckets. Here's a rough guide to what you can and cannot do with Fiddler:

An Incomplete List of Things Fiddler Can Do
- View web traffic from nearly any browser, client application, or service.
- Modify any request or response, either manually or automatically.
- Decrypt HTTPS traffic to enable viewing and modification.
- Store captured traffic to an archive and reload it later, even from a different computer.
- "Play back" previously-captured responses to a client application, even if the server is offline.
- Debug web traffic from most PCs and devices, including Mac/Linux systems, smart phones, and tablet computers.

- Chain to upstream proxy servers, including the Tor network.
- Run as a reverse proxy on a server to capture traffic without reconfiguring the client computer or device.
- Grow more powerful with new features added by FiddlerScript or the .NET-based extensibility model.

An Incomplete List of Things Fiddler Cannot Do

While Fiddler is a very flexible tool, there are some things it cannot presently do. That list includes:

- Debug non-web protocol traffic.
  - Fiddler works with HTTP, HTTPS, and FTP traffic and related protocols like HTML5 WebSockets and ICY streams.
  - Fiddler cannot "see" or alter traffic that runs on other protocols like SMTP, POP3, Telnet, IRC, etc.
- Handle huge requests or responses.
  - Fiddler cannot *buffer* requests or responses larger than 2 gigabytes in size; these may only be *streamed* to their destination.
  - Fiddler uses system memory and the pagefile to hold web traffic. Storing large numbers of Sessions or huge requests or responses can result in slow performance.
- "Magically" remove bugs in a website for you.
  - While Fiddler will identify networking problems on your behalf, it generally cannot *fix* them without your help. I can't tell you how many times I've gotten emails asking: *"What gives? I installed Fiddler but my website still has bugs!"*

With that quick primer out of the way, let's dive in!

Explore Fiddler

GET STARTED

Fiddler is available to download from http://getfiddler.com. It is strongly recommended that you only download Fiddler from this official source, as some unscrupulous websites have repackaged the program using installers that will also install unwanted software (for instance adware or browser toolbars).

System Requirements – Windows

Fiddler is supported on all versions of Windows from XP to Windows 10. The only prerequisite for Fiddler is Microsoft .NET Framework version 2 or later. The .NET Framework is present by default on modern versions of Windows and can be installed using WindowsUpdate if needed. You should prefer to install Fiddler 4 for .NET4, as it offers slightly better performance and better compatibility with modern HTTPS algorithms.

Like most .NET programs, Fiddler will run in 32bit mode on 32bit systems and 64bit mode on 64bit systems. Fiddler runs best on 64bit systems, even if they have less than 4 gigabytes of RAM.

While not required, having Internet Explorer 9 or later installed provides Fiddler with a bit of extra functionality and is strongly recommended. In particular, with IE9+ installed, Fiddler's WebView Inspector can display additional media types, and you will be able to see traffic sent to `http://localhost` without additional configuration steps. Additionally, a configuration change can be made to Internet Explorer to indicate, via the `X-Download-Initiator` request header, why each request was issued.

A basic install of Fiddler requires less than 5 megabytes of disk space, while installing the most popular additional plugins will require another 5 megabytes or so. Fiddler will run on systems with 512 megabytes of RAM, but performance dramatically improves on systems with 2 gigabytes or more of memory.

System Requirements - Mono

The Mono build of Fiddler runs on both Mac and Linux; I regularly test it on Ubuntu, Linux Mint, and the latest version of Mac OS X. Unfortunately, the Mono WinForms implementation on Mac is not very stable; rewriting Fiddler's UI for Mac remains an unfinished project at this time. If you need to run Fiddler on a Mac, your best bet is to run it inside a Linux or Windows virtual machine, pointing the Mac's proxy settings at the Fiddler instance running on the virtual machine.

To run Fiddler on Mono, you first need to install Mono. For Mac, visit `http://mono-project.com/download/` and install the MDK package.

On Linux, running `sudo apt-get install mono-complete` is the best way to ensure that you have all of the necessary Mono packages. After installing Mono, download the ZIP file containing Fiddler's Mono build and extract it to the folder of your choice.

Install Fiddler on Windows

Fiddler's Windows installer is simple—you'll be asked to accept the terms of the End User License Agreement (short summary: don't do anything illegal, and keep in mind that Telerik offers no warranties) and then to select a folder to which Fiddler will be installed. You should accept the default folder location unless there's a strong reason not to—some Fiddler add-ons will blindly assume Fiddler is in the default location and will not install properly if it's not. The default location is %ProgramFiles%\Fiddler2, which on most systems will be C:\Program Files\Fiddler2, or C:\Program Files (x86)\Fiddler2 for 64bit systems. Fiddler installs to the 32bit Program Files folder only because the installer technology is 32bit-- Fiddler itself will run in 64bit mode if the operating system supports it.

After a successful install, a web page will open and display important information about getting started with Fiddler. The tool itself can be launched using the Start Menu or the Fiddler icon in your browser toolbar or menu. Alternatively, you can type fiddler2 in the Windows+R Run prompt.

Permissions and XCOPY Deployment

On Windows, installing Fiddler requires Administrative permissions because it updates machine-wide folder and registry locations. If you don't have administrative permissions on a target machine, you can perform what is commonly called an **XCOPY deployment**. Simply install Fiddler on a different computer, then copy the %ProgramFiles%\Fiddler2\ folder to the target machine or a USB key. While some Fiddler entry points will not be available (e.g. the Internet Explorer toolbar button and the FiddlerHook extension for Firefox), Fiddler itself will run successfully.

Update Fiddler

On startup, Fiddler is configured to make a web-service request to determine if a new version of the tool is available. If a new version is found, an update notice will be shown.

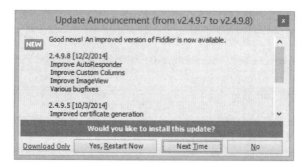

If you choose **Yes, Restart Now**, Fiddler will immediately exit, download the latest version, and install it. If you instead choose **Next Time**, the next time you start Fiddler, it will automatically download and install the latest version. If you choose **No**, the prompt closes and no new version is installed; you will again be notified of the new version the next time you start Fiddler. Choosing **Download Only** will download the installer but will not run it.

Installing Fiddler updates as they become available is strongly recommended, as each update typically adds features, improves performance, and removes bugs. At present, Fiddler Extensions do not participate in the auto-update feature, so you should periodically look for new versions of the Extensions you use on their developers' websites.

Administrators may prevent users from using the **Help** > **Check for Updates** command. To do so, use the Windows Registry Editor to create a new REG_STRING value named BlockUpdateCheck with value True inside the registry key HKLM\SOFTWARE\Microsoft\Fiddler2.

Uninstall Fiddler

If you later wish to uninstall Fiddler, you can do so using the **Add/Remove Programs** applet in your Windows Control Panel. By default, uninstalling Fiddler leaves your existing settings intact and therefore usually will not resolve any configuration problems you may encounter. Instead, see the **Troubleshooting** section in the Appendix of this book for more help.

THE FIDDLER USER-INTERFACE

The Fiddler User-Interface can be overwhelming because it exposes a great deal of information about web traffic and it offers a significant degree of customizability.

On the left side of the Fiddler window is the **Web Sessions** list, and on the right a set of tabbed **Views** that display information about the Sessions which are selected in the Web Sessions list. Above these, the **Main Menu** and **Toolbar** offer quick access to common operations. At the bottom, the **Status Bar** shows key information and exposes important commands. Just below the Web Sessions list is a small command line box called **QuickExec** that permits rapid filtering and command invocation capabilities.

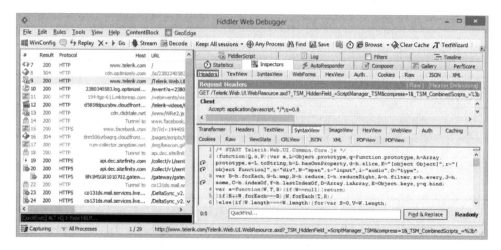

Tips:

- Many UI controls have context menus. Right-click early and often.

- If the mouse cursor turns into a pointing hand, the UI element can be clicked.

- Standard keyboard shortcuts are broadly supported (Use CTRL+C to copy, CTRL+A to select all, CTRL+G to go to a specific line number, F3 to perform a search).

- If a popup message box is shown, pressing CTRL+C will copy its text to the clipboard.

- Press the ESC key to dismiss dialog boxes or clear search boxes.

- To reset Fiddler's UI to its default layout, hold the SHIFT key while starting Fiddler.

- Remove a tab from the Views by middle-clicking the tab title.

- Double-click on a splitter to maximize the display area next to the splitter.

Web Sessions List

The Web Sessions list is the most important feature of Fiddler—it displays a short summary of each Session that Fiddler has captured. Most operations in Fiddler begin by selecting one or more entries in the Web Sessions list and then activating other features. To select more than one Session, hold the CTRL or SHIFT keys while clicking the desired rows. Double-click or press Enter to activate the default **Inspectors** for a single selected Session. When the Inspectors are activated, they will automatically decide which Inspector is best suited to display the selected Session's request and response.

Certain key information is displayed in the columns of the Web Sessions list, including:

- **#** – An identification number generated by Fiddler.
- **Result** – The status code from the response.
- **Protocol** – The protocol (HTTP/HTTPS/FTP) used by the Session.
- **Host** – The hostname and port of the server to which the request was sent.
- **URL** – The URL path, file, and query string from the request.
- **Body** – The number of bytes in the response body.
- **Caching** – Values from the Response's Expires and Cache-Control headers.
- **Content-Type** – The Content-Type header from the response.
- **Process** – The local Windows Process from which the traffic originated.
- **Custom** – Shows any ui-CustomColumn flag value set by FiddlerScript.
- **Comments** – Shows any comment set using the toolbar's Comment button.

You can resize and reorder the columns in the Web Sessions list by adjusting or dragging the column headers. To sort the entries in the Web Sessions list by the values in a specified column, click on that column's header. New columns may be added to the Web Sessions list using FiddlerScript, Extensions, QuickExec, or the Customize Columns screen.

If you ALT+Click a cell in the Web Sessions list, Fiddler will select all Sessions with a matching value in the column of the cell clicked. CTRL+ALT+Click a cell to add all Sessions with that cell's value to the selection; click again to unselect all Sessions with that cell's value.

Drag and Drop Support

You can drag and drop Sessions from the Web Sessions list to another instance of Fiddler (e.g. one running in Fiddler's Viewer Mode). You can also drop Sessions onto the AutoResponder or Composer tabs or a Session Clipboard window.

You can drag and drop files from Windows Explorer to the list and Fiddler will create mock Sessions for those files. If you hold the `Control` key while dropping a file of a type for which an Importer is available (e.g. a `.pcap` file), Fiddler will instead invoke the Importer registered for the dropped file's extension.

Icons and Colors

The default text coloring of each row in the Web Sessions list derives from the HTTP Status (red for errors, yellow for authentication demands), traffic type (`CONNECT`s appear in grey), or response type (CSS in purple, HTML in blue; script in green, images in grey). You can override the font color by setting the Session's `ui-color` flag from FiddlerScript.

Each row is also marked with an icon for quick reference as to the Session's progress, Request type, or Response type:

	Request is being sent to the server.
	Response is being downloaded from the server.
	Request is paused at a breakpoint to allow tampering.
	Response is paused at a breakpoint to allow tampering.
i	Request used the `HEAD` or `OPTIONS` methods, or returned a `HTTP/204` status code. The `HEAD` and `OPTIONS` methods allow the client to acquire information about the target URL or server without downloading the content. The `HTTP/204` status code indicates that there is no response body.
	Request used the `POST` method to send data to the server.
<>	Response is HTML.
	Response is an image.
JS	Response is a script.
css{	Response is a Cascading Style Sheet (CSS).
<x>	Response is Extensible Markup Language (XML).
{js on}	Response is JavaScript Object Notation (JSON).
	Response is an audio file.
	Response is a video file.
	Response is a Silverlight applet.
	Response is a Flash applet.
	Response is a font.
	Response's `Content-Type` is not a type for which a more specific icon is available.
	Request used the `CONNECT` method. This method is used to establish a tunnel through which encrypted HTTPS traffic flows.
SPDY	Session is a `CONNECT` tunnel inside which Google's SPDY protocol is used.
HTTP2	Session is a `CONNECT` tunnel inside which the HTTP2 protocol is used.

⇌	Session is an RPC-over-HTTP tunnel; most commonly used by Microsoft Outlook.
🔲	Session wraps a HTML5 WebSocket connection.
↘	Response is a HTTP/3xx class redirect.
🔑	Response is a HTTP/401 or HTTP/407 demand for client credentials, or a HTTP/403 error indicating that access was denied.
⚠	Response has a HTTP/4xx or HTTP/5xx error status code.
⊘	Session was aborted by the client application, Fiddler, or the Server. This commonly occurs when the client browser began downloading of a page, but the user then navigated to a different page. The client browser responds by canceling all in-progress requests, leading to the Aborted Session state.
▬	Response is a HTTP/206 partial response. Such responses are returned as a result of the client performing a Range request for only a portion of the file at the target URL.
◈	Response has a HTTP/304 status, indicating that the client's cached copy is fresh.
📝	Session is unlocked, enabling modification after normal Session processing has completed.

Keyboard Reference

The following keyboard shortcuts are supported by the Web Sessions list:

Spacebar	Activate and scroll the currently-focused Session into view.
CTRL+A	Select all Sessions.
ESC	Unselect all Sessions.
CTRL+I	Invert selection; selected Sessions are unselected and vice versa.
CTRL+X	Remove all Sessions (subject to the fiddler.ui.CtrlX.KeepMarked preference.)
Delete	Remove selected Sessions.
SHIFT+Delete	Remove all unselected Sessions.
R	Replay the selected requests
SHIFT+R	Replay selected requests multiple times (specified in the subsequent prompt).
S	Replay selected requests sequentially; wait for each to complete before sending the next. If only one request is selected, prompts for a repeat count.
V	Replay selected requests and verify that the responses from the server are unchanged.
U	Unconditionally replay selected requests, sending neither If-Modified-Since nor If-None-Match headers.
SHIFT+U	Unconditionally replay selected requests multiple times (the count is specified in the subsequent prompt).
P	Attempt to select the "parent" request that triggered this request and set focus to it. This feature depends on the HTTP Referer header's value.
C	Attempt to select all "child" requests that were provoked by this response. This feature depends on the HTTP Referer header's value or the Location header on a redirect.
D	Select all "duplicate" requests that have the same request method and URL as the current Session.

ALT+Enter	View the current Session's properties.
SHIFT+Enter	Launch Inspectors for this Session in a new Fiddler window.
Backspace or mouse "Back-button"	Activate the previously selected Session.
I	Indent the icon of selected Sessions.
O	Outdent the icon of selected Sessions.
M	Add a comment to selected Sessions.
SHIFT+M	Add a mock session with a comment.
Insert	Toggle marking of the selected Sessions using a bold red font.
Minus	Toggle selected Sessions' font to strikethrough, like ~~this~~.
ALT+Minus	Select Sessions marked in the ~~strikethrough~~ font.
CTRL+0	Remove all markings on the selected Sessions.
CTRL+1 ... CTRL+6	Mark the selected Sessions in bold and one of the colors: red, blue, gold, green, orange, or purple.
ALT+1 ... ALT+6	Select Sessions that were previously marked using the CTRL+# shortcut.
ALT+0	Select Sessions not previously marked using a CTRL+# shortcut.
=	Add a dividing line at the bottom of the Session list.
CTRL+Z	Restore removed Sessions. This command is only available if the memory used by the removed Sessions has not yet been reclaimed (garbage-collected) by the system.
F3 or .	Select the next search result (after using CTRL+F).
SHIFT+F3 or ,	Select the previous search result (after using CTRL+F).

Web Sessions Context Menu

Right-clicking on the column headers at the top of the Web Sessions list offers a small context menu:

Search this column...	All Sessions that match an expression you supply are selected.
Flag duplicates	Highlight Sessions with duplicate values for the chosen column.
Hide this column	Hide the current column from display, either by shrinking it to zero-width (for built-in columns) or by removing it from Fiddler (for custom columns).
Ensure all columns are visible	Ensure that all columns are visible by resizing each to at least 40 pixels wide.
Customize columns...	Display a dialog box that enables adding new custom columns.

Right-clicking within the body rows of the Web Sessions list shows a large context menu. Many of the options are available only if one or more Sessions are selected in the list. This menu can be extended by FiddlerScript, so it will often contain additional commands that are not listed here.

The **AutoScroll Session List** option controls whether or not Fiddler automatically scrolls to the bottom of the list as new sessions are added.

The **Copy** submenu enables you to copy the information of your choice from the selected Sessions:

Just Url	Copy the URLs of the selected Sessions to the clipboard, one per line. You may also invoke this command by pressing `CTRL+U` when focus is in the Web Sessions list.
This column	Copy the text in the column over which the context menu was opened. The text for each of the selected Sessions is added to the clipboard, one per line.
Terse summary	Copy a terse summary of the selected Sessions to the clipboard. This summary includes the Request Method and URL, and the response status code and status text. If a response is a `HTTP/3xx` redirect, the text will include the target `Location` header. You may also invoke this command by pressing `CTRL+SHIFT+T` when focus is in the Web Sessions list.
Headers only	Copy Sessions' headers to the clipboard. The text is copied in both plaintext and HTML formats, so you will see different results if you paste into an editor that handles only plain text (e.g. Notepad) versus one that handles rich text (e.g. Microsoft Word). You may also invoke this command by double-clicking on the Copy submenu itself, or by pressing `CTRL+SHIFT+C` when focus is in the Web Sessions list.
Session	Copy the entire contents of the selected Sessions. The text is copied in both plaintext and HTML formats, so you will see different results if you paste into an editor that handles only plain text versus one that handles rich text. You may also invoke this command by pressing `CTRL+SHIFT+S` when focus is in the Web Sessions list.
Response DataURI	Copy the response to a DataURI string. Binary data is encoded using base64.
Full Summary	Copy the information shown in the Web Sessions list to the clipboard. The columns are delimited by tabs so you may paste this information into Microsoft Excel or other programs neatly. You may also invoke this command by pressing `CTRL+C` when focus is in the Web Sessions list.

The **Save** submenu exposes options that allow you to save traffic to files:

Selected Sessions	In ArchiveZip	Save selected Sessions to a Session Archive Zip (SAZ) file.
	As Text	Save selected Sessions to a single text file.
	As Text (Headers only)	Save selected Sessions' request and response headers to a single text file.
Request	Entire Request	Save selected Sessions' request headers and bodies to individual files.
	Request Body	Save selected Sessions' request bodies to individual files.
Response	Entire Response	Save selected Sessions' response headers and bodies to individual files. This option is useful if you would like to create response files to later play back using the AutoResponder.
	Response Body	Save selected Sessions' response bodies to individual files. This option is useful if you would like to open the response body (say, an image) in another program that would be confused by the

	presence of HTTP response headers.
...and Open as Local File	Save selected Sessions' response bodies to individual files, then open each file in the registered handler for the response's file type. If you hold the CTRL key while invoking this option, you can choose which application to use to open the file.

The **Remove Submenu** allows you to remove All, Selected, or Unselected Sessions from the Web Sessions list. The CTRL+X, Delete, or Shift+Delete key combinations may be used to activate these commands when focus is in the Web Sessions list.

The **Filter Submenu** allows you to use the attributes of the selected Session as a filter. The filter will be immediately applied to all previously-captured Sessions in the list, and will apply to all subsequent Sessions as they are captured.

Hide '*example*:*'	Hide Sessions whose process name is `example`
Hide Process=#	Hide Sessions originating from the specified Windows Process ID.
Show Only Process=#	Hide Sessions that do not originate from the specified Windows Process ID.
Hide '*example.com*'	Hide Sessions with a hostname of `example.com`.
Hide '*type/subtype*'	Hide Sessions whose response headers include Content-Type: type/subtype.

The **Comment...** menu command allows you to add or update the Comment field for one or more selected Sessions.

The **Mark** submenu allows you to select a color to mark the selected Sessions. The font of the Sessions will be set according to your choice. The **Unmark** option will revert the Sessions' fonts to the default.

The **Replay** submenu offers commands that replay the currently selected requests.

Reissue Requests	Reissue the selected requests as they were originally sent. If you hold SHIFT while invoking this command, Fiddler will prompt you for the number of times the requests should be repeated. You may invoke this command by pressing the R key in the Web Sessions list.
Reissue Unconditionally	Unconditionally replay the selected requests, sending no If-Modified-Since and If-None-Match headers to prevent the server from returning a HTTP/304 response. If you hold SHIFT while invoking this command, Fiddler will prompt you for the number of times the requests should be repeated. You may invoke this command by pressing the U key in the Web Sessions list.
Reissue and Edit	Reissue the selected requests as they were originally sent, setting a request breakpoint on each new Session to allow you to use Fiddler's Inspectors to modify the requests before they are sent to the server.
Reissue and Verify	Reissue the selected requests as they were originally sent. Each reissued request's response will be compared to the original response. If the new response matches, the

	Session will be marked in green. If the response does not match, the Session will be marked in red.
Reissue Sequentially	Reissue the selected requests, waiting for each response before continuing with the next request. If only one request is selected, prompts for a repeat count.
Reissue from Composer	Copy the currently selected request to the Composer tab.
Revisit in IE	For each selected request, navigate to the request URL in Internet Explorer. Note that Internet Explorer will always navigate using a GET request and its own headers and cookies, regardless of what HTTP methods and headers were captured for the sessions you are replaying.

The **Select** submenu allows you to use your currently-selected Session to select other Sessions:

Parent Request	The Parent Request option attempts to use this request's Referer header and Session ID to select the Session that led to this request being sent. For instance, if you invoke this command on a JavaScript request, the Session selected will typically be the HTML page that caused this script to be downloaded. Pressing the P key while focus is in the Web Sessions list will also invoke this command.
Child Requests	The Child Requests option attempts to use this request's URL and Session ID to select any requests sent as a result of this response. For instance, if you invoke this command on a HTML Session, the Sessions selected will typically be the CSS, JS, and image files mentioned in the HTML markup. Pressing the C key while focus is in the Web Sessions list will also invoke this command.
Duplicate Requests	Select all Sessions in the list which share the currently selected Session's URL and HTTP method. Pressing the D key while focus is in the Web Sessions list will also invoke this command.
Matching Values	Select all Sessions with a matching value in the column of the cell over which the context menu was opened. Alternatively, ALT+Click a cell in the Web Sessions list to invoke this command.

The **Compare** command is available only when two Sessions are selected in the Web Sessions list. Running this command saves the two Sessions to temporary files, then launches the configured comparison tool to compare their requests and responses.

The **COMETPeek** command takes a "snapshot" of an in-progress response, allowing you to inspect a partial response before it has been completed. This command is useful in cases where a web application is using the COMET pattern to return a never-ending stream of data to the client. Since the stream is (by-definition) without end, Fiddler wouldn't otherwise be able to show the response until the server terminates the connection.

The **Abort Session** command will terminate the client and server connections for an in-progress Session.

The **Clone Response** command is only available when two Sessions are selected in the Web Sessions list and one of the Sessions is currently paused at a breakpoint and the other Session is completed. The command will copy the response from the completed Session to the paused Session. This feature enables you to easily replicate a previously captured (or modified) response to satisfy a later request.

The **Unlock for Editing** command unlocks a single selected Session, allowing you to edit the completed Session's request and response using the Inspectors. You may invoke this command by pressing F2 when focus is in the Web Sessions list.

The **Inspect in New Window** command opens a Session Inspector window which allows you to view the Session's request, response, and properties in a standalone window.

The **Properties...** command opens the Session Properties window to display information about the currently selected Session, including its timers, session flags, and information about how the request was routed. If two Sessions are selected, two windows will open side-by-side for ease of comparison.

Customize Columns

There are several ways to add new columns to the Web Sessions list, but the easiest is to use the **Customize Columns** screen. To show it, right-click the list's header and choose **Customize Columns...** from the context menu.

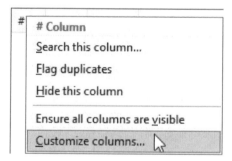

The Customize Columns screen allows you to choose the source of the data, the width of the column, and its title. The first step is to select the data source using the dropdown at the top left:

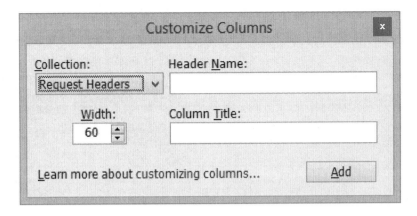

If you choose the **Request Headers**, **Response Headers**, or **Session Flags** collections, supply the name of the header or flag using the textbox to the right. If you select either the **Session Timers** or **Miscellaneous** collections, the textbox is replaced with a dropdown of the datapoints within the selected collection.

The **Session Timers** collection contains each of the timers stored for the Session, as well as several computed timers:

- **TTFB** – Time to first response byte. (`ServerBeginResponse - ClientBeginRequest`)

- **TTLB** – Time to the last response byte. (`ServerDoneResponse - ClientBeginRequest`)

- **Server ThinkTime** – The time the server spent processing the request. (`ServerBeginResponse - ServerGotRequest`)

- **Overall Elapsed** – The total amount of time spent for the Session. (`ClientDoneResponse - ClientBeginRequest`).

The **Miscellaneous** collection contains a wide variety of computed data points:

- **RequestMethod** – The HTTP Method (e.g. `POST`) from the request line.

- **RequestSize** – The size of the request in bytes, including headers and body.

- **RequestBodySize** – The size of the request body (excluding the preceding headers).

- **ResponseSize** – The complete size of the response, including headers and body.

- **CompressionSavings** – If the response is compressed using `Content-Encoding: GZIP` or `DEFLATE`, the number of bytes saved by compression.

- **CompressionSavings%** – If the response is compressed using `Content-Encoding: GZIP` or `DEFLATE`, the percentage of the original response size that was saved.

- **SecurityHeaders** – A terse summary of security-related response headers. The data summarizes the response's `Content-Security-Policy`, `Strict-Transport-Security`, `Public-Key-Pins`,

`Access-Control-Allow-Origin`, `X-XSS-Protection`, `X-Frame-Options`, and `X-Content-Type` options into one succinct string. If any of the headers contains an invalid value or appears in violation of the standards, an exclamation point (!) will be shown in the policy string. You can thus easily search for any resources with invalid policies by simply searching the column for a !.

- **md5(responseBody)** – Displays an MD5 hash value of the response's body bytes. This is primarily useful for identifying duplicate response bodies.

- **ResponseStatusText** – The *status text* portion of the HTTP response headers. For instance, for a `HTTP/200` response, this column will typically display `OK`.

- **ResponseStreamed** – Indicates if the HTTP response was streamed to the client.

- **SentToGateway** – Indicates if the request was sent to an upstream gateway proxy.

- **ClientPipeReuse** – Indicates if the request was received on a connection reused by the client.

- **ServerPipeReuse** – Indicates if the request was sent on a reused connection to the server.

- **ImageDimensions** – The width and height of an image response (e.g. `120, 100`).

- **PixelCount** – The number of pixels contained in an image response (e.g. `12000`).

- **Bytes/Pixel** – The computed number of bytes used for each pixel of the image (e.g. `0.90`). Larger numbers in this column suggest that the image would benefit from optimization.

- **AspectRatio** – The aspect ratio of an image response (e.g. `1.20`).

- **ImageRGB** – A hexadecimal representation of the percentage of red, green, and blue pixels in the image.

- **ImageFingerprint** – A string containing the image's aspect ratio, brightness, and red, blue, and green values. This data is useful for finding duplicate images that have been rescaled.

- **GeoLocation** – If a JPEG image contains geographic location information, it is displayed in this column. Use the ImageView Response Inspector to visualize the location on a map.

After you've selected your data source, provide a title for the column. If the column's data source is a header or Session Flag, choosing a title with a leading # symbol will cause Fiddler to sort that column numerically.

Finally, click **Add** to add your newly defined column to the Web Sessions list. The new column will remain in Fiddler's Web Sessions list for future debugging instances until you remove it using the **Hide this column** command in the list header's context menu.

FIDDLER'S MAIN MENU

The main menu is designed to provide access to almost all of Fiddler's functionality. The menu system can be augmented by FiddlerScript or Extensions, but in this section, we'll discuss only Fiddler's default menu commands.

File Menu

The File menu contains commands to start and stop Fiddler's capture of web traffic, as well as to load and store captured traffic.

The **Capture Traffic** toggle controls whether Fiddler is registered as the system proxy. When Fiddler is registered as the system proxy, applications that respect the WinINET proxy settings (e.g. Internet Explorer and most other browsers) will send their web requests to Fiddler. The FiddlerHook add-on for Firefox also respects this menu option. Even when it is not registered as the system proxy, Fiddler will continue to display and process any requests that are received.

The **New Viewer** command opens a new Fiddler window in Fiddler's Viewer Mode. This mode enables you to view previously-captured traffic and compose new requests, but it does not capture traffic from clients.

The **Load Archive...** command allows you to reload previously-captured traffic stored in a SAZ file.

The **Recent Archives** submenu lists SAZ files that have recently been loaded. You may clear this list or remove outdated references using the commands at the bottom of the submenu.

The **Save** submenu exposes options that allow you to save traffic to files. The options on this menu are the same as those on the Web Sessions list's context menu, except that an **All Sessions...** option is also available.

The **Import Sessions...** command enables you to import previously-captured traffic from another tool or file format.

The **Export Sessions** submenu allows you to export traffic captured by Fiddler to many different file formats. You may choose **All Sessions...** or **Selected Sessions...** from this submenu.

The **Exit** menu command unregisters Fiddler as the system proxy and closes the tool.

Edit Menu

Most of the commands on the Edit menu apply to the currently-selected Sessions in the Web Sessions list, and thus most of the commands are disabled unless one or more Sessions are selected.

The **Copy** submenu enables you to copy the information of your choice from the Sessions selected in the Web Sessions list. The commands on this menu are the same as those on the list's context menu.

The **Remove** submenu allows you to remove All, Selected, or Unselected Sessions from the Web Sessions list. The CTRL+X, Delete, or Shift+Delete key combinations may be used to activate these commands when focus is in the list.

The **Select All** command selects all entries in the Web Sessions list. You may invoke this command by pressing CTRL+A when the focus is in the list.

The **Undelete** command restores the latest removed Sessions. This command is only available if the memory used by the removed Sessions has not yet been reclaimed (garbage-collected) by the system.

The **Paste as Sessions** command will generate one or more mock Web Sessions based on the contents of the clipboard.

If the clipboard contains text and a DataURI can be found starting within the first 64 characters of that text, the DataURI will be parsed out of the text and a new Session will be created and added to the Web Sessions list. This feature is very useful when you are using Fiddler to examine markup containing a DataURI-encoded image, and you want to see what the image looks like. Simply copy the DataURI from the markup and use the **Paste as Sessions** command to generate a new Session that you can then inspect using the ImageView Inspector.

If the clipboard contains a binary image (for instance, if you've used Alt+PrintScrn hotkey to take a screenshot of the active window) the mock Session added to the Web Sessions list will store that image as the response body.

If the clipboard contains one or more files (e.g. copied from Windows Explorer) each file will be used to generate a mock Session that is added to the Web Sessions list. This feature is most useful when you are building a SAZ file to send to someone else and want to include a file that was not transmitted over the network. For instance, a web developer could use this option to include the source code behind a given ASPX page when sending a SAZ file of the output of that page as captured by Fiddler.

If the clipboard contains a cURL.exe command line, the command will be parsed and a mock session will be generated based on the request. You can then reissue this Session to send the request to the server.

The **Mark** submenu allows you to select a color to mark the selected Sessions. The font of the Sessions will be set according to your choice. The **Unmark** option will revert the Sessions' fonts to the default.

The **Unlock for Editing** command unlocks a single selected Session, allowing you to edit the completed Session's request and response using the Inspectors. You may invoke this command by pressing F2 when focus is in the Web Sessions list.

The **Find Sessions…** command opens the Find Sessions window to begin a search of captured traffic. You may press CTRL+F to invoke this command.

Rules Menu

The Rules menu is easily extensible, and most of its commands are provided by FiddlerScript.

The **Hide Image Requests** toggle controls whether Sessions that returned images are shown in the Web Sessions list.

The **Hide CONNECTs** toggle controls whether Sessions that use the CONNECT request method are shown in the Web Sessions list. The CONNECT method is used by a client to establish a "raw" connection to a server, to carry either HTTPS or WebSocket traffic.

The **Automatic Breakpoints** submenu allows you to control whether Fiddler automatically breaks **Before Requests** or **After Responses**. The **Ignore Image** toggle controls whether these breakpoints are applied to requests for images.

The **Customize Rules...** menu command opens your current FiddlerScript file using the configured script editor.

When checked, the **Require Proxy Authentication** menu item will respond to any request that doesn't submit a Proxy-Authorization header by returning a HTTP/407 response demanding proxy credentials. This rule is useful for testing HTTP clients to ensure that they work properly in environments with authenticating proxy servers.

When checked, the **Apply GZIP Encoding** menu item will apply HTTP compression to all responses except images, so long as the request contained an Accept-Encoding header that included the gzip token. This rule is useful to test that clients that advertise GZIP support can actually decompress content. It also allows you to experiment with the performance and bytes-on-wire count for compressed traffic.

When checked, the **Remove All Encodings** toggle removes all HTTP Content-Encodings and Transfer-Encodings from requests and responses. This rule is also exposed by the **Decode** button on the Fiddler toolbar.

The remainder of the commands on this menu are provided by FiddlerScript or extensions, and thus your menu's commands may differ from the commands from those in the default FiddlerScript. You can examine the implementation of these commands (and add your own) by clicking the **Customize Rules...** option in the Rules menu.

The **Hide 304s** option hides all Sessions whose responses bear the HTTP/304 Not Modified status.

The **Request Japanese Content** option will set or replace all requests' Accept-Encoding header value with the ja token, indicating that the client prefers responses in the Japanese language.

The **Automatically Authenticate** option sets each request's X-AutoAuth Session Flag to the value (default). This flag value causes Fiddler to automatically respond to servers' authentication demands using the current Windows user's credentials.

The **User-Agents** submenu allows you to set or replace all requests' User-Agent header with a specified value. You can select among the values provided, or use the **Custom...** option at the bottom of the submenu to specify any value you like.

Performance Submenu

The **Performance** submenu exposes simple options that impact web performance.

When enabled, the **Simulate Modem Speeds** option will set Flags on all subsequent Sessions. The request-trickle-delay flag is set to 300 to delay all network writes by 300ms per kilobyte uploaded. The response-trickle-delay flag is set to 150 to delay all network reads by 150ms/kb downloaded.

When set, the **Disable Caching** option will remove all If-None-Match and If-Modified-Since request headers and add a Pragma: no-cache request header. It will also remove any Expires headers on the response and set the Cache-Control response header to no-cache. Note that this option cannot prevent a browser from reusing a previously cached response that was received *before* this option was enabled. Clear your browser's cache (CTRL+SHIFT+DELETE) after enabling this option for best results.

The **Cache Always Fresh** option will automatically respond to any conditional HTTP request with a HTTP/304 response indicating that the client's cache is up-to-date. This option can dramatically improve performance when visiting sites that fail to set cache expiration dates properly. Pressing CTRL+F5 in the browser is usually enough to force a reload from the server in spite of this option, because browsers will omit the If-Modified-Since and If-None-Match headers on forced-refresh requests.

Tools Menu

The Tools menu is easily extensible, and often many of its commands are provided by FiddlerScript.

The **Fiddler Options...** item opens the Fiddler Options window.

The **WinINET Options...** item opens Internet Explorer's Internet Options window.

The **Clear WinINET Cache** item clears all files in the WinINET cache that is used by Internet Explorer and many other applications.

The **Clear WinINET Cookies** item clears all persistent WinINET cookies used by Internet Explorer and many other applications. Session cookies are not cleared.

The **TextWizard...** item launches the TextWizard window to permit encoding and decoding of text.

The **Compare Sessions** item is enabled only if exactly two Sessions are selected in the Web Sessions list. When clicked, a differencing tool will be used to compare the two Sessions.

The **HOSTS...** item opens Fiddler's Host Remapping tool.

The **Configure AutoSave...** option displays and activates the AutoSave tab, permitting you to automatically save web traffic to a SAZ file according to the schedule you specify.

The **New Session Clipboard...** option displays a new window that provides an auxiliary list for holding Sessions. You can drag and drop Sessions between clipboard windows and the main Web Sessions list.

The remainder of the commands on the Tools menu are provided by FiddlerScript or extensions.

View Menu

The **Show Toolbar** toggle controls whether the Fiddler toolbar is visible.

The **Default Layout** option sets Fiddler to its default window layout, with the Web Sessions list on the left and the Request and Response Inspectors stacked atop one another on the right.

The **Stacked Layout** option reorganizes the Fiddler window such that the Web Sessions list appears atop the Views tabs. This layout is useful when you have added many custom columns and want more space to see those columns.

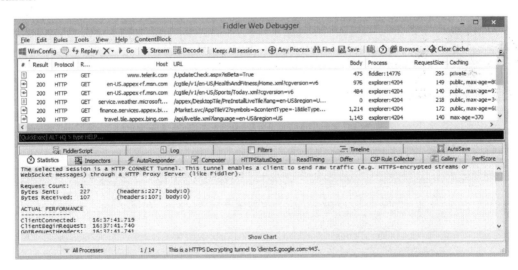

The **Wide Layout** option arranges Fiddler's window in a "pyramid" style, where the Request and Response Inspectors are side-by-side across the bottom of the window, with the Web Sessions list stacked on top.

The **Statistics** item activates the Statistics tab; you can invoke this command by pressing F7.

The **Inspectors** item activates the Inspectors tab; you can invoke this command by pressing F8.

The **Composer** item activates the Composer tab; you can invoke this command by pressing F9.

The **Minimize to Tray** option or CTRL+M will minimize Fiddler to the system tray.

The **Stay on Top** toggle forces Fiddler to remain on top of all other windows.

The **Squish Session List** toggle controls whether the Web Sessions list is collapsed horizontally, giving you more room to view Inspectors and other tabs. This toggle is available only when Fiddler's window is set to the Default Layout. You can toggle this option by pressing the F6 key.

The **AutoScroll Session List** option controls whether Fiddler automatically scrolls to the bottom of the Web Sessions list as new Sessions are added.

The **Refresh** option and the F5 key refresh the information for the currently selected Sessions in the Inspectors or Statistics tab.

Help Menu

The **Fiddler Help** command navigates your browser to the help homepage for Fiddler.

The **Fiddler Discussions** command opens the Fiddler discussion group, where you can ask questions and find answers from other users.

The **Fiddler Book** command opens the Fiddler Book (this one!) in your PDF viewer. This command is only available if Debugging with Fiddler.pdf is stored in Fiddler's program files folder alongside fiddler.exe.

The **HTTP References** command opens a page with links to various references and specifications related to the HTTP protocol.

If you ever find that traffic is "missing" from the Web Sessions list, the **Troubleshoot...** command is your best bet for resolving the problem. When Fiddler's troubleshooting mode is activated, a browser window opens and generates various requests for Fiddler to capture, enabling diagnosis of network configuration problems. Sessions that would otherwise be hidden by filters are instead shown using a strikethrough font— the **Comments** column indicates which filter was responsible for attempting to hide the traffic.

The **Check for Updates...** command contacts a web service to determine whether this is the latest version of Fiddler. If not, you can choose to install the newest version immediately or when Fiddler next starts up.

The **Send Feedback...** command composes an email message to the Fiddler developers and support team.

The **About Fiddler** command opens a window showing Fiddler's version information.

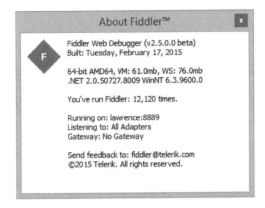

Fiddler's About Box

At the top, the window shows information about the running version of Fiddler, including its version number, whether it's a beta version, and when it was compiled.

The next paragraph indicates whether Fiddler is running in 32bit or 64bit mode, and how much **Virtual Memory** and **Working Set** it is currently using. Below that appear the version information for the Microsoft .NET Framework and the Operating System.

Next, you'll see a counter recording the number of times you've started Fiddler.

Below that, you'll see the hostname and port on which Fiddler is running. The **Listening to** line shows the network connectoids upon which Fiddler registers as the proxy. The **Gateway** line shows information about any upstream proxy server.

Lastly, you'll see contact and copyright information.

You may press Escape or Spacebar to close the window. Hit CTRL+C to copy all of the text, or select a subset of the information with your mouse and press CTRL+C to copy only that text.

FIDDLER'S TOOLBAR

The toolbar provides quick access to popular commands and settings.

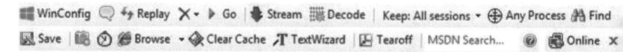

The buttons and their functions are:

WinConfig	*Shown only on Windows 8 and later.* Launches a tool that configures "Immersive" apps to permit sending traffic to Fiddler. Hold the CTRL key while clicking to automatically configure all applications.
Comment icon	Add a Comment to all selected Sessions. The comment appears in a column of the Web Sessions list. Hold the SHIFT key while clicking to add a new mock Session to the list with the comment of your choice.
Replay	Reissue the selected requests to the server. Hold the CTRL key while clicking to reissue the requests without any Conditional Request headers (e.g. If-Modified-Since and If-None-Match). Hold the SHIFT key while clicking to be prompted to specify the number of times each request should be reissued.
Remove icon	Show a menu of options for removing Sessions from the Web Sessions list: • **Remove all** removes all Sessions from the list. • **Images** removes all Sessions that returned an image. • **CONNECTs** removes all CONNECT tunnels. • **Non-200s** removes all non-HTTP/200 responses. • **Non-Browser** removes all requests that were not issued by a web browser. • **Complete & Unmarked** removes Sessions in the Done or Aborted states that are unmarked and have no Comment set. • **Duplicate response bodies** removes any Session which has no response body or has a response body identical to one received in an earlier Session.
Go	Resume all Sessions which are currently paused at a Request or Response breakpoint. Hold the SHIFT key while clicking to resume only selected Sessions.
Stream	Enable the Stream toggle to deactivate response buffering for all responses except those for which a breakpoint is set.
Decode	Enable the Decode toggle to remove all HTTP Content and Transfer encodings from requests and responses.
Keep: *value*	Control how many Sessions are stored in the Web Sessions list. When the limit is reached, Fiddler will begin removing older Sessions to attempt to limit the list to the desired value. Incomplete Sessions and those with comments, markers, or open Inspector windows are not removed.
Process Filter	Drag and drop the Process Filter icon to an application to create a filter that hides all traffic except that originating from the selected process. Right-click the Process Filter icon to clear a previously set filter.

Find	Open the Find Sessions window.
Save	Save all Sessions to a SAZ file.
Camera icon	Add a JPEG-formatted screenshot of the current desktop to the Web Sessions list. By default, a five-second countdown is observed. Hold `CTRL` or `SHIFT` while clicking to skip the countdown.
Timer icon	Start a simple timer; click to start and stop, or right-click to clear.
Browse	If one Session is selected, open Internet Explorer to the target URL. If zero or multiple Sessions are selected, open Internet Explorer to `about:blank`. Additional browsers can be added to the list using the `fiddler.ui.toolbar.BrowserList` preference.
Clear Cache	Clear the WinINET caches. Hold `CTRL` while clicking to also purge persistent cookies stored by WinINET.
TextWizard	Open the Text Encoding / Decoding Wizard which can be used to transform text between various encodings.
Tearoff	Create a new window into which all Views are placed; the Web Sessions list expands to the full width of the main Fiddler window.
MSDN Search	Perform a search in the Web Content area of MSDN.
Help icon	Open Fiddler's help.
Online Indicator	Indicates whether the system is currently online or offline. When online, hovering over the indicator will show a tooltip containing the local computer's hostname and IP addresses. Double-click the indicator to open the system's Network Connections control panel.
X	Remove the toolbar. To display it later, click **View** > **Show Toolbar**.

Hover over any element of the toolbar to show a tooltip that tersely explains the element's function.

You can reorganize the toolbar by holding the `ALT` key and dragging individual toolbar elements to a new location. To remove a command, drag it to the Web Sessions list. Please note that toolbar changes are not currently saved and are reset when Fiddler restarts.

If you're using Fiddler on a small display, the narrow toolbar will overflow some of the commands into a dropdown menu on the far right. If you'd like, you may set the preference `fiddler.ui.toolbar.ShowLabels` to `false` to hide the toolbar's text labels, decreasing the toolbar's width.

Fiddler's Status Bar

The status bar along the bottom of Fiddler's main window shows a set of panels that display information about the current Fiddler configuration. Several of these panels can be clicked to quickly change the configuration. From the left, the panels are:

Capturing Indicator	Indicates whether Fiddler is currently configured as the system proxy. Click the panel to toggle the capturing state.
Process-type Filter	Indicates whether Fiddler is currently configured to capture traffic from only one type of process. Click the panel to show a menu of process-type filtering options.

Breakpoint Indicator	Indicates whether Fiddler is configured to breakpoint all requests, all responses, or neither. Click the panel to quickly toggle breakpoint functionality.
Session Counter	Displays the number of entries in the Web Sessions list. If one or more Sessions are selected, the indicator will show the selected and the total number of Sessions, e.g. "2 / 5". Click this panel to scroll the first selected Session into view.
Status Information	By default, shows the URL of the first selected Session. This panel is also used to show succinct information about the results of actions; for instance, when a SAZ file is loaded or saved, that fact is mentioned here.

QUICKEXEC

The QuickExec box below the Web Sessions list provides keyboard access to common and advanced operations. Use the Alt+Q hotkey to set focus to the QuickExec box when Fiddler is active—if Fiddler isn't active, first press CTRL+ALT+F to activate the Fiddler window.

While QuickExec is focused, pressing CTRL+I will insert the URL of the first selected Session from the Web Sessions list. You can also drag/drop one or more Sessions from the list to insert their URLs in the QuickExec box, or you can drag/drop one or more files from your file system to insert their file paths. Press ESC to clear the QuickExec box. Press the Up or down arrow keys to scroll through the list of previously-used commands. After typing one or more characters, hitting ALT+L will show the list of previously-used commands that start with the text you've typed. Hit CTRL+Delete to clear the command history, or hit Shift+Delete to remove just the current command from history. Set the fiddler.QuickExec.AutoComplete preference to false if you'd like to disable autocompletion.

QuickExec Selection Commands

QuickExec allows you to quickly select traffic of interest based on search criteria you specify. After typing a selection command, hitting Enter will set focus to the Web Sessions list if the search returned any matches.

Command	Action	Example
?search	Select Sessions whose URLs contain the specified search text. This is the only *find-as-you-type* search feature in the QuickExec box. All other search types require that you press Enter to begin the search. For ?-prefixed searches, hitting Enter will set focus to the Web Sessions list.	?example.com/pathchars
select type	Select Sessions whose response Content-Type header contains the chosen type.	select css select image/jp
select header-col-or-flag value	Select Sessions where the named SessionFlag, Column, or Header case-insensitively contains the specified value string. Unless preceded by a slash, asterisk means *any value*. Use * to match a literal asterisk.	select ui-comments slow select ui-bold * select ui-backcolor red select ui-comments * select @col.Process chrome select @Request.Accept html

		`select @Response.Set-Cookie` `httponly`

`>size`	Select Sessions whose response size is greater than *size* bytes.
	
	 Note: the character "k" is converted to "000", allowing you to easily specify sizes in kilobytes or megabytes.
		`>40000000`
		 `>4000k`
		 `>4KK`

`<size`	Select Sessions whose response size is less than *size* bytes. Note: the character "k" is converted to "000".	`<5k`
`@host`	Select Sessions whose request `Host` header contains the specified *host*.	`@example.com` `@.gov`
`=ResponseCode`	Select Sessions where the response's status code matches the provided value.	`=200` `=404`
`=Method`	Select Sessions where the request's HTTP method matches the provided value.	`=GET` `=POST`

Beyond selecting traffic, QuickExec also has built-in support for other commands:

`cols add flagname`
 	
 `cols add title flagname`
	Add a new column to the Web Sessions list (for this instance only). The `title` parameter is optional; if not present, the column will be titled with the `flagname` parameter. The `flagname` can either represent a Session Flag, or a request or response header name.
	
	 After a column is added, it will be filled automatically for all subsequent Sessions. To update the columns of already completed Sessions, select them and hit F5.
		`cols add x-clientIP`
		
		 `cols add Server`
		 `  @Response.Server`
		
		 `cols add Accept`
		 `  @Request.Accept`

`!listen port`
 `[SubjectCN]`
	Start a new proxy listener object on the specified *port*. This listener's Sessions will be added to the Web Sessions list. The listener instance is automatically configured to permit remote connections.
	
	 If the `CN` parameter is present, all inbound connections on this listener will automatically invoke a HTTPS handshake;
		`!listen 8889`
		
		 `!listen 4443`
		 `  secure.example.com`

	Fiddler will present a certificate containing the specified *SubjectCN*. This feature is useful when Fiddler is being used as a reverse proxy for a HTTPS site.	
`!dns hostname` `!nslookup hostname`	Perform a DNS lookup (or consult Fiddler's cache) for the specified *hostname*, showing the results in the Log tab.	`!dns example.com`
`!ping hostname`	Performs a network ping request to the target host or IP and records its progress in the Log tab.	`!ping example.com`
`!lm [substring]`	Log information about all of the loaded .NET assemblies. If a *substring* is provided, only assemblies whose filenames contain the specified string are shown.	`!lm formats`
`prefs show [substring]`	Display all of Fiddler's configured Preferences in a message box. If a *substring* is provided, only preferences containing that substring are shown.	`prefs show` `prefs show composer`
`prefs remove name`	Delete a Preference with the specified *name*. The next time the Preference is consulted, the default value will be used.	`prefs remove` `  fiddler.ui.font.size`

`prefs set name value`	Update or create a Preference with the specified *name* and *value*.	`prefs set`
		`  fiddler.differ.UltraDiff`
		`  False`

`prefs log`	Write all of Fiddler's configured Preferences to the Log tab, enabling you to easily copy them.	
`!spew`	Toggle "DebugSpew" mode, used mostly for debugging problems with Fiddler itself. In DebugSpew mode, Fiddler will log verbose logging information (including all raw traffic) to the system's debug port. You can monitor this information using SysInternals' DebugView tool. Fiddler will also log some additional information to Fiddler's Log tab while this mode is active. Type `!spew` again or restart Fiddler to disable DebugSpew.	
`about:cache`	Log information about Fiddler's listening port number and the contents of its connection-reuse and DNS caches to the Log tab.	
`about:config`	Display Fiddler's Preference configuration tab, which lists all configured preferences and their values.	
`about:connectoids` `about:network`	Add information about the WinINET-configured connections to the Log tab.	
`toolbar`	Show the Fiddler Toolbar if it was hidden.	
`tearoff`	Remove the Inspectors from the main Fiddler window and show them in a	

	floating window instead.

If the command entered in QuickExec does not match any of the intrinsic commands listed above, Fiddler-Script and Fiddler Extensions have the opportunity to respond to the command.

Default FiddlerScript Commands

The default FiddlerScript file used by Fiddler adds a number of useful commands that can be launched from the QuickExec box.

Command	Action	Example
bold *urltext*	Apply font bolding to any future Session whose URL contains the specified text. Type bold with no parameter to disable this formatting.	bold uploaddata.asp
bps *status*	Create a response breakpoint for any Session whose response status code matches the specified value. Type bps with no parameter to disable the breakpoint.	bps 404
bpm *method*	Create a request breakpoint for any Session whose HTTP Method matches the specified value. Type bpm with no parameter to disable the breakpoint.	bpm POST bpm OPTIONS
bpu *urltext*	Create a request breakpoint for any Session whose URL contains the specified text. Type bpu with no parameter to disable the breakpoint.	bpu uploaddata.asp
bpafter *urltext*	Create a response breakpoint for any session whose URL contains the specified text. Type bpafter with no parameter to disable the breakpoint.	bpafter dodownload.cgi
nuke	Clear the WinINET cache and cookies.	nuke
tail ####	Trim the Web Sessions list so that it contains no more than the specified number of Sessions.	tail 200
log *string*	Send the specified text or macro to the Log tab.	log "At this point, requests start failing" log @Log.Save
cls	Clear the Web Sessions list.	cls
dump	Store all captured traffic to dump.saz in the \Captures\ folder.	dump
g	Immediately resume all Sessions currently paused at breakpoints.	g
help	Show online help for QuickExec.	help
urlreplace	Replace the specified substring in later	urlreplace jQuery.min jQuery.dbg

`oldtext` `newtext`	requests' URLs with the provided string. Type `urlreplace` with no parameters to stop replacements.	

`overridehost`
`oldhost`
`newhost`
	Retarget requests so that they are sent to a different host. Type `overridehost` with no parameters to stop retargeting.	`overridehost`
		`production.example.com`
		`dev.internal.example.com`

`start`	Enable capturing mode, registering Fiddler as the system proxy.	`start`
`stop`	Disable capturing mode, unregistering Fiddler as the system proxy.	`stop`
`keeponly` `MIMEtype`	Clear the Web Sessions list of all Sessions whose responses do not specify the supplied MIMEtype.	`keeponly video/`
`quit`	Exit Fiddler.	`quit`

You can see the full list of FiddlerScript commands (and add your own) by editing your FiddlerScript. Simply click **Rules** > **Customize Rules**, and scroll to the `OnExecAction` method.

Many of the commands above are provided to permit lightweight automation of Fiddler using the `ExecAction.exe` utility included with Fiddler and discussed later in this book.

Extensions often add support for additional commands to QuickExec—check your extensions' documentation for more information.

APPLICATION HOTKEYS

The QuickExec feature provides powerful keyboard support, but Fiddler offers additional hotkeys for keyboard lovers.

Fiddler registers a system-wide hotkey, CTRL+ALT+F to activate Fiddler regardless of what application is active. This hotkey may be changed to another using the **Tools > Fiddler Options** > **General** tab.

Beyond its global hotkey, Fiddler supports a number of hotkeys that should always be available when Fiddler is active:

ALT+Q	Set focus to the QuickExec box
CTRL+R	Open the FiddlerScript Rules editor
CTRL+E	Open the TextWizard
CTRL+Down	Select the next Session in the Web Sessions list
CTRL+Up	Select the previous Session in the Web Sessions list
CTRL+T	Activate the TextView Inspectors
CTRL+H	Activate the Headers Inspectors
CTRL+0	Set the font size to 8.25pt (the default)
CTRL+Plus	Increase the font size by 1pt (up to 32pt)
CTRL+Minus	Decrease the font size by 1pt (down to 7pt)
CTRL+M	Minimize Fiddler
CTRL+SHIFT+DEL	Clear the WinINET cache
F12	Toggle registration as the system proxy

FiddlerScript and Extensions may add new system-wide hotkeys using the RegisterCustomHotkey method, which binds a hotkey to a QuickExec command.

STATISTICS TAB

Fiddler's Statistics tab shows basic information about the currently selected Web Sessions. Textual information is shown at the top of the tab, while the bottom contains a pie chart showing a MIME-type breakdown of the traffic.

When multiple Sessions are selected, the data shown includes:

Request Count	Number of Sessions selected.
Unique Hosts	Count of unique hosts to which this traffic was sent. This field will not be shown if all selected traffic was sent to the same server.
Bytes sent	Total number of outbound bytes in the HTTP Request headers and bodies. The number of bytes for each is shown parenthetically after the total count.
Bytes received	Total number of inbound bytes in the HTTP Request headers and bodies. The number of bytes for each is shown parenthetically after the total count.
Requests started at	Time that the first byte of the first request was received by Fiddler.
Responses completed at	Time that the last byte of the last response was sent by Fiddler to the client application.
Sequence (clock) duration	"Clock time" between the start of the first request and the end of the last response.
Aggregate Session duration	Sum of all selected Sessions' overall time from request to response. Because sessions are usually running in parallel, this time can be longer than the amount of "clock time" taken. Similarly, because Sessions may be selected that were started and finished with idle time between them, this time can be much shorter than the amount of "clock time" between the first and last Session.
DNS Lookup time	Total amount of time spent in DNS resolution for all selected Sessions. This field is not shown if no time was spent on DNS resolution because the DNS cache handled all requests, or all connections had already been established.
TCP/IP Connect duration	Total time spent in establishing TCP/IP connections for all selected Sessions. This field is not shown if no time was spent on TCP/IP connections because all requests were sent on reused connections.
HTTPS Handshake duration	Total time spent in HTTPS handshaking for all selected Sessions. This field is not shown if no time was spent on HTTPS handshakes because all Sessions were HTTP, decryption is disabled, or all requests were sent on previously-secured connections.

Response Codes	List of unique HTTP response codes with a counter of how many times each was received.
Response Bytes by Content-Type	Count of bytes for each response Content-Type in the selected Sessions. This information is also presented in a pie chart at the bottom of the tab.
Requests Per Host	List of unique hosts with a counter of requests sent to each. This field will not be shown if all selected traffic was sent to the same server.
Estimated Performance	Very rough estimates of how long the selected traffic would spend on the network from different locales or when utilizing a variety of connection types. This data is simply calculated by looking at the number and size of the selected Sessions. There are many factors that impact real-world network performance, so the estimates shown here may be wildly inaccurate.

If only a single Session is selected, the Timers for that Session are shown. If the selected Session was recorded on a previous day, the date that the traffic was captured will also be listed-- this can be helpful when examining SAZ files captured by automated logging tools.

If a single CONNECT tunnel is selected, the number of bytes sent and received on that tunnel will be shown (unless the tunnel is configured for HTTPS decryption, in which case this information can be approximated using the decrypted HTTPS Sessions in the Web Sessions list.)

Hidden by default, the bottom of the tab contains a pie chart. Click the **Show Chart** link to show a chart that categorizes the response content of the selected Sessions. A slice is shown for the headers and each MIME type in the selected traffic; the size of the slice is based on the number of bytes of that type.

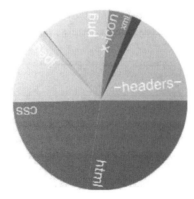

The **Copy this chart** link at the bottom-left copies the chart image to your clipboard as a bitmap, suitable for pasting into reports or presentations.

FILTERS TAB

The Filters tab provides a "point-and-click" means of applying simple filters against traffic as it is captured. Every setting on the tab can be mimicked in FiddlerScript (usually more precisely or powerfully) but for simple jobs, the Filters tab will probably meet your filtering needs.

The **Use Filters** checkbox at the top-left of the tab enables the filters listed below to run against traffic as it is captured. When **Use Filters** is checked, the options below it can be adjusted to control whether a given Session:

- Is hidden
- Is flagged in the Web Sessions list
- Is breakpointed for manual tampering
- Is blocked from being sent
- Has its headers modified automatically

Note that Fiddler continues to modify and proxy traffic from hidden Sessions, even though they aren't shown in the Web Sessions list. After processing is completed, hidden Sessions are removed from Fiddler (and cannot be recovered) in order to limit memory usage.

The **Actions** button at the top-right of the tab allows you to save the currently selected filters as a Filterset, to load a previously saved Filterset, and to run the *current* Filters against *previously-captured* traffic in the Web Sessions list. The Help option launches a help topic about the Filters tab.

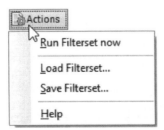

Each group of filtering options is described below.

Hosts
The Hosts box provides filters that are based on the hostname of the request.

The **Zone Filter** dropdown allows you to show traffic only to your Intranet (e.g. dotless hostnames) or only to the Internet (e.g. dotted hostnames). This is a useful option when debugging a site in one zone while referencing web-based documentation from the other zone.

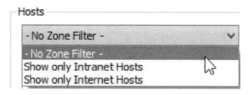

The **Host Filter** dropdown enables you to flag or hide traffic to domain names specified in the textbox under the dropdown.

You may specify multiple hosts by including a semicolon between each.

Subdomains are not wildcarded automatically. That means that if you have "Show only the following Hosts" set and only `fiddler2.com` is in the list, you will not see traffic to `www.fiddler2.com`. To instead see traffic to subdomains, add a wildcard like `*.fiddler2.com`. This wildcarded entry will include traffic to `test.fiddler2.com` and `sub.fiddler2.com`, and so on. If you also want to see traffic to the root domain `fiddler2.com`, change the wildcard to `*fiddler2.com`— this will include traffic to any domain that ends with `fiddler2.com` without requiring a leading dot.

When the background of the text box is yellow, it means your changes have not yet been applied. Click anywhere outside the box to save changes to the list.

Client Process

Process filters allow you to control which processes' traffic is shown within Fiddler. Fiddler can only determine which process issued a given request when the application process is running on the same computer as Fiddler itself.

The **Show only traffic from** dropdown contains a list of all currently-running processes on the system; select a process to show only traffic from that specific process.

The **Show only Internet Explorer** traffic option hides traffic unless the process' executable name begins with `IE` or the request bears a User-Agent header containing `compatible; MSIE`.

The **Hide traffic from Service Host** option will hide traffic from `svchost.exe`, a system process that synchronizes RSS Feeds and performs other background network activity.

Note that some client security software may interfere with Fiddler's Process Filtering options by routing all outbound requests through the security software's own process first (e.g. `tmproxy.exe` or `avp.exe` are common culprits).

Request Headers

Using these options, you can add or remove request headers, or flag requests that contain certain headers.

The **Show only if URL contains** box allows you to hide requests whose URL does not contain a required string. You can demand case-sensitivity using the `EXACT` prefix:

```
EXACT:example.com/q=Case+Sensitive+String
```

…or you can use a regular expression:

```
REGEX:(?inx).*\.(gif|png|jpg)$ #only show image requests
```

You may enter multiple strings delimited by a space:

```
Term1 EXACT:Term2 REGEX:.*term3$
```

The **Hide if URL contains** box allows you to hide requests whose URL contains a given string. You can use the `EXACT` and `REGEX` prefixes, and delimit multiple terms using a space.

The **Flag requests with headers** option allows you to specify one or more HTTP request header names, that if present, will cause the Session to be bolded in the Web Sessions list. Header names can be delimited by a space, comma or semicolon.

The **Delete request headers** option allows you to name one or more HTTP headers that, if present, will be removed from the request headers.

The **Set request header** option allows you to create or update a request header with the value you specify.

Breakpoints

The breakpoints box enables you to break requests or responses that match the specified attributes.

Break request on POST option will set a request breakpoint for any request whose method is `POST`. The **Break request on GET with QueryString** option will set a request breakpoint for any `GET` request whose URL contains a query string.

The **Break on XMLHttpRequest** option will set a request breakpoint for any request that can be determined to have been issued by the XMLHttpRequest object. Because requests issued by the XMLHttpRequest object are generally not distinguishable from other types of traffic, this feature looks for an `X-Requested-With` header (added by the jQuery framework). It will also check for an `X-Download-Initiator` header which Internet Explorer 10 and later can be configured to send.

The **Break response on Content-Type** option will set a response breakpoint for any response whose Content-Type response header contains the specified text.

Response Status Code

Using these options, you can filter display of Sessions based on the response's status code.

The **Hide success** option will hide any response whose status code is between 200 and 299 inclusive. These response codes are used to indicate a successful request. The **Hide non-2xx** option will hide any response whose status code is not between 200 and 299 inclusive.

The **Hide Authentication demands** option will hide responses with the 401 and 407 status codes used to prompt the client for credentials.

The **Hide redirects** option will hide HTTP/30x responses that redirect the request.

The **Hide Not Modified** option will hide responses with the 304 status code. This status is sent in response to a conditional validation request to indicate that the client's cached entity remains fresh.

Response Type and Size

Using these options, you can control what types of responses appear within the Web Sessions list, and block responses matching certain criteria.

The **Type dropdown** list allows you to hide Sessions whose response does not match a specified type.

- **Show all Content-Types** performs no filtering.
- **Show only IMAGE/*** hides Sessions whose Content-Type header does not specify an image type.
- **Show only HTML** hides Sessions whose Content-Type does not specify an HTML type.
- **Show only TEXT/CSS** hides Sessions whose Content-Type does not specify the text/css type.
- **Show only SCRIPTS** hides Sessions whose Content-Type does not specify a script type.
- **Show only XML** hides Sessions whose Content-Type does not specify an XML type.
- **Show only JSON** hides Sessions whose Content-Type does not specify a JSON type.
- **Hide IMAGE/*** hides Sessions whose Content-Type specifies an image type.

The **Hide smaller than** option allows you to hide responses whose bodies are smaller than the specified number of kilobytes. The **Hide larger than** option allows you to hide responses whose bodies are larger than the size specified.

The **Time HeatMap** checkbox sets a background color for each Session based on how long the server took to return a given response completely (computed using the Timers object: ServerDoneResponse - FiddlerBeginRequest). Responses that take less than 50 milliseconds show in shades of green. Responses that take between 50 and 300 milliseconds are not colored. Responses that take between 300 and 500 milliseconds show in yellow. Responses that take more than 500 milliseconds show in shades of red.

The **Block script files** option will return a HTTP/404 response instead of the returned response if the response declared a script Content-Type. The **Block image files** option will return a 404 response if the response declared an image type. The **Block SWF files** option will return a 404 response if the response declared an Adobe Flash (application/x-shockwave-flash) type. The **Block CSS files** option will return a 404 response if the response declared a CSS type.

Response Headers

Using these options, you can add or remove response headers, or flag responses that contain certain headers.

The **Flag responses that set cookies** option will mark in bold any response that contains a Set-Cookie header.

The **Flag responses with headers** option allows you to specify one or more HTTP header names that, if present, will cause the Session to be bolded in the Web Sessions list. Header names can be delimited by a space, comma or semicolon.

The **Delete response headers** option allows you to name one or more HTTP headers that, if present, will be removed from the response headers.

The **Set response header** option allows you to create or update a HTTP response header with the value you specify.

TIMELINE TAB

This tab renders the timing of between 1 and 500 selected Sessions as a "waterfall" diagram, useful both for Performance analysis and to understand how requests relate to one another. The bulk of the tab is the timeline of the selected traffic. Across the top of the tab is the title which displays the mode ("Transfer Timeline", by default). The Help link at the top-right opens a help topic about the feature.

Right-click in the body of the tab to see the context menu. It exposes the following options:

AutoScale Chart	When enabled, the chart is scaled such that the entire chart fits in the horizontal width of the tab without a horizontal scrollbar.
Copy Chart	Click to copy the chart to the clipboard in bitmap format, suitable for pasting into reports or presentations.
Mode (dropdown)	Control what information the chart displays: • **Timeline** – display each Session on its own line, with a colored bar representing its duration. • **Client Pipe Map** – Display each connection between a client program and Fiddler on its own line. • **Server Pipe Map** – Display each connection between Fiddler and an up-stream server on its own line. The Client Pipe Map and Server Pipe Map modes show how the client and server reuse connections, which can be useful in identifying performance bottlenecks. Connections which were reused for multiple Sessions will display multiple bars on a single line.

The Timeline tab does not presently display any CONNECT tunnels because the traffic flowing through such tunnels is either opaque or tracked by one or more decrypted HTTPS Web Session entries.

Mode: Timeline

In this mode, Fiddler will show each selected Session on its own line, with filename extracted from the URL written to the left of the transfer bar. Hovering over any entry will show more information about the entry in the status bar at the bottom of the tab. Hold SHIFT while clicking an entry to inspect the Session in a new window. Double-click an entry to unselect all others and inspect the single chosen Session using the main window.

The color of the text is green if the request was conditional (e.g. revalidating a cached response), or black if the request was unconditional. The bar's color is determined by the MIME type of the response; light-green for images, dark-green for JavaScript, purple for CSS, and blue otherwise.

TRANSFER TIMELINE

The start of the transfer bar is drawn at the time when the client sends the request to Fiddler (Timers.ClientBeginRequest). The end of the bar is drawn at the time when the response to the client is completed (Timers.ClientDoneResponse). If the bar is "hatched" rather than smooth, this indicates that the response was buffered by Fiddler rather than being streamed to the client as it was read from the server. Buffering alters the waterfall diagram, as you can see in the Timeline below— when buffering is enabled, none of the images begin to download until their containing page completes:

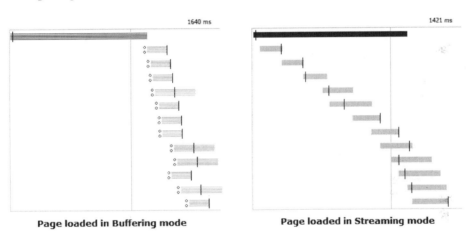

Page loaded in Buffering mode   Page loaded in Streaming mode

The black vertical line in the bar indicates the time to first byte of the server's response (Timers.ServerBeginResponse). The two small circles before the bar indicate whether the Session was transmitted on reused connections. The top circle represents the client's connection to Fiddler; the bottom circle represents Fiddler's connection to the server. A green circle shows that a connection was reused while a red circle means that the connection was newly created.

A red X icon ˣ after the bar indicates that the server sent a Connection: close header (or failed to send a Connection: Keep-Alive header for a HTTP/1.0 response), preventing subsequent reuse of the connection. The gray arrow icon 🔽 indicates that the server's response was a redirect (302). The red ! icon ⚠ indicates that the server returned an error code (4xx, 5xx). The green lightning bolt icon ⚡ indicates that the response was generated by Fiddler (for instance, as the result of an AutoResponder or script rule, or a connection failure).

Note: In an upcoming release of Fiddler, selecting just one Session will instead chart the arrival times of each of the chunks of response data read from the server. This feature is not yet complete.

Mode: Client Pipe Map

In this mode, the Timeline will show each inbound connection from a client on its own line. At the left edge of the chart is the connection identifier, which shows the process name, process ID, and client port number. For instance, `iexplore:1364(p14421)` identifies that the client was Internet Explorer process number 1364, using port 14421 to connect to Fiddler. Connections reused for multiple Sessions will display multiple bars on the same line:

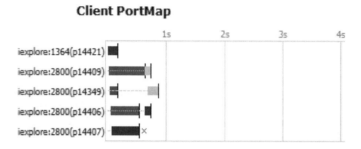

Mode: Server Pipe Map

In this mode, the Timeline will show each outbound connection from Fiddler to a server on its own line. At the left edge of the chart is the connection identifier, which shows the outbound port number and the hostname of the target server. For instance `p14357->twimgs.com` indicates that Fiddler used local port 14357 to establish a connection to port 80 on `twimgs.com`. Connections reused for multiple Sessions will display multiple bars on the same line:

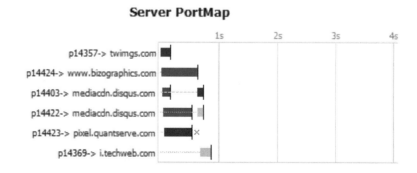

Using the Timeline for Performance Analysis

The Timeline tab provides an information-rich view of how your application is using the network. You can easily identify slow requests (long bars), bottlenecks where requests are blocked due to connection limits (stair-step groups of six parallel requests), and cases where connections were unnecessarily closed (red X icons). Using this information, you may be able to adjust your application to better order requests and optimize network performance.

AUTORESPONDER TAB

This tab exposes some of the most powerful functionality in Fiddler. It permits you to create **rules** that will automatically trigger in response to requests, typically reacting by returning a previously-captured response without hitting the server. This capability enables you to quickly test changes to web code without updating the production server, reproduce bugs previously captured in SAZ files, or even run website demos while entirely offline.

Across the top of the tab are a set of options which control the AutoResponder's behavior, while most of the tab contains the **Rules List** that maps inbound **Match Conditions** to **Actions**.

The **Enable automatic responses** checkbox controls whether the AutoResponder is active. When this option is unchecked, the rest of the tab is disabled.

The **Unmatched requests passthrough** option controls what happens when a Session does not match any of the specified rules. When ticked, unmatched requests are sent to the server normally, without interference from the AutoResponder. When unticked, Fiddler will generate a HTTP/404 Not Found response for any *unconditional* request that does not match any of the rules. If a client sends an unmatched *conditional* request containing If-None-Match or If-Modified-Since headers, the AutoResponder will instead return a HTTP/304 Not Modified response.

The **Enable Latency** option controls whether requests that match a rule are acted upon immediately, or if the action is delayed by the number of milliseconds specified in the rule's **Latency** column. The Latency column is hidden when latency is disabled. Enable the option to more accurately simulate a real-world server's response times, or disable the option for faster performance.

The **Add Rule** button adds a new rule to the AutoResponder list. By default, the Match Condition is the URL of the currently-selected Session in the Web Sessions list.

The **Import** button allows you to import a previously-captured SAZ file; each Session in the imported file will be used to generate a new rule in the Rules list. You can also import a FARX file which contains rules exported from the AutoResponder tab.

The center of the tab is a list that contains the rules. The first column specifies the **Match Condition** used to determine if an incoming request matches the rule. The checkbox preceding the Match Condition's text controls whether the rule is enabled. The second column contains the action to undertake if the rule is matched. The **Action Text** may specify a local filename to return, or may specify another type of action.

When a rule is selected, the **Rule Editor** box at the bottom of the tab enables you to adjust the rule's Match Condition and Action Text. The **Test** link allows you to test your Match Condition against the sample URL of your choice; this feature can be helpful if your regular expression skills are rusty. The **Match only once** checkbox controls whether the rule will automatically disable itself after it triggers once; this is useful for scenarios where a single URL returns different results if it is requested more than once.

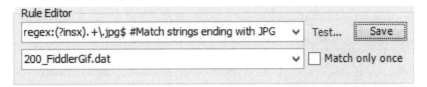

After making any changes to the Match Condition or Action Text, click the **Save** button to update the rule. If you select multiple rules, the Rule Editor will hide the Match Condition box and provide the option to set all selected rules' Action Text at once. This capability allows you to easily specify multiple rules that trigger the same response.

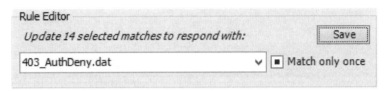

Specify the Match Condition

By default, the Match Condition performs a case-insensitive match against the request URL. So, if you want a rule to match any request whose URL contains the word `fuzzle`, simply type `fuzzle` in the box. The rule will match any of the following URLs:

```
http://fuzzle.bunnies.com
http://bunnies.fuzzle.net
http://example.com/Fuzzle/
http://example.com/search?q=FuZzLe
```

A Match Condition of * will match all inbound requests.

By specifying the `NOT:` prefix, a rule will match any request URL that does not case-insensitively contain the provided string. So, if you want a rule to match any URL that does not contain the word `fuzzle`, simply type `NOT:fuzzle` in the box. Unless the text `fuzzle` is found anywhere in the request's URL (case-insensitively), the rule will match.

By specifying the `EXACT:` prefix, you can require that the URL exactly match the Match Condition, case-sensitively. So, a rule of `EXACT:http://example.com/a/` will match:

```
http://example.com/a/
```

…but it will not match any of the following URLs:

```
http://example.com/A/
```

```
https://example.com/a/
http://example.com/b/
http://example.com/a/otherstuff
```

By specifying the `REGEX:` prefix, you can provide a regular expression against which the request URL will be evaluated. Expressions are evaluated using the .NET regular expression engine.

There are many great books that explain how to develop powerful regular expressions; this book is not one of them. I recommend `http://fiddler2.com/r/?RegExHelp` to get started. A few sample regular expression rules are:

Rule	Matches
`REGEX:.+`	Any URL of one or more characters
`REGEX:.+\.jpg.*`	Any URL that contains `.jpg` after at least one other character
`REGEX:.+\.jpg$`	Any URL that ends with `.jpg`
`REGEX:.+\.(jpg|gif|png)$`	Any URL that ends with `.jpg` or `.gif` or `.png`
`REGEX:^https.+$`	Any URL that begins with `https`
`REGEX:(?inx).*\.(jpg|gif|png)$`	Any URL that ends with `.jpg` or `.gif` or `.png`, case-insensitively

You can specify regular expression options (like case-sensitivity) by prefixing the expression with an appropriate declaration. The option string (`?inx`) works well; it turns on case-insensitivity, requires explicit capture groups, and enables comments after the # character. Comments are useful to combat regular expressions' "write once, read never" nature. Without an informative comment, you may quickly forget what your carefully-crafted regular expression was meant to match.

Match Request Method

Rules may be constrained to apply to only particular methods. For instance, to take action only when a HTTP Request using the `DELETE` method is sent to `Manage.aspx`, use the following Match Condition:

```
Method:DELETE Manage.aspx
```

The URL component may be a partial string, or an `Exact`, `Not`, or `RegEx` expression, like so:

```
Method:DELETE REGEX:.+\.cgi.*
```

To apply a rule to all requests that use the `DELETE` method, simply omit the URL component.

```
Method:DELETE
```

Match Session Flags

Rules may be constrained to match only Sessions with a particular flag set. For instance, to take action only when the `X-ProcessInfo` flag contains `iexplore`, use the Match Condition:

```
Flag:X-ProcessInfo=iexplore
```

To apply the rule if the flag is present with *any* value, omit the flag's value:

```
Flag:X-ProcessInfo
```

Match Request Headers

Rules may require that the Request contain a specified header value. For instance, to take action only when a Request contains the ACCEPT header and whose value contains image/, use the Match Condition:

```
Header:Accept=image/
```

To apply the rule to all requests bearing an ACCEPT header, simply omit the value:

```
Header:Accept
```

Match Request Bodies

In some cases, a site may use the same request URL for many unrelated operations, specifying the operation desired in the request's body instead of the URL. You may extend your Match Condition to examine a POST or PUT request's body by specifying the URLWithBody: prefix for your Match Condition. When this prefix is used, the portion of the string up to the first space character is used as the Match Condition for the request's URL, while the remainder of the string is used as a Match Condition for the string-representation of the request's body. For performance reasons, you should specify the URL portion of the Match Condition as narrowly as possible to minimize the number of request bodies that the AutoResponder needs to evaluate. If a request has no body, it will not match any URLWithBody rule.

Your Match Condition may specify the EXACT:, NOT:, and REGEX: prefixes for both the URL and the body. For example:

```
URLWithBody:upload.php TextToFindInBody
URLWithBody:login.php EXACT:Action=Login
URLWithBody:ping.php NOT:POST Data I Do Not Care About
URLWithBody:EXACT:https://example.com/upload.php REGEX:^.+TextToFind.*$
URLWithBody:REGEX:^.+/upload.php.*$ REGEX:^.+TailOfPOST$
```

Keep in mind that most POSTs from Web Forms encode the body text, so you should ensure that your Match Condition accounts for such encoding. For instance, to match the following POST:

```
POST http://www.enhanceie.com/sandbox/FileForm.asp HTTP/1.1
Content-Type: application/x-www-form-urlencoded
Content-Length: 54

2=This+is+some+text&fileentry2=&_charset_=windows-1252
```

Your Match Condition should be:

```
URLWithBody:/sandbox/FileForm.asp This+is+some+text
```

"Dice Roll" Matches

By prefixing your Match Condition with a percentage (1% to 99%) you can randomly apply the rule to just the specified percentage of matching requests. This feature is useful to simulate random network failures or slowness. For instance, you could create a rule with a Match Condition of

```
25%Example.com/Script.js
```

...and Action Text of *delay:1000 to delay one in four requests for the specified script. Or, you could create a rule of 5%* with Action Text *drop to cause one in twenty requests to fail.

Specify the Action Text

The Action Text defines the behavior when a Match Condition is hit. The Action may involve returning content, redirecting the request, or performing some other action.

Any Action may be either **Final** or **Non-Final**. Non-Final Actions allow a request to match multiple rules. As soon a rule specifying a Final action is reached, the matching process exits and no further rules are processed for that Session. Rules are evaluated in the order that they appear, so you should adjust the order of the rules to match your needs.

The available Actions are:

Action Text	Explanation	Final?
filename	Return contents of *filename* as the response.	yes
http://targetURL	Return the contents of the *targetURL* as the response. This action retargets the request to a different URL without informing the client application.	yes
redir:http://targetURL	Return a HTTP/307 Redirect to the target URL. Unlike a plain URL, using the *redir prefix ensures that the client knows where its request is going, so it can send the correct cookies, etc.	yes
*bpu	Set a request breakpoint.	no
*bpafter	Set a response breakpoint.	no
*delay:####	Delay sending request to the server by the specified number of milliseconds.	no
*CORSPreflightAllow	Respond to a Cross-Origin-Resource-Sharing (CORS) preflight request, granting the client permission to access the target resource. Use with a Match Condition like: METHOD:OPTIONS *example.com*	yes
*ReplyWithTunnel	Respond with a HTTP/200 tunnel, through which subsequent HTTPS requests will flow. Use with a Match Condition that limits to CONNECT requests, like so:	yes

	METHOD:CONNECT *secure.example.com*	
*header:*name=value*	Set a *Request* header to a specified value. For instance, use `*header:Cache-Control=no-cache` to indicate that a server or proxy should not return a cached response. Leave the `value` blank to delete the named header.	no
*flag:*flagname=value*	Set a Session Flag to a specified value. For instance, use `*flag:ui-bold=1` to bold the item in the Web Sessions list. Leave the `value` blank to delete the specified Session Flag.	no
*drop	Close the client connection immediately without sending a response. The closure is *graceful* at the TCP/IP level, returning a `FIN` to the client.	yes
*reset	Close the client connection immediately without sending a response. The closure is abrupt at the TCP/IP level, returning a `RST` to the client.	yes

*script:*funcname*	Invokes a function of the specified name in the FiddlerScript file. For example:
	
	`public static function RunAsARFilter(oS: Session)`
	`{`
	`   oS["ui-backcolor"] = "red";`
	`}`
	
	Functions whose names contain the word `filter` cause the rule to be treated as non-Final, allowing subsequent rules to apply.
		maybe

*exit	Stop processing rules.	yes

The **Find a file...** option in the Actions dropdown displays a file picker to allow you to select a filename that should be returned. The **Create New Response...** option will display a standalone Inspector window to allow you to compose a new response to return to the client.

The AutoResponder is most commonly used to return a local file from disk. When the specified file is loaded, Fiddler looks for a set of HTTP headers at the start of the file. If present, those headers are used as the response headers, with the remainder of the file returned as the response body. If no headers are found, Fiddler automatically generates a set of default headers and returns the entire file as the response body.

When the AutoResponder returns a response, the Session is shown with a Lavender background in the Web Sessions list.

Use RegEx Replacements in Action Text

Fiddler's AutoResponder permits you to use regular expression group replacements to map text from the Match Condition into the Action Text. For instance, the rule:

Match Text	Action Text
REGEX:.+/assets/(.*)	http://example.com/mockup/$1

…will map a request for `http://example.com/assets/Test1.gif` to `http://example.com/mockup` `/Test1.gif`.

The following rule:

Match Text	Action Text
REGEX:.+example\.com.*	http://proxy.webdbg.com/p.cgi?url=$0

…will rewrite the inbound URL so that all URLs containing `example.com` are passed as a URL parameter to a page on `proxy.webdbg.com`.

Many sites serve up "crunched" or "minified" versions of their scripts on production servers, but also keep the original version of the script available for debugging purposes. For instance, the crunched version of a script will be at the URL:

    http://example.com/main/js/main_c.js

…and the uncrunched version will be available at:

    http://example.com/main/js/main.js

You can write a RegEx replacement rule that maps requests for the crunched version to the original version like so:

Match Text	Action Text
REGEX:(?inx)^http://example.com(?'path'.+)_c\.js$	http://example.com${path}.js

This rule captures the path to the file in the variable named `path`. That variable is later used to replace the `${path}` token in the Action Text. Beyond changing the URL's host or path, you can create similar rules that modify, add, or remove query string parameters.

When mapping URLs to local files, the replacement functionality is smart enough to swap forward-slashes for backslashes, so the rule:

Match Text	Action Text
REGEX:(?inx).+/assets/(?'fname'[^?]*).*	C:\src\${fname}

…maps a request for `http://example.com/assets/img/1.png?bunnies` to `C:\src\img\1.png`.

Drag-and-Drop support

The AutoResponder allows you to easily create new AutoResponder rules using drag-and-drop. You can drag-and-drop files or folders full of files from Windows Explorer to automatically generate rules for those files. Alternatively, you can drag-drop Sessions from the Web Sessions list to reuse responses captured previously. You may edit a rule's stored response by selecting the rule and hitting `Enter` or by selecting the **Edit Response** item on the rule's context menu.

Work with the Rules List

The context menu on the Rules list exposes the following commands:

Remove	Delete the selected rules. Alternatively, select one or more rules and press `Delete`.
Promote	Move the rule one slot earlier in the list. Alternatively, select one rule and press the `Plus` key.
Demote	Move the rule one slot later in the list. Alternatively, select one rule and press the `Minus` key.
Clone	Append a copy of the current rule the list.
Set Latency…	Prompts you for a number of milliseconds to use as a latency value when the rule is matched. For instance, if you specify `50` for a rule where the Action Text is a local filename, Fiddler will wait 50 milliseconds before returning the specified file as the response. You may specify a leading + or - indicator if you wish to adjust the rule's current latency value rather than setting it to an absolute value; this capability is useful when adjusting the latency of multiple rules simultaneously.
Set Comment…	Assign a comment to describe the current rule.
Edit Response…	If the rule is backed by a file, open that file for editing. If the rule is backed by a previously-captured response, open a standalone Inspectors window to enable editing.
Generate File	If the rule is backed by a previously-captured response, save that response to a file and adjust the rule to point to it. Use this command when you want to edit a response using a standalone editor like Expression Web or Visual Studio.
Edit File With…	Edit the rule's response using an editor you select. Use this command to edit a response using a standalone editor which is not the default program for handling the saved response's file type.
Open URL…	Open the URL specified in the Match Condition using the default web browser.
Find…	Highlight in yellow any rules containing the specified Action or Match Condition text.
Export All…	Save the current set of rules to a FARX file. This file can be later imported to reload the rules.

Press `CTRL+C` to copy the Match Condition and Action Text for the selected rule(s). Press `CTRL+U` to copy only the URL specified in the Match Condition (if any) from the first selected rule. Press `CTRL+A` to select all of the rules.

FARX Files

Fiddler AutoResponder XML (FARX) files contain a set of AutoResponder rules. Your current set of AutoResponder rules is automatically saved on exit and reloaded when you restart Fiddler. This automatically-saved file is named `AutoResponder.xml`, but if you use the Export command to save a separate file, it will have a `.farx` file extension.

FARX files contain the full set of rules, including any previously captured responses used for playback.

Binary responses are base64-encoded and compressed to help reduce the size of the file, but a large set of AutoResponder rules (or a small set of rules with large responses) can cause a FARX file to grow very large. Because your default set of AutoResponder rules is automatically reloaded when Fiddler starts up, a large default FARX file can make Fiddler slow to start. To avoid problems with slow startup, export large rule sets to a FARX file of your choosing and then remove those rules from your default list before closing Fiddler.

Playback Mode

When using the AutoResponder to "play back" captured traffic, you might prefer not to play back *exactly* the same responses. For instance, if the traffic capture contains HTTP/401 or HTTP/407 authentication challenges, you may not want those responses to play back as they could interfere with debugging. Similarly, you probably wish to permit CONNECT tunnels to succeed even if the target server is unreachable from your PC, since subsequent rules may supply the necessary HTTPS responses.

To increase the success rate of using the AutoResponder to playback previously captured traffic, use **SAZ for Playback** Mode when importing a previously-captured SAZ file. To import a SAZ file in Playback mode, click the **Import...** button in the AutoResponder. In the **Import File** dialog box, choose **SAZ for Playback** from the Type dropdown:

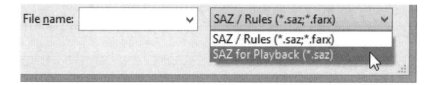

In addition to handling authentication and tunnels, the Playback mode importer also sets the **Match only once** option for Rules where more than one response for a given URL was imported, and it generates more precise Match Conditions when generating rules for requests bearing a SOAPAction header.

If necessary, you may further tweak the Rules generated by the import process in order to create a successful simulation.

TextWizard

When interacting with web content, text is often encoded using one or more formats. The TextWizard allows you to quickly transform text to and from popular formats.

The TextWizard can be opened by clicking **Tools > TextWizard** or by pressing CTRL+E. You may open multiple copies of the TextWizard at the same time.

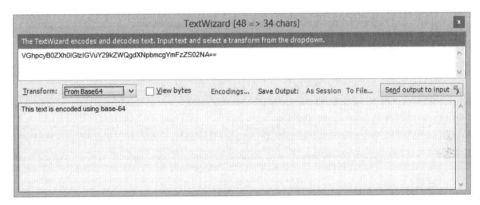

At the top of the TextWizard is the **Input box** into which you can type or paste the input text. A dropdown box below the Input box contains a set of **Transformations** you can apply to generate the output text, which is shown in the read-only **Output box** at the bottom right.

The list of available transformations is hardcoded, and only one transformation can be applied at one time. If you'd like to "chain" multiple transformations, use the **Send output to input** button to copy the last operation's Output into the Input box, then select the next transformation to apply.

As the tool opens, if text (32kb or less) is present on the clipboard, it is automatically pasted into the Input box.

The selected transformation is applied immediately as the text in the Input box is updated. The title bar indicates the number of characters in the input and the number of characters of output generated. If any transformation results in creation of a `null` character (which would terminate the string prematurely), the TextWizard will replace the `null` character with the Unicode Replacement Character (0xFFFD, ◆).

The **View bytes** checkbox allows you to view the output in hexadecimal, which can be useful when decoding binary content that is not renderable as text.

The **Encodings...** link opens a panel that allows you to select the **Input** and **Output** text encodings that are used when converting text to and from binary formats. By default, **UTF-8** is assumed.

The **Save Output** links can be useful if a binary body (like an image) results from the decoding process. The **As Session** link generates a new Web Session whose response body contains the output of the transformation. The **As File…** link prompts you for a filename to which the output will be saved.

The **Send output to input** button allows you to replace the input text with the output text, useful when chaining a series of transformations.

Available transformations include:

To Base64	Convert the Input string into UTF-8 then encode the result as a 7-bit ASCII string using Base64 encoding.
To Base64URL	Encode in Base64 and replace + and / with - and _ respectively.
From Base64	Decode the Input string from Base64-encoded (7-bit) ASCII to a byte array, then interpret the result as a UTF-8 string.
URLEncode	Apply URL Encoding to the Input string.
URLDecode	Reverse the **URLEncode** operation by decoding escape sequences.
HexEncode	Convert each character of the input string into its hexadecimal equivalent preceded by a % character.
To C# byte[]	Represent the string as a C# byte array definition.
To JS string	Replace \ with \\, Carriage Returns with \r, Line Feeds with \n, " with \", and any character over ASCII 127 with \u*XXXX* where *XXXX* is the Unicode code point.
From JS string	Reverse the **To JS string** operation.
HTML Encode	Encode the Input string using HTML Entities; for instance < becomes <.
HTML Decode	Reverse the **HTML Encode** operation.
To UTF-7	Convert the Input string into a UTF-7 string preceded by a byte-order marker.
From UTF-7	Convert the Input string from a UTF-7 string.
To Deflated-SAML	Convert the Input string to UTF-8 bytes, then DEFLATE compress the bytes, Base64 encode the compressed data, and URLEncode the final result.
From Deflated-SAML	URLDecode the string into Base64, convert to a byte array, decompress the array, and convert the resultant array into a UTF-8 string.

COMPOSER TAB

This tab enables you to manually build and send HTTP, HTTPS, and FTP requests. Alternatively, you can drag a Session from the Web Sessions list to the Composer tab to copy the request from that Session into the interface. Clicking the **Execute** button sends the request to the server.

The Composer tab contains four sub-tabs: **Parsed**, **Raw**, **Scratchpad**, and **Options**.

Request Options

The **Options** tab provides the following controls:

Inspect Session	After the request is sent, activate the Inspectors tab to show the results of the request.
Fix Content-Length header	This option controls whether the Composer will automatically add or update the `Content-Length` request header to reflect the actual size of the request body. In many cases, requests that lack a proper `Content-Length` header will hang or result in a HTTP error response.
Follow Redirects	This option controls whether the Composer will automatically follow a `HTTP/3xx` redirection using the response's `Location` header. When this option is enabled, the Composer will follow a maximum of 10 redirects before failing.
Automatically Authenticate	This option controls whether the Composer will automatically respond to a server's `HTTP/401` or `HTTP/407` authentication demands. When this option is enabled, the Windows credentials of the account that Fiddler is running under will be used to automatically respond to such challenges. To supply a different set of credentials, set the `fiddler.composer.AutoAuthCreds` preference. If the server requires credentials that are different than those provided, the request will fail, typically with a `HTTP/403` response.
Tear off *button*	Press to remove the Composer from the main Fiddler window and show it in a separate floating window. This option is especially useful when you have the **Inspect Session** option enabled, as it permits you to see both the Composer and Inspectors tabs at the same time.
Help link	Launch Help for the Composer.

Scratchpad Requests

The Composer's **Scratchpad** tab allows you to easily store a collection of requests for later reuse—it's great for iterative development or public demonstrations of web APIs. Simply select the desired text on the tab and click the Execute button, and the text will be parsed into a request and sent to the server. You can easily add new requests to the Scratchpad by dragging and dropping existing Sessions from the Web Sessions list.

Triple-clicking within a text block automatically selects the adjacent text of the entire request, including the headers and body, if any.

The Scratchpad can interpret cURL command lines strings. Simply select the full cURL command line and click **Execute** to send the request cURL would have generated.

The text in the tab is automatically saved each time Fiddler exits and reloaded each time Fiddler restarts.

Raw Requests

The **Raw** tab provides a simple text box into which you must enter a single HTTP request. If your request is not well-formed (say, because you forgot the trailing CRLF after the request headers) then clicking the Execute button will not issue a request.

This tab is rarely useful—most requests should be composed using the Parsed tab instead.

Parsed Requests

The **Parsed** tab allows you to construct a request using separate boxes for each component of the request.

Across the top of the tab are three boxes: The first allows you to specify the HTTP Method (e.g. POST). The second allows you to specify the full URL of the request (it must begin with http://, https://, or ftp://). The third box allows you to specify the HTTP Version (typically HTTP/1.1).

Below the top line are two large text areas: the top box allows you to edit the request headers, and the bottom box allows you to edit the request body. If the currently selected HTTP Method is one that typically does not allow a body (e.g. GET) the body box will turn red if any text is entered into it.

The Composer History List

The Parsed tab of the Composer stores a list of Composer-sent requests so that you may easily reuse them. Simply double-click any item in the list to repopulate the Parsed tab's fields with the values copied from the previously-sent request.

Right-click in the history list to display its context menu:

Comment	Add a Comment to describe the request. The comment will be shown instead of the default URL.
Remove	Remove the request from the list.
Select All	Select all requests in the list.
Remove Duplicates	When this option is enabled, any duplicate requests in the History will be removed each time a new entry is added.
Load…	Load a SAZ or RAZ file. A RAZ file is similar to a SAZ file, except that it only stores the requests (no responses).
Save All…	Save the History list to a RAZ file.
AutoSave on Exit	When this option is enabled, Fiddler will automatically save the History on exit and reload it upon restart. Note that a large History list can slow down Fiddler's startup and shutdown.
Hide History	Hide the History list. The operation can be reversed using the Options tab.

Send Sequential Requests

In some scenarios, it is useful to send multiple requests that are identical except for a single number. For instance, when trying to download a series of sequentially-named images, each request might differ by only one number in the URL. The Composer can generate a series of sequentially-numbered requests – simply include a # symbol in the URL where the number should appear.

When the request is executed, Fiddler will prompt you for the first number. You can enter a simple number (e.g. 8) or if the all numbers must be the same length in digits, pad the number with leading zeros. For instance, to ensure that all URLs' numbers contain two digits, use 08:

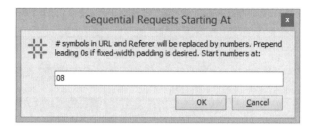

Next, you'll be prompted for the number at which you would like Fiddler to stop issuing requests:

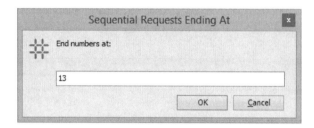

After providing the Start and End numbers, Fiddler will then issue the sequential requests for the range you specified:

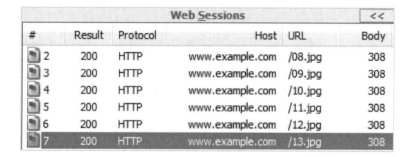

Some servers will not return responses unless an expected `Referer` header is present. Placing a # in your request's `Referer` header will instruct Fiddler to replace that character with the current request number.

The Sequential Requests feature is only available when using the **Parsed** tab; the # is treated as a plain character if the request is composed using the **Raw** or **Scratchpad** tabs.

File Upload Requests

You can construct a file upload by clicking the **Upload File** link near the top-right of the tab. A **Select File for Upload** file picker window will appear. You may only choose one file if your request's Method is PUT, or you may choose multiple files if the Method is POST.

After you select the files for upload, the Composer will construct a request with the proper format; all @INCLUDE references in the body will be replaced with the contents of the specified files when the request is executed.

File uploads are typically conducted using either the PUT or POST methods. When uploading a file using the PUT method, the Request Body typically contains the raw content of the file.

In contrast, uploads using the POST method usually format the Request Body using Content-Type: multipart/form-data.

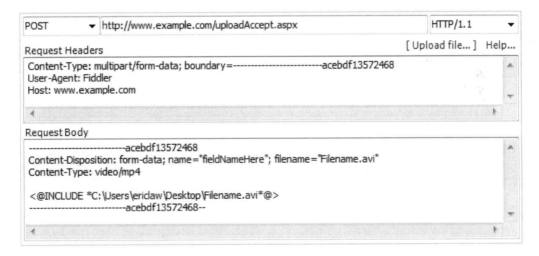

For POST uploads, you may need to edit the Name attribute to ensure that it matches the form field name expected by the server.

If the server expects to receive the file encoded as base64 text (for instance, as the content of an XML tag), add a base64 token within the @INCLUDE directive, like so:

```
<@INCLUDE base64 *C:\users\ericlaw\desktop\Filename.avi*@>
```

Edit with an Automatic Request Breakpoint

In some cases, Fiddler's Request Inspectors provide a better request-editing experience than the Composer. Hold the Shift key while clicking the Execute button to set a breakpoint on the new request. The new Session will be immediately paused at a breakpoint and the Request Inspectors will become active. You can then use the Inspectors to modify the request before it is sent to the server.

Send Binary Body Data

If you wish to include any binary data directly in the request body, you will need to encode it in base64 to avoid corruption by the text box. After adding the encoded data, in the headers box, add a custom header named Fiddler-Encoding with value base64. Fiddler will decode the body and omit this pseudo-header when sending the binary body to the server.

Override the Host Header

In some scenarios, you may wish to violate the HTTP protocol and send a request with a Host header that does not match the target to which the request is sent. To do so, supply the target IP address or hostname in a custom header named Fiddler-Host.

The Composer will propagate the value to an X-OverrideHost Session flag and drop the pseudo-header.

Log tab

The Log tab collects logged messages that are generated by extensions, FiddlerScript, or Fiddler itself. Fiddler logs a message in response to various application events (e.g. when a SAZ file is saved or loaded) as well as system events (e.g. when the system's network connectivity is lost or restored).

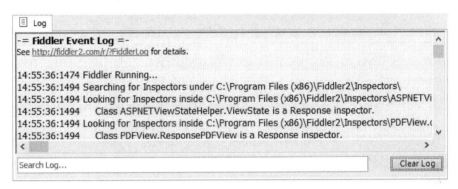

Right-click on the Log textbox to display a context menu offering commands for interacting with the log:

Copy	Copies selected text to the clipboard.
Save…	Saves the current Log to a file on disk. You may save in plaintext (.txt) or formatted RichText format (.rtf).
Clear	Clears all text in the Log.

You can search the Log using the box at the bottom of the tab, and clear its messages by pressing the **Clear Log** button.

The Log tab supports simple macro commands that you can invoke from the QuickExec box.

Command	Action
`log @Log.Clear`	Clear the log
`log @Log.Save`	Generate a new Session in the Web Sessions list whose response body contains the Log tab's text.
`log "@Log.Export \"log.txt\""`	Save the Log tab's text to the specified file. Use a filename ending in `.rtf` to save in Rich Text Format, preserving font size and weight, or ending in `.txt` to save as plaintext.

Logging from FiddlerScript or an Extension is as simple as:

```
FiddlerApplication.Log.LogFormat("Got HTTP/{0} for {1}",
                                 oSession.responseCode, oSession.url);
```

FIND SESSIONS WINDOW

Fiddler's Find Sessions window searches requests and responses to flag those that contain text of interest. Open the Find Sessions window using the command on the Edit menu, or press the CTRL+F hotkey anywhere in Fiddler.

Specify the text to search for using the **Find** text box at the top of the window. Previously searched terms appear in a drop-down and autocomplete as you type.

The **Options** box controls how the search is conducted. The **Search** dropdown determines what gets searched; choices are **Requests and responses** (the default), **Requests only**, **Responses only**, and **URLs only**. Unless you choose **URLS only**, the **Examine** dropdown specifies whether to search the Session's **Headers**, **Bodies**, or both (the default).

Below the dropdowns are a set of checkboxes. When ticked, the **Match case** box makes the search case-sensitive. The **Regular Expression** box causes Fiddler to treat the search text as a regular expression. The **Search binaries** option instructs Fiddler to perform the search even inside Sessions with a Content-Type header that suggests the body is of a binary type like audio, video, images, Flash objects, etc.

The **Decode compressed content** option instructs Fiddler to remove HTTP Transfer- and Content-Encodings from requests and responses as it searches. This option can significantly slow the search and will permanently remove the encoding from the affected bodies.

The **Search only selected sessions** box is enabled (and ticked by default) if multiple Sessions are selected in the Web Sessions list when the Find Sessions window is opened. This option restricts the search to only those Sessions that were selected when the search began.

The **Select matches** option causes Fiddler to automatically select any Sessions which contain the search text. The **Unmark old results** option will remove the highlight color from any Sessions highlighted as a result of a prior search. The **Result Highlight** dropdown allows you to select the background color which should be set for all Sessions that contain the search text. If the **Unmark old results** option is disabled, this color is automatically cycled every time the Find Sessions operation is performed-- that way, when performing multiple searches, the results of each search will be highlighted in a different color.

After configuring the search, press the **Find Sessions** button to perform the search. The Find Sessions window will close and matching search results will be highlighted (and selected, if that option was chosen) in the Web Sessions list. Fiddler's status bar will indicate the number of matches found. You may hit F3 or . (period) to navigate to the next match, and Shift+F3 or , (comma) to navigate to the previous match.

Press Cancel or hit Escape to close the window without performing a search.

SESSION CLIPBOARDS

Session Clipboards provide one or more independent lists of Sessions you can keep open alongside the primary Web Sessions list in Fiddler's main window. To display a new Session Clipboard, click **New Session Clipboard...** on Fiddler's **Tools** menu.

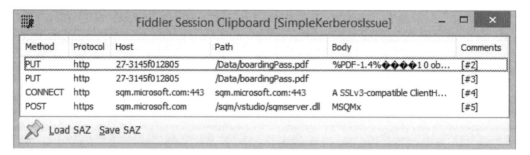

Use the **Load SAZ** and **Save SAZ** buttons at the bottom of the window to add Sessions to the list or save all of the listed Sessions to an archive.

You can drag Sessions to and from the Web Sessions list in Fiddler's main window. You can also drag Sessions from the Session Clipboard to the Composer or AutoResponder tabs, to another Session Clipboard, or to the Web Sessions list in a Fiddler Viewer Mode window.

Click the pin icon at the bottom left of the window to keep it on top of all other windows.

SAZ AutoSave

In some circumstances, you may want to configure Fiddler to periodically save traffic to Session Archive files; use the AutoSave tool to do so on the schedule of your choice. To show the AutoSave tab, click **Configure AutoSave...** on Fiddler's **Tools** menu.

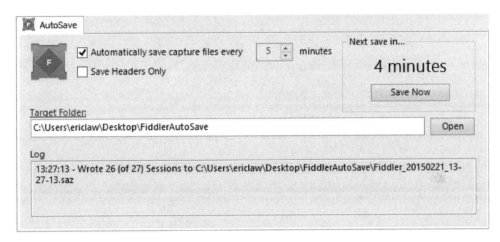

You can configure automatic saves to take place at an interval ranging from 1 minute to 12 hours. Check the **Automatically save capture files** box to enable the timer, which will be displayed to the right.

Check the **Save Headers Only** box if you only wish to preserve the request and response headers in the SAZ file; this option can be useful for minimizing the size of the archive if only headers are needed.

Click the **Target Folder** link to display a folder picker dialog box. Click the **Open** button to open Windows Explorer to the specified folder.

The **Log** box at the bottom of the tab records information about the files as they are saved.

After the SAZ file is saved, its Sessions are removed from the Web Sessions list and a garbage collection operation is initiated to reclaim as much memory as possible.

HOST REMAPPING TOOL

The **Hosts Remapping** tool allows you to easily reroute requests from one host to another, overriding the normal DNS association between a hostname and its IP address list. To enable the feature, click the **HOSTS...** item on Fiddler's **Tools** menu. The **Host Remapping** window will appear.

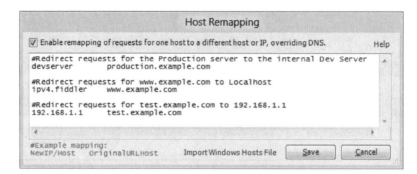

Use the **Enable remapping** checkbox to enable or disable the feature. In the textbox, enter a list of overrides, one per line. Type the new host or IP address in the first column, then one or more whitespace characters, and finally the corresponding hostname to override. Any line may be preceded by a pound character (#) to indicate that the line represents a comment.

You may import the system's HOSTS file (%SYSTEMROOT%\System32\drivers\etc\hosts) using the link at the bottom of the window. Unlike the Windows HOSTS file, this feature does not require that you specify the IP address of the new target; you may specify a host instead. If needed, you can even specify a target port. The rule:

    127.0.0.1:8088   meddler

... sends all requests for http://meddler/ to http://127.0.0.1:8088/ instead. A leading wildcard is also permitted on the original host, so you can use:

    127.0.0.1:8088   *example.com

...to remap traffic from example.com, www.example.com, and test.example.com using just one override.

Sessions rerouted from one hostname to another using the Host Remapping tool are rendered with a light blue background in the Web Sessions list. HTTPS Sessions that have been rerouted have the X-IgnoreCertCNMismatch and X-OverrideCertCN Session Flags set to avoid raising "Certificate Name Mismatch" errors. As explained in the upcoming section "Retarget Traffic with Fiddler", you can also use this tool to rewrite or redirect requests by specifying the operation as a third parameter.

    127.0.0.1:8088   example.com   redirect

Techniques and Concepts

RETARGET TRAFFIC WITH FIDDLER

Fiddler offers three different mechanisms you can use to change the target of a request. These mechanisms all have different implications for the client and server, and understanding the differences will allow you to choose the proper mechanism for your needs.

Method #1 - Rewrite

A *rewrite* occurs when you use Fiddler to change the request's headers (either the target URL or the Host header) such that a request targeted to Server A is instead sent to Server B.

The client will be unaware that the request it sent has been changed underneath it, so any cookies sent with the request will belong to the original URL instead of the new one. Similarly, if you look at the resource's URL in the browser's address bar or in the DOM, you will see the original URL and not the rewritten one.

Since the URL and HOST header of network request itself are updated, rewritten requests can safely flow through an upstream proxy server without problems. The target server will see its own Host header in the inbound request.

If the request uses HTTPS and decryption is enabled, you may want to control the certificate the client computer receives to avoid seeing "Certificate Name Mismatch" errors. To do so, use the Session's X-OverrideCertCN flag to supply the Subject CN value Fiddler will send to the client.

Method #2 - Reroute

A *reroute* sends a request meant for Server A to Server B without changing the request itself. Instead, before Fiddler connects to the server to send the request, it notices that the request is marked to be rerouted. Rather than connecting to the host specified by the request's Host header, Fiddler instead connects to the new target host specified within the Session's X-OverrideHost flag. (Note: Using the X-OverrideHostName flag instead allows you to preserve the original request's target port number).

Because the client is unaware that the target has been changed underneath it, the Host header, URL, and Cookies of the request will be those intended for the original host, not the new target host. Request rerouting only works when Fiddler itself determines the target IP address to which the request will be sent. If an upstream gateway proxy is in use, it will be unaware of Fiddler's desire to reroute the request and will instead use the request's original Host header for routing. Therefore, the Host Remapping tool sets the X-OverrideHost flag *and* the bypassGateway boolean to ensure that rerouted requests bypass any upstream gateway proxy.

When the web server receives the request, it will find the original server's unmodified hostname in the Host request header. Depending on its configuration, the server may reject the request with a HTTP/400 error message complaining that "No such host is known."

When HTTPS requests are rerouted to a different server, either the client or Fiddler is likely to complain about a "Certificate Name Mismatch." For instance, when using the following remapping FiddlerScript:

```
if (oSession.HTTPMethodIs("CONNECT") && oSession.HostnameIs("example.com"))
{
  oSession["X-OverrideHostName"] ="www.fiddler2.com";
}
```

…loading `https://example.com/` will show a certificate warning complaining that the server presented a certificate for `www.fiddler2.com` instead of the expected `example.com` certificate:

You can avoid the Certificate Error message by setting the `X-IgnoreCertCNMismatch` flag:

```
if (oSession.HTTPMethodIs("CONNECT") && oSession.HostnameIs("example.com"))
{
  oSession["X-OverrideHostName"] ="www.fiddler2.com";

  // Set flag to suppress Fiddler's HTTPS Name Mismatch errors
  oSession["X-IgnoreCertCNMismatch"] = "no worries mate";
}
```

If you would prefer that Fiddler ignore *all* certificate errors for a Session, because the target site is using an expired or self-signed test certificate, set the `X-IgnoreCertErrors` flag instead.

The Host Remapping tool sets the `X-IgnoreCertCNMismatch` flag automatically. When the Certificate Name Mismatch error is ignored, you will see the `https://www.fiddler2.com/` page while the browser's address bar shows `https://example.com/`.

Method #3 - Redirect

A *redirect* occurs when you use Fiddler to return a `HTTP/307` redirection response to the client so that it will resend its request to a new URL. Because the client is responsible for resending the request, it is aware that the request target has changed, and the new request will be sent with an updated `Host` header and URL. The client will send the proper cookies for the new target URL, and if the request is over HTTPS, the client will expect the target server to use the correct certificate for the new target hostname. Since the new request is sent with the new target URL and matching `Host` header, the request will safely flow through an upstream gateway proxy to the desired server.

Features to Retarget Requests

Fiddler allows use of any of these three different retargeting mechanisms via several independent features:

1. Use the **HOSTS...** command on the **Tools** menu to reroute traffic from one IP address to another.

2. Using FiddlerScript or an extension, you can set the `X-OverrideHost` flag on the `Session` object to reroute traffic from one IP address and port to another address and port. Using the `X-OverrideHostName` flag
   allows you to reroute from one IP address to another without changing the port.

3. Using FiddlerScript or an extension, you can set the `Session` object's `host` property or `fullUrl` property to rewrite a request from one URL to another.

4. You can use the AutoResponder to rewrite a request from one URL to another by supplying the new URL as the Action text.

5. You can use the AutoResponder to redirect a request from one URL to another using the `*redir:` prefix on the Action text.

6. You can use the `utilCreateResponseAndBypassServer` method from FiddlerScript or an extension to generate a redirect from one URL to another.

7. You can use the AutoResponder to reroute a request from one host to another by using `*flag:X-OverrideHostName=targethost` as the Action text.

COMPARE SESSIONS

One of the most common debugging tasks is to determine why one request was successful while another failed in some way. The ability to compare one Session to another is a powerful tool for accomplishing this task.

To compare two Sessions, simply select both in the Web Sessions list and choose **Compare** from the context menu (or hit CTRL+W). When you invoke the comparison command, the two selected Sessions will be saved to temporary files and then the file comparison tool will be launched and passed the paths of the two files.

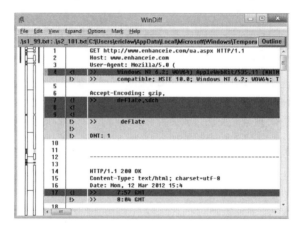

Fiddler does not itself install a file comparison tool, although most developers already have WinDiff, Odd, Beyond Compare, WinMerge or a similar utility installed. If you have WinDiff, copy it to the \Program Files\Fiddler2 folder, or put it somewhere within your system's PATH (e.g. C:\Windows\System32) in order for Fiddler to find it. If you *don't* already have a comparison tool, grab WinMerge from http://WinMerge.org.

To direct Fiddler to launch a tool other than WinDiff, specify its path inside the **Tools** > **Fiddler Options** > **Tools** tab. If the tool requires non-default command line arguments, specify these Preferences using the QuickExec box or the **about:config** tab.

Configure the command line arguments, where {0} and {1} are replaced by the path to each temporary file:

```
PREFS SET fiddler.differ.Params "/diff \"{0}\" \"{1}\""
```

You can also set an "alternate" command line that will be invoked if you hold SHIFT while invoking the comparison:

```
PREFS SET fiddler.differ.ParamsAlt "/diff /p \"{0}\" \"{1}\""
```

The alternate command-line feature works with file comparison utilities that support multiple modes. For example, WinDiff exposes the -p command line flag to break each line of the comparison at the first instance of punctuation. When you hold SHIFT while invoking the **Compare** command, Fiddler will pass the -p flag to WinDiff and a new line will appear after each character of punctuation. This is useful to observe deltas within long lines of text (e.g. a URL's query string).

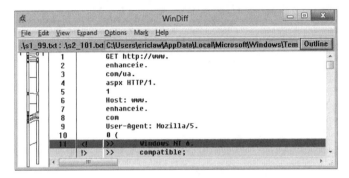

You can set the fiddler.differ.DecodeFirst preference to false if you don't want Fiddler to automatically unchunk and decompress both Sessions before comparing them.

UltraDiff

By default, Fiddler reformats the temporary files for easier viewing in line-oriented comparison tools like WinDiff. Called UltraDiff, this feature reorders the headers of both files such that headers that are exactly the same in both Sessions are listed first, then headers with different values are listed, then headers that are entirely different are listed last. UltraDiff reformats request URLs to ensure that if the URLs are only slightly different (e.g. a single character differs in the middle of a 512-character URL) then that difference is made obvious.

You can set the fiddler.differ.ultradiff preference to false if you don't want Fiddler to modify the headers and URL when saving the temporary files.

Compare Multiple Sessions at Once

If you want to compare multiple Sessions (or even entire SAZ files) at one time, you should use the **Traffic Differ** extension, described in the Extensions chapter. The extension allows you to compare lists of Web Sessions and then perform text-comparisons of individual Sessions within those lists.

DEBUG WITH BREAKPOINTS

In a traditional debugger, you can select instructions in your program at which you would like execution to pause; these are called **breakpoints**. While paused at a breakpoint, you can examine the state of the program and modify memory or the flow of execution to change the behavior of the program.

Fiddler offers similar breakpoint-based debugging functionality for web requests. Sessions may be paused at two points during their execution:

1. After the request is read from the client, before it is sent to the server

2. After the response is received from the server, before it is returned to the client

These are known as **request breakpoints** and **response breakpoints**.

When paused at a request breakpoint, you can change any aspect of the request, including the URL, headers, or body. You may prevent the request from being sent to the server at all by returning a response of your choosing. With rare exceptions, the client application will never know that Fiddler has modified its request.

Similarly, when paused at a response breakpoint, you can change any aspect of the response, including the headers or body. You may also generate a new response and substitute it in place of the response received from the server. At a response breakpoint, you *can* also change any aspect of the *request*, but since the request has already been sent, the change is only reflected in Fiddler—the server will never see your changes.

Set Breakpoints
There are many different ways to set breakpoints; under the covers, all of them set the Session's X-BreakRequest or X-BreakResponse flag.

You can easily break on all requests or responses using the **Rules** > **Automatic Breakpoints** menu, or by clicking into the 3rd panel from the left on Fiddler's status bar. The downside of using such broad breakpoints is that you will likely find it tedious to unpause each Session that you are not interested in debugging.

Instead, consider using the Filters or AutoResponder tabs to more precisely target your breakpoints. The Filters tab allows you to set breakpoints on Sessions that use the POST method, those sent with a Query String, those sent by XMLHttpRequest, or those that returned a particular Content-Type. The AutoResponder tab allows you to set a request or response breakpoint for any request whose URL matches the text or regular expression you provide. Set the rule's Action text to *bpu to create a request breakpoint, or *bpafter to create a response breakpoint.

If you need to define more elaborate breakpoint conditions, use **Rules** > **Customize Rules** to set the `X-BreakRequest` or `X-BreakResponse` flags within your FiddlerScript's `OnBeforeRequest`, `OnPeekAtResponseHeaders`, or `OnBeforeResponse` methods. When setting a response breakpoint, if the breakpoint criteria depend only upon the response headers, prefer the `OnPeekAtResponseHeaders` handler over `OnBeforeResponse` because the former always executes at the appropriate time. If a Session is configured to stream to the client, the `OnBeforeResponse` handler only runs *after* the complete response was returned to the client.

The default FiddlerScript file allows you to easily set a single request breakpoint and a single response breakpoint using the QuickExec box. Simply type:

```
bpu TextFromURL
```

…to set a request breakpoint for any Session whose URL contains the specified text. Similarly, type:

```
bpafter TextFromURL
```

…to set a response breakpoint for any Session whose URL contains the specified text.

You can also set a request breakpoint for any request using a specified HTTP Method:

```
bpm POST
```

… and you can set a response breakpoint for any response returning a specified HTTP Status code:

```
bps 307
```

Typing any of the breakpoint commands (`bpu`, `bpafter`, `bpm` or `bps`) with no parameter following will clear the specified breakpoint.

Restarting Fiddler will also clear any FiddlerScript breakpoints set using QuickExec.

Tamper Using Inspectors
When paused at a breakpoint, you can use Inspectors to edit the request or response. As discussed in the Inspectors chapter, many Inspectors support Read/Write functionality that you can use to change the request and response headers or body. Changes you make while paused at a breakpoint are committed automatically by the Inspector.

In addition to using the Inspectors, you can clone a previously-captured response into a Session paused at a breakpoint. The **Clone Response** command is available from the Web Sessions list's context menu when two Sessions are selected in the Web Sessions list and one of the Sessions is currently paused at a breakpoint and the other is completed. The command will copy the response from the completed Session to the paused Session. This feature enables you to easily reuse a previously captured (or modified) response to satisfy a later request.

The Breakpoint Bar

When a Session is paused at a breakpoint, a red Breakpoint Bar will appear between the Request and Response Inspectors. This bar includes two buttons and one dropdown.

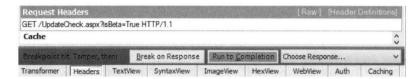

The yellow **Break on Response** button is enabled only when paused at a request breakpoint. Click the button to set a response breakpoint for the current Session and send the (potentially modified) request to the server. The green **Run to Completion** button sends the request without setting a response breakpoint.

The dropdown at the right side of the Breakpoint Bar allows you to select a template response or the file of your choice to return as the response to a request.

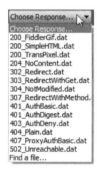

When you select a file from the dropdown, it will be immediately loaded into the response Inspectors so that you may further modify the response (without changing the file on disk) before it is returned to the client. If you use the dropdown to select a response while paused at a request breakpoint, the request will never be sent to the server.

Resuming Multiple Sessions

If your breakpoints are not targeted specifically enough, you may have many requests paused at break-points that you wish to resume quickly:

Simply click the **Resume** button on the Fiddler toolbar, or type g in the QuickExec box to immediately resume all paused Sessions.

Configure Fiddler and Clients

FIDDLER OPTIONS

The Fiddler Options window, shown by clicking **Tools > Fiddler Options**, exposes many settings to control Fiddler's behavior. Changes to some settings require a restart of Fiddler to take effect, but some changes take effect immediately or when Fiddler's **Capture Traffic** option is toggled. After adjusting settings, click the **OK** button at the bottom of the window to save the changes or **Cancel** to abandon your updates. Click the **Help** link at the bottom left to learn more about the available settings.

General Tab

The General tab allows you to adjust settings related to Fiddler's general operation.

The **Check for updates on startup** option controls whether Fiddler will consult a web service on startup to determine whether a new version of Fiddler is available. If you disable this option, you may manually check for new versions by clicking **Check for Updates...** on Fiddler's Help menu.

The **Offer upgrade to Beta versions** option controls whether beta versions are offered when update checks are performed.

The **Enable IPv6 (if available)** option controls whether Fiddler will listen on and attempt to connect to IPv6 endpoints. Even if this option is disabled, Fiddler will still attempt to connect to an IPv6 server endpoint if DNS only returned IPv6 addresses.

The **Map requests to originating application** option controls whether Fiddler will attempt to determine which locally-running process issued each request. The process information is shown in the **Process** column in the Web Sessions list, and is stored in the Session's LocalProcess property. This feature works by querying Windows for the list of open network connections and checking each inbound connection against that list. Some requests may not be successfully mapped back to their original process; in particular, process information is not available for requests from mobile devices or remote client PCs and virtual machines. Note: Disabling this option is not recommended, as it will break many features around Fiddler.

The **Enable high-resolution timers** option instructs Fiddler to configure Windows to use a timer resolution of 1 millisecond instead of the default 15.6 millisecond resolution. While this option improves the accuracy of timestamps recorded by Fiddler, the use of higher-frequency timers decreases mobile PCs' battery life.

The **Automatically stream audio & video** option controls whether responses with audio/* and video/* MIME types are automatically streamed to the client without buffering the entire response within Fiddler. When this option is set, you cannot use Fiddler's Inspectors or FiddlerScript to modify audio or video response bodies. The advantage in setting this option is that streamed responses are available to begin playback immediately in the client browser or application. To stream *all* responses in Fiddler, click the **Stream** button in the Fiddler toolbar.

The dropdown **If client aborts while streaming** controls Fiddler's behavior when streaming a response to a client that closes the connection prematurely. The options are:

- Finish downloading anyway – Continue the download to completion, even if the Session is no longer visible in Fiddler's Web Sessions list.

- Finish if Session is visible – Continue the download only if the Session has not been deleted from Fiddler's Web Sessions list. Use this setting if you are using Fiddler to collect content (e.g. web audio or video) and don't care whether the browser gets it.

- Close the server connection – Immediately close the connection to the server without completing the download. Use this setting if you don't care whether Fiddler has a complete copy of the requested file.

The dropdown **If protocol violations are observed** controls whether Fiddler will show a popup message when malformed web traffic is encountered. Protocol violations can cause problems for clients and servers, so this option should be left enabled when you are debugging your own clients and sites. Your choices include:

- Do nothing – Fiddler will not display protocol violation warnings.

- Warn on critical errors – Fiddler will only warn about serious violations of the HTTP protocol that are likely to cause problems (e.g. an incorrect `Content-Length` header value).

- Warn on all errors – Fiddler will warn about any observed violations of the HTTP protocol (e.g. a non-absolute `Location` header value).

Sessions with protocol violations are shown in the Web Sessions list with a yellow background and the Session's Properties contain a copy of the protocol violation message.

The **Systemwide Hotkey** setting enables you to select a hotkey to restore and activate Fiddler when it is minimized or inactive.

HTTPS Tab

The HTTPS tab controls settings related to Fiddler's interception of secure traffic.

The **Capture HTTPS CONNECTs** option controls whether Fiddler registers as the system proxy for secure requests; clients use the HTTP `CONNECT` method to *tunnel* secure traffic through proxies like Fiddler. If this option is disabled, most of the other HTTPS-related options are unavailable.

The **Decrypt HTTPS traffic** option controls Fiddler decrypts HTTPS requests and responses. When you first enable the decryption option, Fiddler will generate a new self-signed root certificate and ask whether you would like to configure Windows to trust that certificate.

When decryption is enabled, a dropdown box permits you to select which processes will have their traffic decrypted by default. You can select between:

- **All processes** – Decrypt regardless of where the traffic originates.
- **Browsers only** – Decrypt only when the process name identifies a web browser.
- **Non-Browsers** – Decrypt only when the process name is not a browser.
- **Remote clients** – Decryption only when the process name is unknown (suggesting that the request is from a remote computer or mobile device).

Use the Decryption Process Filter to avoid decrypting traffic that you do not care about—for instance, you may not care about the background HTTPS requests made from a file-synchronization program like Dropbox.exe, and you can exclude such traffic easily using this filter.

The **Certificates generated using** text shows what module is being used to generate interception certificates. On Windows, the default is **Fiddler.DefaultCertificateProvider** which relies upon makecert.exe or the Windows Certificate API. If you are instead using a certificate generation plugin, it will be listed here. If the active module exposes a configuration UI, its name will be shown as a clickable hyperlink.

The **Ignore server certificate errors** checkbox controls whether Fiddler will warn you when a server presents an invalid security certificate. If checked, Fiddler will ignore any certificate errors encountered when handshaking with a HTTPS server. Errors would otherwise be "hidden" from the client application because Fiddler always generates valid security certificates. You should leave this option disabled unless you use Fiddler exclusively on a trusted network where you expect to encounter innocuous invalid server certificates (e.g. self-signed development servers).

The **Check for certificate revocation** checkbox controls whether Fiddler will attempt to contact the certificate authority for each received certificate to determine whether the certificate has been revoked. Enabling this option slightly improves security but it entails a performance cost for the HTTPS handshake.

Click the **Enabled Protocols** link to control which SSL and TLS protocol versions that Fiddler offers when connecting to servers. The defaults are ssl3;tls1.0. When running Fiddler 4 on Windows 7 or later, you may add tls1.1 and tls1.2 to the list, but buggy or outdated HTTPS servers may fail to handshake when these higher-security protocol versions are offered.

The **Learn more...** link launches a help page that explains how traffic decryption works.

The **Skip decryption for the following hosts** box allows you to specify that traffic bound to selected servers should not be decrypted, allowing you to skip decrypting traffic you do not care about. For instance, you may not care about the HTTPS requests made to Exchange RPC-over-HTTPS endpoints and this filter allows you to easily exclude such traffic. Use semicolons to delimit the list, and use * as a wildcard. For instance, to skip decryption of traffic to `example.com` and any of its subdomains, as well as traffic to `fiddler2.com`, specify the filter `*example.com; fiddler2.com`.

The **Export Root Certificate to Desktop** button copies Fiddler's root certificate to the file `FiddlerRoot.cer` on your desktop. This certificate file can then be easily copied to another device or imported to Firefox's Trusted Certificates store.

The **Remove Interception Certificates** button is enabled only when the **Decrypt HTTPS traffic** box is unchecked. Click the button to remove the Fiddler root certificate and the server certificates that chain to it. If you later re-enable HTTPS decryption, Fiddler will generate a new root certificate and prompt you to trust that new root certificate.

Connections Tab

The Connections tab exposes options to control Fiddler's network settings.

The **Fiddler listens on port** box controls the port number that Fiddler uses to listen for web traffic; the default is port **8888**.

The **Copy Browser Proxy Configuration URL** link copies a Proxy Configuration Script URL that you can paste into a client's proxy configuration screen. This feature is rarely used.

The **Capture FTP requests** checkbox controls whether Fiddler registers as the system proxy for FTP requests. This option is off by default.

Check the **Allow remote computers to connect** box to listen for requests from other computers or devices. Under the hood, this option causes Fiddler to listen on all network interfaces instead of just the loopback interface. After changing this option, you must restart Fiddler. Upon restarting, you may see a prompt from your system firewall confirming that Fiddler should be allowed to receive inbound connections.

 Warning: Do not enable this option on a hostile network, as an attacker could send his traffic through your Fiddler instance, making it appear that the traffic was originating from your computer. This illusion could circumvent IPsec or other security protections.

The **Reuse client connections** option controls whether Fiddler will reuse client connections (client keep-alive). Similarly, the **Reuse server connections** box controls whether Fiddler will reuse server connections (server keep-alive). The connection reuse options should be left enabled for performance reasons; only disable them for troubleshooting purposes.

The **Act as system proxy on startup** option controls whether or not Fiddler registers as the system's proxy on startup. Internet Explorer and many other applications use the system proxy by default and are notified when it changes.

The **Monitor all connections** checkbox controls whether Fiddler will register as the proxy for all WinINET Connections. This option should be enabled if you are connected to a VPN, RAS, or dialup connection because WinINET will always use the proxy settings for any such connections if they are active.

The **Use PAC Script** checkbox controls how Fiddler registers as the system proxy; specifically, when this box is ticked, Fiddler will tell the browser to use a proxy configuration script (which can be found by clicking the Copy Browser Proxy Configuration URL link) instead of using the default fixed proxy configuration of `127.0.0.1:8888`. This option is rarely useful except on IE8 and below when attempting to capture loopback traffic (e.g. `http://localhost` or http://127.0.0.1); such traffic is not sent to Fiddler when configured as a fixed proxy, but is sent if a PAC Script is used instead.

The **WinINET Connections** list shows what network connections are configured for this machine. This may be useful if you are connected to the Internet via dialup or VPN and want Fiddler to automatically hook a connection other than your LAN connection. Notably, the list is readonly; to specify a single Connection to hook, use the `HookConnectionNamed` registry key. The checkboxes beside the connection names indicate whether Fiddler expects that connection's proxy settings to be pointed at Fiddler; if Fiddler is not currently in Capturing mode, for instance, all of the checkboxes are unchecked.

The **Bypass Fiddler for URLs** list controls which requests should not be sent through Fiddler at all when it is registered as the system proxy. Note that this list is generally only respected by WinINET clients like Internet Explorer. This box accepts a semicolon delimited list of hostnames, and supports * as a wildcard. For instance, to specify that you would like all traffic (including loopback traffic) to go to Fiddler except for secure traffic bound for `example.com`, and any traffic bound for `fiddler2.com`, use the string:

```
<-loopback>;https://example.com;*fiddler2.com
```

The default `<-loopback>` token tells IE9 and later that loopback requests *should* be sent to Fiddler; when this token is not present (and on IE8 and lower) WinINET will automatically bypass the system proxy for loopback traffic. Fiddler automatically adds this token if missing; to prevent that, add a `<loopback>` token (without the leading - character).

You must detach and reattach Fiddler (click File > Capture Traffic) for changes in the proxy bypass list to take effect.

Gateway Tab

The Gateway tab allows you to easily configure how Fiddler accesses the network. On Windows, Fiddler defaults to **Use System Proxy**, adopting the WinINET/Internet Explorer proxy settings as an upstream gateway. If you choose **Automatically Detect Proxy using WPAD**, Fiddler will attempt to automatically discover the upstream proxy server using the Web Proxy Auto Detection algorithm. If you select **Manual Proxy Configuration,** you can specify the upstream proxy and proxy bypass list. The proxy configuration string takes either the form:

```
proxyserver:8080
```

…if all requests should be sent to the same gateway proxy, or the protocol-specific form:

```
http=httpproxy:8080;https=httpsproxy:8080
```

The proxy bypass list supports wildcards and the special tokens `<local>` (meaning any hostname which does not contain a period) and `<-loopback>` which *removes* the default bypass for `127.0.0.1`, `::1`, and `localhost` hostnames.

If you select **No Proxy**, Fiddler will not use an upstream gateway and will send all traffic directly to the origin server.

If your gateway needs are more elaborate, you can use the FiddlerScript `OnBeforeRequest` method to adjust the `bypassGateway` property on each individual Session object, or set its `X-OverrideGateway` flag.

The **Show Current Gateway Info** link shows information about any known upstream gateway proxy.

Appearance Tab

The Appearance tab exposes options that control how Fiddler is displayed.

The **Font size** box allows you to select the size of text in Fiddler. The **Choose Font** button enables you to select a different font face than the default. For font changes to take full effect, you must restart Fiddler.

The **Hide Fiddler when minimized** checkbox will show the Fiddler icon in your system tray rather than the taskbar when Fiddler is minimized.

When **Always show tray icon** is checked, Fiddler's icon will remain visible in the system tray even when Fiddler is not minimized.

The **Use SmartScroll in Session List** option controls Fiddler's behavior when new Sessions are added to the Web Sessions list. When this option is disabled, Fiddler will respect the **View** > **AutoScroll Session List** option; by default, the list will automatically scroll to show the newest Sessions added to the list as they appear. When this option is enabled, Fiddler will only scroll to show the newest Sessions *if* the Web Sessions list is already scrolled to the bottom. Leave this option enabled to help avoid losing your place when inspecting and capturing traffic simultaneously.

Enabling the **Reset Session ID counter on CTRL+X** option causes Session ID numbering to restart from 1 when the Web Sessions list is cleared via the CTRL+X hotkey or the **Remove** > **All Sessions** menu command. When this option is not set, Session IDs will start at 1 and continually increment until Fiddler is restarted.

The **Set Readonly Color** button sets the background color for readonly textboxes. This setting exists because gray is the default readonly color for Windows but the lack of contrast between grey and black can be hard on the eyes. A restart is required to complete this change.

Extensions Tab

The Extensions tab exposes options to control FiddlerScript and lists loaded Extensions.

The **Automatically reload script when changed** option controls whether Fiddler will automatically reload the FiddlerScript `CustomRules.js` file when it detects that the file has been changed.

The **References** box allows you to specify any additional .NET assemblies that your FiddlerScript depends upon. Learn more about this option in the chapter on FiddlerScript.

The **Extensions** box shows all loaded Extensions except Inspectors and Transcoders. You can copy the information from this textbox to include in bug reports or support queries. To list *all* loaded assemblies, instead use the `!lm` command in the QuickExec box.

The **Find more extensions…** link opens the Fiddler Add-ons directory webpage.

Tools Tab

The Tools tab allows you to set the path to external tools invoked by various features. The "..." button adjacent to each box launches a file picker dialog box.

The **Text Editor** box controls the editor launched by the "View in Notepad" button shown on the Raw and TextView Inspectors.

The **FiddlerScript Editor** box controls which text editor is used to edit your FiddlerScript when you press CTRL+R or click **Rules** > **Customize Rules**.

The **File Diff Tool** box controls what tool is invoked when you compare two Sessions by pressing CTRL+W or clicking **Compare** on the Web Session list's context menu.

HEADERENCODING SETTING

When transmitting text, both the client and the server must agree on how to convert between text strings and the raw bytes that are transmitted over the wire. The HTTP specification uses the `charset` attribute of the `Content-Type` header to convey the character set used within the request and response bodies.

Unfortunately, HTTP does not provide a broadly-respected mechanism for representing non-ASCII characters within the HTTP headers themselves. Instead, the HTTP specification indicates that only ASCII characters *may* be used. Some clients and servers respect this directive (usually by percent-encoding non-ASCII characters) but others will emit and accept non-ASCII characters. There are some instances where bytes-to-characters conversion discrepancies will exist between the client application (e.g. a browser), an intermediary (e.g. a proxy like Fiddler) and the server (e.g. Apache or IIS).

To support the broadest range of clients and servers, Fiddler assumes that HTTP headers are transmitted in UTF-8 encoding. There are some locales (particularly in Asia) where, by convention, a different encoding is used (e.g. `EUC-CN`). You can manually configure Fiddler to utilize a different default encoding for headers by creating a new registry string named `HeaderEncoding` inside `HKCU\Software\Microsoft\Fiddler2`. The string value provided must be an `Encoding` name recognized by the .NET Framework; valid values can be found at `http://fiddler2.com/r/?EncodingNames`.

You must restart Fiddler for any change to `HeaderEncoding` to take effect.

PREFERENCES

Fiddler supports an extensible list of Name/Value-paired settings called Preferences that are used by extensions and other components of Fiddler. Many Preferences can be adjusted using menus or checkboxes in the Fiddler user-interface, but some Preferences are not exposed and can *only* be viewed or changed using the Preferences system.

Using the QuickExec box below the Web Sessions list, you can use the PREFS command to interact with Preferences. Typing prefs log will log all Preferences to Fiddler's Log tab. You can type prefs set [prefname] [prefvalue] to create or update a Preference's value; wrap the value in quotation marks if it contains any spaces. Type prefs remove [prefname] to delete a Preference; the next time Fiddler queries the value of the Preference, its absence will be noted and the default value for that Preference will be used. Type prefs show [partialname] to show the list of Preferences whose name contains the provided string. Preference names are case-insensitive and may not contain spaces.

You can see all of the configured Preferences by typing about:config in the QuickExec box; this will create or activate the **about:config** tab in the Fiddler UI to list all Preferences sorted alphabetically by name.

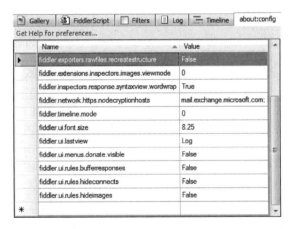

You can remove a Preference by selecting its row and tapping the Delete key. Press CTRL+C on a cell to copy its value, or select a row and press CTRL+C to copy both the name and value. You may modify a Preference's value by clicking into the Value column and entering a new value. You can add a new Preference by clicking into the last row (marked with an asterisk in the left margin) and typing a new Name and Value.

A partial list of Preferences supported by Fiddler and the Extensions I've created may be found in Appendix D.

Configure Clients

As a proxy server, Fiddler is only able to observe traffic that is sent to it. By default, web traffic from most applications will automatically flow through Fiddler because it registers itself with Windows as the default proxy when running. Most client programs will use the registered system proxy when sending network traffic. In the few cases where this doesn't happen automatically, configuration changes can be made to either the client or to Fiddler to capture traffic. As a proxy, Fiddler is also able to capture traffic from remote computers and network devices that support proxy servers (e.g. tablet computers and phones that support Wi-Fi).

In this chapter, I'll explain the myriad ways in which Fiddler can be configured to capture traffic.

Capture Traffic from Browsers

Internet Explorer, Chrome, Firefox and Safari for Windows automatically send traffic to the system proxy server by default, meaning that Fiddler will capture their traffic automatically.

Note that some browser add-ons may cause the browser to ignore the system proxy settings; if you find your traffic isn't captured, examine your add-ons list paying special attention to any entries related to proxies, privacy, security or geographic location.

Chrome

By default, Chrome adopts the system proxy settings. You can also manually specify the proxy using a command line argument:

```
chrome --proxy-server=127.0.0.1:8888
```

Firefox

The latest versions of Firefox default to **Use system proxy settings**, meaning that Fiddler will capture their traffic automatically. In Firefox 4 and later, you can verify the settings by clicking **Tools** > **Options** to open Firefox's Options window. Click the **Advanced** icon, and click the **Network** tab. On that tab, click the **Settings** button in the **Connections** area. Select the **Use system proxy settings** option from the list.

Fiddler also installs **FiddlerHook**, a Firefox add-on to simplify use of Fiddler with Firefox. You may need to enable the add-on using **Firefox's Tools > Add-ons > Extensions** screen. When enabled, FiddlerHook adds a **Monitor with Fiddler** command to Firefox's **Tools** menu.

The menu offers the ability to change whether Fiddler is used as Firefox's proxy, and permits you to launch Fiddler directly. If the **Show StatusBar item** option is ticked, and Firefox's **View > Toolbars > Add-on Bar** option is also ticked (this option is only present in the latest Firefox versions when add-on "The Add-on Bar (restored)" is installed), Firefox's status bar will show the current state of FiddlerHook at the bottom right:

Fiddler: ON (auto)

If you click on this status bar panel, a popup menu enables you to change your FiddlerHook settings, as well as providing one-click commands to clear the Firefox cache and cookies.

When FiddlerHook is enabled, you can also add a button to Firefox's toolbar that launches Fiddler. Right-click the Firefox toolbar and choose **Customize**. Drag the **Fiddler** button to the desired location:

Even if you disable or cannot use the FiddlerHook plugin, it is simple to reconfigure Firefox to use Fiddler.

Opera

To configure Opera to use Fiddler, click **Preferences** on the **Tools** menu. Click the **Advanced** tab, and click **Network** in the list at the left. Click the **Proxy Servers** button, and set the **HTTP** and **HTTPS** proxy server fields to 127.0.0.1 and the Port for each to 8888.

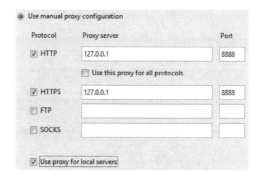

Other Browsers

Of the dozens of minor browsers that run on Windows, most will pick up the default proxy settings automatically. For the few that do not, you can usually follow configuration steps similar to those used for Opera—use whatever UI the browser provides to set the HTTP and HTTPS proxy to point at Fiddler's proxy endpoint, which runs on 127.0.0.1:8888.

Alternatively, you can also configure many browsers to use a Proxy Configuration script. Fiddler automatically generates such a script and updates its contents as the Capture Traffic setting is toggled. Use the **Copy Browser Proxy Configuration URL** link on the **Tools** > **Fiddler Options** > **Connections** tab to copy the proxy configuration script URL to your clipboard for easy pasting into the browser's configuration settings.

Capture Traffic from Other Applications

The most-commonly used HTTP/HTTPS/FTP network stack in Windows is called WinINET, and it is used by Internet Explorer and tens of thousands of other client applications. These applications generally work seamlessly with Fiddler because Fiddler sets the WinINET proxy settings directly when capturing is started.

However, Windows includes several other networking stacks that are not based on WinINET, and some other applications, like Firefox, ship with their own networking components. In many cases, those components will automatically adopt the WinINET proxy settings on application launch; in some cases, you will need to manually configure the component or application to point at Fiddler.

WinHTTP

WinHTTP is similar to WinINET except that it is designed for silent operation in Windows Services and other contexts. It is used by Windows components like BITS (background intelligent transfer service) and by features like Windows Update and the CryptoAPI certificate validation code. Depending on how it is being used, WinHTTP may automatically chain to Fiddler if Fiddler is running *before* the WinHTTP-based application is started. If your application is calling into WinHTTP, you may use the WinHttpOpen or WinHttpSetOption APIs to direct requests through Fiddler. If you cannot change the application's code, you can change the default WinHTTP proxy settings using command line tools.

On Windows XP & Windows 2003 or earlier:

```
proxycfg -p http=127.0.0.1:8888;https=127.0.0.1:8888
```

On Windows Vista and later, use:

```
netsh winhttp set proxy 127.0.0.1:8888
```

If you follow these configuration steps, you should manually change the proxy settings back when you close Fiddler, otherwise WinHTTP-based applications may subsequently fail to connect to the network.

.NET Framework

The Microsoft .NET Framework provides implementations of the HTTP/HTTPS and FTP protocols using the System.Net assembly. In some cases, .NET-based applications will automatically adopt the WinINET proxy when the application starts, so starting Fiddler before the application can ensure that its traffic is captured.

If that doesn't happen, the application's code can be temporarily modified to point at Fiddler by setting the proxy configuration as follows:

```
GlobalProxySelection.Select = new WebProxy("127.0.0.1", 8888);
```

Alternatively, you can manually specify the proxy on an individual WebRequest object like so:

```
objRequest = (HttpWebRequest)WebRequest.Create(url);
objRequest.Proxy= new WebProxy("127.0.0.1", 8888);
```

If you don't have access to the application's source, you can specify the proxy inside the application's configuration manifest. Edit (or create) the yourappname.exe.config file in the application's folder, adding or updating the following section:

```
<configuration>
  <system.net>
    <defaultProxy>
      <proxy
        usesystemdefault="true"
        bypassonlocal="false"
        proxyaddress="http://127.0.0.1:8888"
      />
    </defaultProxy>
  </system.net>
</configuration>
```

Instead of modifying an individual application's manifest, you might also adjust the machine-wide settings in the machine.config file's configuration section. The advantage of updating machine.config is that the change will apply to .NET code running in *any* application in *any* user-account, including the service accounts used by ASP.NET applications running atop IIS.

Regardless of how you specify your proxy settings, .NET will always bypass the Fiddler proxy for URLs that point to the current machine (also known as "loopback"). Debugging of loopback traffic requires additional configuration, as described later in this chapter.

Java

Some Java Runtime Environments (JREs) will automatically adopt the WinINET proxy settings automatically. Otherwise, the mechanism to set the default proxy server may depend on which JRE you use; one JRE includes an applet in the Windows Control Panel that enables proxy selection.

If neither of the following two command lines works for your JRE:

```
jre -DproxySet=true -DproxyHost=127.0.0.1 -DproxyPort=8888 MyApp

jre -DproxySet=true -Dhttp.proxyHost=127.0.0.1 -Dhttp.proxyPort=8888
```

…please consult the documentation for your JRE to learn how to configure its proxy.

PHP / cURL

To proxy traffic from cURL running inside PHP, add the following line of code before you send your web requests, where $ch is the handle returned by curl_init():

```
curl_setopt($ch, CURLOPT_PROXY, '127.0.0.1:8888');
```

Capture Traffic from Services

Fiddler only registers as the system proxy for the current user running Fiddler. That means that system services running in different accounts, including ASP.NET and IIS Worker Processes, will not send their traffic to Fiddler by default.

Unfortunately, the configuration steps to proxy traffic from system accounts are generally scenario-specific. For instance, to capture Web Service calls from ASP.NET pages, edit the web.config or machine.config files for the ASP.NET installation, or modify the code to manually specify a web proxy using the steps in the .NET Framework configuration section.

For Windows Services that utilize other networking stacks (e.g. Java or WinHTTP), you will need to find the configuration settings for those services and configure their proxy manually.

Capture Traffic to Loopback

You may need to take special configuration steps to capture traffic that is sent to a server running on the same computer as the client application and Fiddler are both running on. Such traffic is called "loopback" traffic because it never leaves the machine; loopback traffic typically includes traffic sent to the loopback addresses of 127.0.0.1, [::1], the hostname localhost, and sometimes to any of the current computer's TCP/IP addresses.

There are three scenarios that can cause problems with loopback traffic:

1. Many client applications and frameworks are hardcoded to bypass the proxy server for loopback traffic.

2. On Windows Vista and later, HTTP authentication behaves different when the client and server are on the same computer.

3. On Windows 8, Metro-style applications are not able to connect to loopback listeners (like Fiddler) running outside of the app package.

Let's explore each of these in turn.

Loopback Bypasses

Many clients automatically bypass the proxy for loopback traffic with the expectation that a remote proxy server wouldn't know what to do with traffic bound for "127.0.0.1", since the proxy server's definition of that address is different than the client's. However, these clients failed to consider the case where the proxy server is running on the same computer as the client (like Fiddler), in which case both the client and the proxy have the same definition for such addresses.

Prior to Internet Explorer 9, all traffic sent via the WinINET networking stack (used by IE, Office, etc.) would bypass the proxy server if it was sent to addresses of 127.0.0.1, [::1], or the hostname localhost. Current versions of Opera do the same, and Firefox's **No Proxy For** setting is set to localhost, 127.0.0.1 by default. Microsoft .NET Framework versions 1 through 4.5 also bypass the proxy for loopback requests.

If you attempt to use one of these clients to connect to a loopback server, the client ignores the proxy setting.

The simplest way to capture such traffic in Fiddler is to change the hostname requested by the client so that the client doesn't recognize it as bound for a loopback address. One option is to simply use the current computer's DNS hostname (e.g. http://mymachinename), but this requires that you know the current computer's hostname and can make it complicated to build test cases that work across multiple machines.

To help mitigate that shortcoming, Fiddler supports several "virtual hostnames" that alias the loopback addresses:

Rather than:	Instead use:
127.0.0.1	ipv4.fiddler
[::1]	ipv6.fiddler
localhost	localhost.fiddler

By using these virtual hostnames, the client will send the traffic to Fiddler, and Fiddler will automatically substitute the correct hostname in the request URL and Host header.

In Internet Explorer 9, WinINET was enhanced with a new feature that allows the client to configure WinINET to proxy loopback traffic. To opt-in to this behavior, the Proxy Bypass List is configured with the special token `<-loopback>`; Fiddler sets this token automatically by default, ensuring that you can easily see traffic sent to the local computer. Starting in Windows 8, the WinHTTP stack also respects the `<-loopback>` token. Hopefully, Opera and the .NET Framework will permit loopback proxying in future versions.

Loopback Authentication

Windows Vista and later attempt to protect the user against "loopback authentication" attacks, in which a client thinks it is authenticating with a remote server but is actually authenticating back to the local computer. Such attacks are usually attempting to elevate privilege against the local computer. When Windows encounters an unexpected attempt to authenticate to the local machine, the authentication request will be blocked.

To disable loopback protection, set `DisableLoopbackCheck=1` as described here: `http://support.microsoft.com/kb/926642`.

Loopback Blocked from Metro-style Windows 8 Apps

Windows 8 introduced a new application-isolation technology known as AppContainer. This technology is used by new "Metro-style apps" including the Immersive mode of Internet Explorer, as well as all applications you download from the Windows Store. In order to prevent inter-process communication between the isolated AppContainer processes and other processes (most of which run at higher privilege) Metro-style applications are prevented (by the firewall) from making network connections to servers running on the local computer. This blockage occurs no matter what hostname is used-- attempts to connect to `http://localhost`, `http://127.0.0.1`, and `http://machinename` will all fail. Using the `CheckNetIsolation.exe` tool, an end-user may exempt a single process from this restriction for debugging or development purposes only. Debugging an application with the latest version of Visual Studio will also temporarily allow it to connect to loopback.

By default, if you run Fiddler on Windows 8 and launch the Immersive browser or any Metro-style application, you will find that the app is unable to connect to any site, including Internet sites. That's because Fiddler is running on the local computer and the firewall will block the application from proxying its traffic to Fiddler. Because Fiddler is the configured proxy server, the app will conclude that the network is unavailable and abort the request.

To resolve this problem, a utility called **EnableLoopback** allows you to exempt one or more AppContainers from Loopback restrictions. Users of the v4 builds of Fiddler will find the `EnableLoopback.exe` utility installed by default; it can be launched using the **WinConfig** toolbar button at the left edge of the Fiddler toolbar:

Users of the v2 builds of Fiddler can download the utility from `http://fiddler2.com/r/?Win8EL`. The tool requires Administrative privileges to adjust the Loopback Exemptions list, and will prompt for permission to run as an Administrator when launched.

If you `CTRL+Click` the WinConfig toolbar button, the utility will automatically exempt all AppContainers and exit. Otherwise, as the utility starts, it will enumerate all of the AppContainers on the local computer and display them in a list. A checkbox before each entry indicates whether the AppContainer is exempted from loopback restrictions. You can individually change the setting on a per-AppContainer basis, or you may use the buttons at the top of the tool to adjust all AppContainers' exemptions together. After making changes, click the **Save Changes** button to commit the list back to Windows.

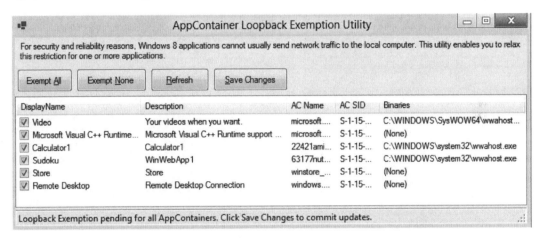

After exempting an app's AppContainer from loopback restrictions, you will find that Fiddler can successfully debug its traffic, just like any other desktop application.

Run Fiddler in a Virtual Machine on Mac OS X

As a Windows Application, Fiddler cannot run on Mac OS X natively. However, virtualization products like Oracle's **VirtualBox**, **VMWare Fusion** and **Parallels Desktop** permit you to run Windows applications like Fiddler in a virtual machine on your Mac.

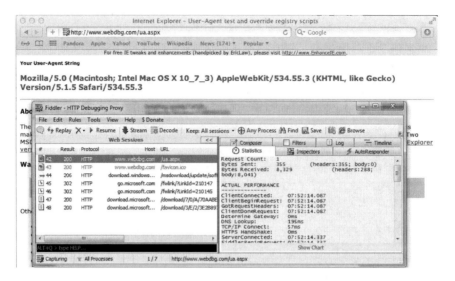

To run Fiddler under Parallels, only minor configuration changes are needed. Install Parallels and reconfigure the Windows Virtual Machine's **Hardware** > **Network 1** Type setting to use **Bridged Network** mode:

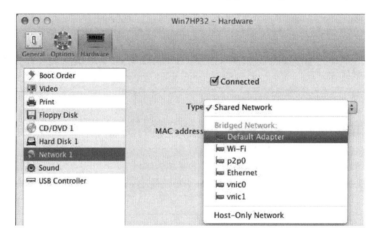

This configuration will enable your Mac to send network traffic into the Virtual Machine. Restart the Virtual Machine and install Fiddler. To configure Fiddler, click **Tools** > **Fiddler Options** > **Connections** and check the box labeled **Allow remote computers to connect**. You will need to restart Fiddler for the change to take effect, and you may need to reconfigure your firewall to allow incoming connections to the Fiddler process. These steps allow Fiddler to accept connections from the Mac environment. Now, you must manually configure your Mac to direct its web traffic through Fiddler running in your Virtual Machine.

First, you must learn the IP address of the virtual machine. To do so, hover over the **Online** indicator at the far right of the Fiddler toolbar. A tooltip will show you the IP addresses assigned to the virtual machine:

Next, click the Apple Menu and click **System Preferences**. Click the **Network** icon, select the active network connection, and click the **Advanced** button. Click the **Proxies** tab. Enable the **Web Proxy (HTTP)** and **Secure Web Proxy (HTTPS)** options to point to the IPv4 address of the virtual machine; also specify that the proxy runs on port 8888.

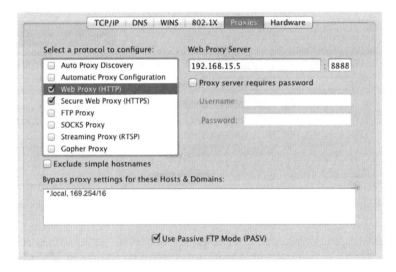

After configuring the Mac's proxy, Fiddler will begin capturing traffic from Safari and other applications. When you're done using Fiddler, return to the OS X System Preferences and disable the proxy settings.

Capture Traffic from Other Computers

You can use Fiddler to capture traffic from any application running on another computer if that application supports a proxy server; after all, that's how proxy servers normally work. To capture traffic in this configuration, you must first configure Fiddler and then configure the other computer.

To configure Fiddler, click **Tools** > **Fiddler Options** > **Connections** and check the box labeled **Allow remote computers to connect**. You will need to restart Fiddler for the change to take effect, and you may need to reconfigure your firewall to allow incoming connections to the Fiddler process.

You should verify the client computer can successfully reach Fiddler without problems caused by the firewall or routing by opening its browser and visiting http://IPOfTheFiddlerPC:8888. If you see the "Fiddler Echo Service" webpage, then you know that the client and Fiddler are able to communicate.

After verifying connectivity, your next step is to configure the proxy settings on the other computer, using the techniques described in the Capturing Traffic from Other Applications section above. The one difference is that instead of using 127.0.0.1:8888 as the proxy address, you must instead use IPOfTheFiddlerPC:8888. So, for instance, the other computer's **Internet Explorer** > **Tools** > **Internet Options** > **Connections** > **LAN Settings** screen might look like this:

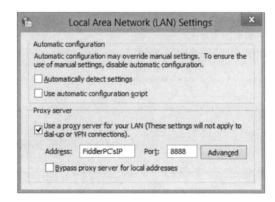

A few tips:

- When traffic is from another computer, filters that rely upon the process name (e.g. "Show only Web Browser traffic") will not work, as the process name cannot be determined for remote traffic.
- If you plan to decrypt HTTPS traffic from a client not running on the same computer as Fiddler, see the HTTPS Configuration chapter for configuration steps.
- When you stop debugging by closing Fiddler, you will need to clear the other computer's proxy settings. Otherwise, all of its subsequent requests will fail because the proxy server is not running.

Capture Traffic from Devices

Most computing devices that support Wi-Fi or Ethernet can be configured to send their traffic to Fiddler; this includes iOS devices like the iPhone, iPad, and iPod Touch, many Android devices, and all Windows Phone and Windows RT devices.

Begin by following the steps in the previous section to configure Fiddler to allow traffic from remote computers. Next, it's best to test the connection between the device and the computer running Fiddler—use the device's browser to visit http://IPOfTheFiddlerPC:8888 and verify that the device's traffic appears in the Web Sessions list. You may need to disable the device's cellular (3G) connection in order to ensure that traffic is sent only over Wi-Fi. If you don't see traffic from the device and it shows a connection error, you may need to configure your Wi-Fi network. Two common configuration issues are encountered:

1. Wi-Fi Isolation

2. IPsec

Many home routers offer a **Wi-Fi Isolation** feature, in which Wi-Fi-connected devices may not connect to devices that are attached directly to the router's Ethernet ports. Some routers even offer the ability to block one Wi-Fi client from connecting to another Wi-Fi client. If your router offers such features, you will need to disable them to allow your device to reach Fiddler.

Some corporate networks use **IPsec** for security; IPsec prevents connections from non-IPsec clients to IPsec clients. Most devices do not support IPsec, so when you need to send traffic from such a device, you must configure the machine running Fiddler with an "IPsec Boundary Exception" to permit inbound traffic not protected with IPsec. On many networks, such exceptions can only be created by a Network Administrator.

After you've successfully connected your device to Fiddler, you will need to configure it to proxy its HTTP and HTTPS traffic.

Apple iOS Proxy Settings

To access the proxy settings on an iPhone, iPad, or iPod, click the **Settings** icon on the home screen. In the Settings list, pick **General** and then choose **Network** from the list. Click **WiFi** and push the small blue arrow at the right of the Wi-Fi network's name to configure its settings. Click the **Manual** option in the **HTTP Proxy** section. In the **Server** box, enter the IP address or hostname of your Fiddler instance. In the **Port** box, provide the port Fiddler is listening on. You should leave the **Authentication** slider set to Off.

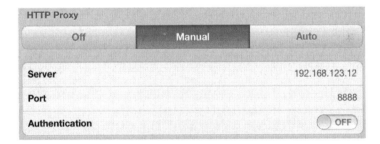

Windows Phone Proxy Settings

To access the proxy settings on your Windows Phone, open the **Settings** app and click the **Wi-Fi** entry. Tap and hold the Wi-Fi network's name and click **Edit**. Set the **Proxy** slider to On. In the **Server/URL** box, enter the IP address or hostname of your Fiddler instance. In the **Port** box, provide the port Fiddler is listening on. Leave the **Proxy authentication** slider set to Off.

Windows RT Proxy Settings

The new Windows RT operating system only runs Metro-style applications; this blocks Fiddler from running directly on the device. However, you can configure your Windows RT device to send its traffic to a traditional Windows 8 desktop or laptop computer. From the Windows RT Start screen, type **proxy** and click the **Settings** option to show the **Configure Proxy Server** tile. Click the tile to launch the **Internet**

Properties dialog box on the desktop. Click the **LAN Settings** button and adjust the settings as in the following screenshot, placing the IPv4 address of the Fiddler PC in the **Address** box:

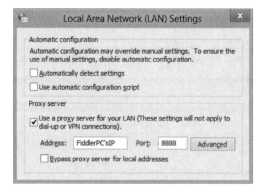

Other Devices

Most other devices that support Wi-Fi offer a way to configure a proxy using a Settings applet. However, a small number of devices, like some versions of Amazon's Kindle Fire, do not provide a supported mechanism to configure the proxy server. To use Fiddler with these devices, you may need to "jailbreak" the device to get access to non-public configuration settings, or utilize Fiddler in reverse-proxy mode, described later in this chapter.

Tips:

- If you don't see all traffic, ensure that you've disabled the device's cellular features to force all traffic to use the Wi-Fi network.

- Most devices will require special configuration to allow Fiddler to decrypt their HTTPS traffic. Configuration details can be found in the chapter on HTTPS decryption.

Use Fiddler as a Reverse Proxy

Sometimes, you may want to use Fiddler to capture traffic but cannot configure the client to use a proxy server. To address this need, Fiddler can operate as a "reverse proxy." In the reverse proxy configuration, Fiddler runs on a server and forwards inbound requests to a different port or even a different computer.

For instance, say you're running a website on port 80 of a machine named WEBSERVER. You're connecting to the website using a Kindle Fire, for which you cannot configure the web proxy. You want to capture the traffic from the tablet, and the server's response.

1. Start Fiddler on the WEBSERVER machine, running on the default port of 8888.

2. Click **Tools** > **Fiddler Options**, and ensure the **Allow remote computers to connect** checkbox is checked. Restart if needed.

3. Choose **Rules** > **Customize Rules**.

4. Inside the `OnBeforeRequest` handler, add a new line of code:

    ```
    if (oSession.HostnameIs("webserver")) oSession.host = "webserver:80";
    ```

5. On the Kindle, navigate to `http://webserver:8888`

Requests from the tablet will appear in Fiddler. The requests are forwarded from port 8888 to port 80 where your webserver is running. The responses are sent back through Fiddler to the device, which has no idea that the content originally came from port 80.

If you'd like, you can use Fiddler as a reverse proxy without changing the port that the client application targets. To do so, you must reconfigure both your web server software and Fiddler. First, reconfigure your web server to listen on a new port. For instance, if your web server runs on port 80, you must reconfigure it to run on port 81. Then, configure Fiddler to listen on port 80 using the box on the **Tools** > **Fiddler Options** > **Connections** tab.

Acting as a Reverse Proxy for HTTPS

One problem with running as a reverse proxy is that the client never knows that its traffic is really flowing through a proxy server. That means that if the client makes a HTTPS request to Fiddler, it does not establish a `CONNECT` tunnel first, it instead attempts to begin a HTTPS handshake immediately. Fiddler, expecting a HTTP request, will consider the binary HTTPS handshake as malformed traffic and will abort the connection.

This problem can be solved by creating an additional network listener for Fiddler to receive HTTPS connections. In the QuickExec box, type

```
!listen 444 WebServer
```

This will create a new network listener on port 444 which will expect all inbound connections to start with a HTTPS handshake. Fiddler will act as the server, returning a certificate for whatever hostname was specified in the second parameter to the listen command. In the example above, the certificate would match any request to `https://WebServer`.

After the secure connection is established, the `OnBeforeRequest` handler in FiddlerScript may route the inbound secure requests to the actual server. You can examine the `oS.oRequest.pipeClient.LocalPort` property to identify requests that were sent to the secure listener.

Chain to Upstream Proxy Servers

By default, Fiddler will adopt the current system's proxy settings and use those settings as the default upstream gateway proxy for all outbound requests:

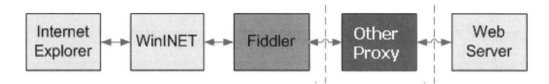

Fiddler supports all types of proxy settings, including manually specified proxies, proxy scripts, and automatically detected (WPAD) proxies. Any proxy bypass list will also be respected.

Your system's default proxy settings (see Internet Explorer's **Tools** > **Internet Options** > **Connections** > **LAN Settings** screen) are used as the upstream gateway by default. That's true even if you don't normally use Internet Explorer for anything else, or you rely upon a dialup modem or VPN connection that has a different default proxy. If you wish to prevent Fiddler from automatically chaining to your system's default proxy, adjust the settings inside the **Tools** > **Fiddler Options** > **Gateway** tab.

If required, you may use FiddlerScript to override the default gateway proxy for an individual Session. To do so, set the X-OverrideGateway flag. If you set the flag's value to DIRECT, Fiddler will bypass the gateway and send the request directly to the target server. If you set the value to an *address:port* combination like myproxyserver:80, Fiddler will instead use the specified proxy for that Session.

Chain to SOCKS / TOR

By default, Fiddler expects a proxy specified by the X-OverrideGateway flag to use the CERN proxy protocol used by nearly all proxies. However, one less popular proxy standard exists, called SOCKS. In the SOCKS protocol, the client sends the proxy a binary preface which specifies the target address to which a TCP/IP connection should be made. After the SOCKS proxy confirms that the requested connection tunnel has been generated, the client sends its web traffic through the tunnel.

The SOCKS protocol is occasionally used by corporate Virtual Private Networking (VPN) software, but it is also used to make connections into the Tor Project. The Tor Project can be thought of a global proxy network designed to provide anonymity for users of the project. Tor network requests are bounced between world-wide endpoints in an attempt to prevent network monitors from determining the origin of any given request. SOCKS protocol version 4a also allows the proxy server to perform DNS lookups, enhancing privacy. When connected to Tor using SOCKS v4a, DNS resolution happens privately in the cloud rather than from your local computer.

Beyond enhancing privacy, one other interesting aspect of the Tor network is that it allows you to experience your site as if you were coming from a different location. For instance, when using Tor, I visited a page with advertising. The ads were in Dutch because my request exited the Tor network in Amsterdam.

When setting the X-OverrideGateway flag, use the socks= prefix to indicate that Fiddler should use the SOCKS v4a protocol when speaking to the upstream server. For instance, the Tor Browser sets up an entry point to the Tor network using a SOCKS proxy on port 9150. You can add the following inside your

FiddlerScript's OnBeforeRequest method to route any request to test.example.com through the Tor network:

```
if (oSession.HostnameIs("test.example.com")) {
  oSession["x-OverrideGateway"] = "socks=127.0.0.1:9150";
}
```

If you'd instead prefer to send *all* of your web traffic via Tor, you can simply set the X-OverrideGateway flag unconditionally for each Session, and even block non-Tor traffic, as shown in the following example:

```
// Option inside FiddlerScript's Handlers class:
public static RulesOption("Use &Tor")
BindPref("fiddlerscript.rules.ephemeral.UseTor")
var m_EnableTOR: boolean = false;

// Script inside OnBeforeRequest
if (m_EnableTOR)
{
  oSession["X-OverrideGateway"] = "socks=127.0.0.1:9150";

  // Boolean controls whether we disallow non-TOR URLs
  var bRequireONION: Boolean = false;
  var sProc = oSession.LocalProcess;

  if ((!oSession.isAnyFlagSet(SessionFlags.RequestGeneratedByFiddler)
      && !sProc.StartsWith("firefox"))
      || (bRequireONION && !oSession.hostname.EndsWith(".onion")))
  {
    oSession.utilCreateResponseAndBypassServer();
    oSession.responseCode = 504;
    oSession["ui-strikeout"] = "not onion";
    return;
  }

  oSession["ui-backcolor"] = "#EFEF9F";
}
```

VPNs, Modems, and Tethering

When you establish a VPN, 3G tethering, or dial-up modem connection in Windows, WinINET will use that connection's proxy settings for all requests. To ensure that such traffic is captured by Fiddler, ensure that the **Monitor all connections** box is checked inside **Tools > Fiddler Options > Connections**.

Some uncommon network software products operate outside of the WinINET layer. When connected using such software, your web traffic may not be visible to Fiddler because it is being captured and routed using mechanisms beyond WinINET's control.

DirectAccess

Recent versions of Windows support a technology known as DirectAccess (`http://technet.microsoft.com/en-us/network/dd420463`) that permits remote access to a corporate network without establishing a VPN. DirectAccess is integrated into WinINET so that requests which flow over DirectAccess are never sent to the system default proxy.

Unfortunately, this behavior means that Fiddler cannot observe traffic when DirectAccess is in use.

It appears that individual DirectAccess configuration entries can be updated in the registry to specify a per-target proxy server, but debugging via this mechanism would prove very cumbersome. Instead, when using Fiddler in such an environment, engineers typically use Remote Desktop to access a desktop PC running inside the corporate network, then run Fiddler and the client application on that PC.

Windows Phone Tethering

Unfortunately, the Windows Phone team decided to configure their `IPOverUsbSvc.exe` service to operate on port 8888, the same port used by Fiddler. As a consequence, when you plug a Windows Phone device into your PC, you may find that Fiddler doesn't show any traffic and all clients' web requests fail. This problem occurs because all requests are being sent to the Phone's service process instead of the Fiddler proxy.

To resolve the conflict, you can simply change Fiddler's listening port inside **Tools** > **Fiddler Options** > **Connections** from 8888 to any other available port, like 8899.

MEMORY USAGE AND FIDDLER'S BITNESS

Fiddler stores the entire request and response in memory; this means that Fiddler can use large amounts of random access memory (RAM) while it is running. The Operating System's memory manager is designed to manage the use of memory by applications and ensures that even if Fiddler is using a large amount of memory, rarely-accessed objects are swapped out of the system's physical memory into the disk-based pagefile.

However, even with lots of RAM and disk space, Fiddler may occasionally show a warning message:

```
Exception of type 'System.OutOfMemoryException' was thrown.
  at System.IO.MemoryStream.set_Capacity(Int32 value)
  at System.IO.MemoryStream.EnsureCapacity(Int32 value)
  at System.IO.MemoryStream.Write(Byte[] buffer, Int32 offset, Int32 count)
  at Fiddler.Session.Execute(Object objThreadstate)
```

This message is misleading because the system isn't usually *out of memory*—the memory manager could not find a *contiguous* block of address space large enough to store the request or response. This problem most often occurs when downloading large files (e.g. a video over a hundred megabytes in size). No matter how much RAM you have, a 32bit process is limited to an address space of 2 gigabytes in size. Each object in that address space can cause "fragmentation" that could prevent storage of large objects by splitting available memory into chunks that are too small to store an entire response within one contiguous block.

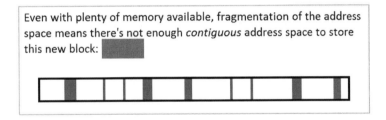

On a 32bit computer, if you have thousands of Sessions in Fiddler's Web Sessions list, fragmentation can prevent a response as small as a few megabytes from being stored. You can reduce the incidence of this problem by clearing Fiddler's Web Sessions list periodically. Alternatively, use the **Keep Only** box on the toolbar to automatically trim the Web Sessions list to a fixed number of Sessions to free up space.

Out-of-memory errors are rarely encountered when Fiddler runs on a 64bit version of Windows because the 64bit address space is so large that you cannot possibly fill it or fragment it enough to prevent storage of even giant Sessions. However, even on 64bit computers, each individual request and response is limited to 2 gigabytes due to an underlying limit within the .NET Framework; larger requests or responses cannot be buffered or stored.

You can help avoid out-of-memory errors when downloading huge files by adding the following code to your FiddlerScript inside the OnPeekAtResponseHeaders function. This snippet will cause files larger than 5 megabytes to stream to the client and Fiddler will not keep a copy:

```
// This block enables streaming for files larger than 5mb
if (oSession.oResponse.headers.Exists("Content-Length"))
{
  var sLen = oSession.oResponse["Content-Length"];
  if (!isNaN(sLen)) {
    var iLen = parseInt(sLen);
    if (iLen > 5000000) {
      oSession.bBufferResponse = false;
      oSession["ui-color"] = "yellow";
      oSession["log-drop-response-body"] = "save memory";
    }
  }
}
```

If you're building on FiddlerCore or writing a Fiddler Extension, you can use similar logic:

```
FiddlerApplication.ResponseHeadersAvailable += delegate(Fiddler.Session oS)
  {
    if (oS.oResponse.headers.Exists("Content-Length"))
    {
      int iLen = 0;
      if (int.TryParse(oS.oResponse["Content-Length"], out iLen))
      {
        // File larger than 5mb? Stream and don't save content
        if (iLen > 5000000)
        {
            oS.bBufferResponse = false;
            oS["log-drop-response-body"] = "save memory";
        }
      }
    }
  };
```

By default, Fiddler will always run in 64bit mode when running on a 64bit version of Windows. In rare instances, you may prefer to run Fiddler in 32bit mode. You must run in 32bit mode when you're using an extension that requires native binaries that are only available as 32bit modules (e.g. Silverlight 4) or your FiddlerScript depends upon other modules unavailable in 64bit. For example, the Microsoft.Jet. OLEDB.4.0 database provider used to write to Microsoft Access .MDB database files is not available in 64bit mode. To force Fiddler to run in 32bit mode on 64bit Windows, use the ForceCPU.exe tool located in the Fiddler installation folder.

Buffering vs. Streaming Traffic

In order to enable modification of requests and responses, Fiddler must buffer messages before passing them along to their destinations. HTML5 WebSockets automatically stream all messages bi-directionally and audio/video responses are streamed automatically.

Request Buffering

When a client connects to Fiddler, Fiddler will, by default, read the entire HTTP request from the client. If a breakpoint is set, the request is then paused to allow tampering using the Inspectors. After the request is resumed, the server connection is established and Fiddler transmits the entire request to the server.

Fiddler offers a mechanism to stream a HTTP request body to the server as it is read from the client. This is primarily useful if you need to use Fiddler to transmit uploads larger than 2 gigabytes, because .NET is unable to buffer arrays of that size.

To activate request streaming, you must set the `BufferRequest` property on the Session's Request object to `false` before the request body is read. Inside FiddlerScript's `OnPeekAtRequestHeaders` function (you may need to uncomment it), add code similar to the following:

```
if (oSession.host.Contains("whatever.com") &&
    oSession.oRequest.headers.ExistsAndContains("Transfer-Encoding", "chunked"))
{
  oSession["ui-backcolor"] = "orange";
  oSession["log-drop-request-body"] = "streamingThisRequest";
  oSession.oRequest.BufferRequest = false;
}
```

Streamed requests cannot be modified using Fiddler's Inspectors.

Response Buffering

After sending the request to the server, Fiddler begins reading its response. Some common web scenarios (particularly streaming audio and video) are impacted negatively by response buffering, so Fiddler permits streaming of responses. Streamed responses cannot be modified using Fiddler's Inspectors. By default, only audio and video responses are configured to stream. You can configure all responses to stream using the toggle on the Fiddler toolbar, or you may stream selectively on a per-response basis by setting the Session's `bBufferResponse` property to `false` using FiddlerScript.

When streaming is enabled for a response, each block of data read from the server is immediately passed to the client application. By default, if the client application closes its connection to Fiddler, Fiddler will continue to read the response from the server to permit collection of the entire response. If you'd prefer Fiddler to abort the download if the client disconnects, set the `fiddler.network.streaming.AbortIfClientAborts` preference to `true`.

When buffering is disabled for a response, FiddlerScript's `OnBeforeResponse` method runs *after* the response is fully returned to the client. This (perhaps surprising) behavior allows operations that don't modify the response (e.g. logging the response body to a database) to work properly for all Sessions. If your code needs to determine whether a given response was streamed, it can test the Session's `BitFlags`:

```
bool bWasStreamed = oSession.isFlagSet(SessionFlags.ResponseStreamed);
```

If you need to modify the response body before it is sent to the client, you must disable streaming by setting `oSession.bBufferResponse=true` in either the `OnBeforeRequest` or `OnPeekAtResponseHeaders` handlers.

COMET

Fiddler's Inspectors will only show the response's body after the response data has been completely read from the server. But what happens if the server's response never ends? Such responses occur with streaming radio stations and on sites that use a web programming technique called COMET.

With COMET, a server uses a "hanging frame" or other mechanism to push data to the client using a long-held HTTP connection that trickles data to the client as needed. HTML5 introduces a similar mechanism called "Server Sent Events" which works using the same general mechanism. Because a server's COMET response never really "finishes," the response body data is not normally visible to Fiddler's Inspectors until the connection closes.

To enable such data to be inspected, Fiddler offers the **COMETPeek** command on the Web Session's context menu. When you invoke the command, Fiddler will take a "snapshot" of the in-progress response, allowing you to inspect the partial response data read from the server.

Fiddler's default behavior of buffering responses wreaks havoc with sites that depend on COMET. That's because the server's response never ends and therefore Fiddler's buffering of a COMET stream will usually cause the web application to stall. Fiddler automatically streams Server Sent Events responses that bear the Content-Type `text/event-stream`, but unfortunately, most COMET responses aren't marked in any way. You will need to manually exempt such responses from buffering if you do not wish to enable the Streaming option globally.

HTML5 WebSockets

The HTML5 specification introduces WebSockets, a technology that enables real-time socket communication between a client and server. To create a WebSocket, the client first establishes a HTTP(S) connection to the server. Next, the client and server handshake and agree to use the WebSocket protocol for subsequent traffic on the connection. The `ws://` and `wss://` URI schemes are used for plaintext and secure WebSockets respectively, even though the initial handshakes take place over HTTP or HTTPS.

To help ensure that WebSocket traffic flows unimpeded through a proxy (like Fiddler), clients will first establish a `CONNECT` to the proxy, requesting a tunnel to the destination server. If the WebSocket URI uses the `wss://` scheme, a HTTPS handshake then occurs. If the unsecure `ws://` scheme is used, then the HTTPS handshake is skipped.

The client then uses the newly-established connection to send a HTTP `GET` request with an `Upgrade` header proposing a switch to the `WebSocket` protocol. If the server agrees to change protocols, it sends a `HTTP/101 Switching Protocols` response. You can easily observe this process using the Web Sessions list and Inspectors:

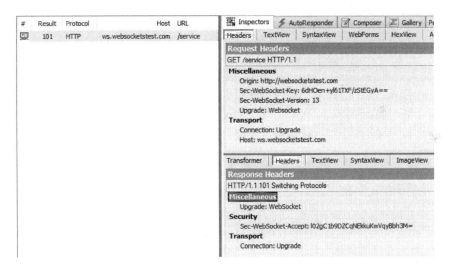

After the handshake, the client and server may send one another WebSocket messages in any order. Unlike HTTP's request-response pattern, the server may send WebSocket messages to the client without the client first sending a WebSocket message to the server. HTTP messages are no longer exchanged on a connection which has been upgraded to the WebSocket protocol, and you will not see the WebSocket messages in the Web Sessions list or the request or response Inspectors.

To view WebSocket messages, double-click or hit Enter on a `HTTP/101` WebSocket entry in the Web Sessions list to display and activate the **WebSockets** tab:

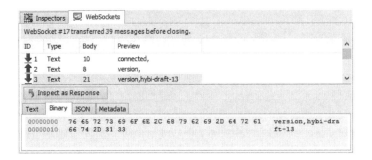

At the top of the WebSockets tab, text shows the current status of the WebSocket (active or closed). Below the status text is a simple list of the messages transmitted on the WebSocket connection. Each list entry shows an icon indicating whether the message was sent by the client or the server, and an auto-generated identification number. The **Type** column indicates the type of the message (Text, Binary, Continuation, and Close are common types). The **Body** column shows the length of the message body in bytes. The **Preview** column shows up to 64 characters of the message body.

Select a message in the list to inspect it using the Message Inspector subtabs at the bottom of the window. The **Text** tab interprets the message payload as text; the **Binary** tab will show the hexadecimal values of the binary payload, and the **JSON** tab attempts to interpret the payload as JSON, displaying it in a treeview. The **Metadata** tab shows information about the message, including the timestamps at which the message was received and resent.

These Message Inspectors may not sufficient for all needs; for instance, a message's payload might consist of a JPEG that you wish to view as an image. Push the **Inspect as Response** button to send the current message's payload to the main Web Sessions list as the body of a mock response. You can then use any of Fiddler's existing Response Inspectors to view the message's payload.

Today, the WebSockets tab does not expose functionality to manually modify messages as they pass through Fiddler; this capability will be added to future versions.

For now, you can modify WebSocket messages using FiddlerScript and the OnWebSocketMessage handler:

```
static function OnWebSocketMessage(oMsg: WebSocketMessage) {
  // Conditionally modify message content
  var sPayload = oMsg.PayloadAsString();
  if (sPayload.Contains("time")) {
    oMsg.SetPayload(sPayload + "... bazinga!");
  }
  // FiddlerApplication.Log.LogString(oMsg.ToString());
}
```

In this silly example, as each message is captured, Fiddler checks its payload for the string "time"; if found, the suffix "...bazinga!" is appended to the payload of the message before it is transmitted to its destination.

WebSocketMessage Objects

As with Fiddler's Session objects, each WebSocketMessage object contains a wealth of properties and methods that reveal information about the message and enable modifications to it.

The ID property returns the numeric identifier for the message.

The IsOutbound property returns true if the message is being sent by the client or false if it has been received from a server.

The PayloadAsString() method returns the message's payload interpreted as a string. For Text messages, this is simply the *unmasked* payload bytes interpreted as a UTF-8 string. If the message is not of the Text type, the method will return a hexadecimal string representing the unmasked bytes of the payload.

The PayloadLength property returns the length of the message body in bytes. The PayloadAsBytes() method returns a byte[] containing the unmasked payload bytes.

Use either of the SetPayload() methods to overwrite the body of the message using either a string or an array. If necessary, the bytes will be masked according to the message's masking key.

Payload Masking

To help prevent attacks against transparent proxies and other buggy but well-meaning intermediaries, a client's WebSocket messages are typically "masked" by XOR'ing the message bytes against a 4 byte masking key that is not visible to JavaScript running in a browser client. The MaskingKey property returns a byte[4] masking key, or null if the message is not masked.

The PayloadData property returns a byte[] containing the payload bytes *without* unmasking them.

FIDDLER AND HTTPS

When visiting a HTTPS site in Fiddler, there's not a lot to see by default. Instead of the expected list of requests and responses, you'll only see one or more CONNECT tunnels:

#	Result	Protocol	Host	URL	Body
🔒	200	HTTP	Tunnel to	www.fiddler2.com:443	0
🔒	200	HTTP	Tunnel to	www.telerik.com:443	0
🔒	200	HTTP	Tunnel to	www.facebook.com:443	0

The HTTPS protocol sandwiches an encrypted (SSL or TLS) connection between HTTP requests and the underlying TCP/IP network connection upon which those requests are sent. Network intermediaries or observers are thus prevented from viewing or modifying the HTTP traffic thanks to the use of the crypto-graphic protocols. If you use Fiddler's TextView Inspectors to look at these Tunnel Sessions, you'll only see basic information about the HTTPS handshake (such as the TLS protocol version, ciphers offered and selected, etc), but no request or response data.

You might then be surprised to learn that Fiddler can both view and modify HTTPS traffic if configured appropriately. Fiddler achieves this by using a "man-in-the-middle" approach to intercepting HTTPS, which means that when talking to the client, it pretends to be the server, and when talking to the server, it pretends to be the client.

The HTTPS protocol is explicitly designed to block this attack by using digital certificates to authenticate the identity of HTTPS servers (and optionally the client). When a client receives a certificate from the server, it validates that the certificate itself is trustworthy by determining whether it is chained to a **Root Certification Authority** that is trusted by the client or the operating system. Since you are typically running Fiddler on your own computer, you can reconfigure your browser or operating system to trust Fiddler's root certificate. After you do so, the client application will not complain when it encounters Fiddler-generated certificates.

To enable HTTPS traffic decryption in Fiddler, click **Tools** > **Fiddler Options**. On the **HTTPS** tab, tick the box labeled **Decrypt HTTPS traffic**.

When you enable HTTPS decryption, Fiddler will generate a self-signed root certificate and a matching Private Key. Fiddler will use this root certificate to generate HTTPS server certificates (also called "End Entity" certificates) for each secure site that you visit.

Trust the Fiddler Root Certificate

After generating the root certificate, Fiddler gives you the opportunity to add it to Windows' Trusted Root Certificate Authorities store. Adding the root to the Trusted Store will allow the HTTPS server certificates Fiddler later generates to be deemed valid by browsers and other applications. This will help stop browsers from showing warning screens and prevent applications from failing to connect due to "trust errors."

Fiddler and Windows show prompts to warn off users who might not understand the implications of trusting a certificate:

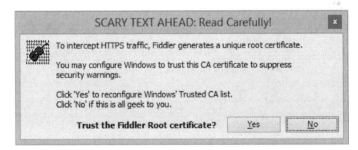

If you click **Yes**, Windows will then prompt you to confirm the change:

These warnings are deliberately verbose and scary, but the actual level of risk is minimal. Each Fiddler root certificate is generated uniquely per-computer, which improves security by ensuring that no other Fiddler user has the same root certificate. As such, the root certificate could only really be abused by malware running on the local computer, and if your computer is already infected by malware, you have bigger problems to worry about.

Machine-wide Trust on Windows 8+

On Windows 8 and later, Metro-style applications will not trust Fiddler's root certificate unless it is in the per-Machine Trusted Root certificate store. Therefore, after the prior steps add the certificate to your per-User Trusted Root certificate store, Fiddler will then launch an administrative program to add the certificate to the Machine store:

If you click **Yes** to launch the utility, it will confirm the operation:

After you click through this flurry of prompts, Fiddler's root certificate will be installed and applications that rely on the Windows certificate store will no longer present security errors when Fiddler is decrypting their traffic.

To later remove all Fiddler-generated certificates, untick the **Decrypt HTTPS traffic** checkbox and then press the **Remove Interception Certificates** button.

Manually Trust the Fiddler Root

If you'd prefer to manually trust the FiddlerRoot, launch `certmgr.msc` and drag the `DO_NOT_TRUST_FIDDLERROOT` certificate from the **Personal** folder to the **Trusted Root Certification Authorities** folder. If you wish to make this change on a machine-wide basis:

1. In Fiddler's Tools > Fiddler Options > HTTPS tab, click **Export Root Certificate to Desktop**.
2. Launch `mmc.exe`.
3. Click **File > Add/Remove Snap-In.**
4. Select the **Certificates** snap-in and press **Add.**
5. When prompted **This snap-in will always manage certificates for:** choose **Computer Account**
6. Click **Local Computer**, then **Finish**, then **OK.**
7. Open the **Certificates (Local Computer)** node.
8. Right-click the **Trusted Root Certificate Authorities** folder and choose **All Tasks > Import**.
9. Choose the file you exported in step #1 and import it.

Additional HTTPS Options

Before closing the Fiddler Options window, consider using the dropdown to configure which processes should have their traffic decrypted:

If you only plan to decrypt browser traffic, choose that option to avoid decrypting traffic from other applications that aren't of interest to you. Beyond saving CPU cycles and memory, doing so can prevent problems with applications that are not using HTTPS in standard ways (e.g. Outlook uses RPC-over-HTTPS tunnels to connect to Exchange Server) or that do not respect the Fiddler root certificates' presence in the Windows Trusted store (e.g. Dropbox).

You may also use the textbox to list servers for which HTTPS traffic should not be decrypted. For instance, I use the following settings to prevent decryption of Outlook Web Access and Dropbox traffic:

Skip decryption for the following hosts:
```
*.exchange.microsoft.com;*dropbox.com
```

Use semicolons to delimit the hostnames in the list, and use * as a wildcard character.

CONFIGURE CLIENTS FOR HTTPS DECRYPTION

While most applications (Internet Explorer, Microsoft Office, Chrome, Safari, etc.) use the Windows Certificate Store to validate certificate chains, some applications maintain their own certificate stores. For instance, Java Runtime Environments often have their own certificate stores, and the Firefox and Opera browsers also maintain their own certificate lists.

To configure such clients to trust Fiddler-generated certificates, you must first obtain Fiddler's root certificate as a `.CER` file. You have two options to do so:

1> Click the **Export Root Certificate to Desktop** button on the **HTTPS** tab of the **Fiddler Options** window.

2> While Fiddler is running, visit `http://127.0.0.1:8888/` in the browser and click the **FiddlerRoot Certificate** link to download the `.CER` file.

After you have the root certificate file, you can add it to the client application's Trusted Certificates list.

Browsers

Firefox
If you have the FiddlerHook add-on installed in Firefox, simply click Tools > Monitor with Fiddler > Trust FiddlerRoot certificate. Alternatively, click Firefox's **Tools** > **Options** menu. Click the **Advanced** button, and switch to the **Encryption** tab. Click **View Certificates** to open the **Certificate Manager**. Click the **Authorities** tab and click the **Import** button. Select the `FiddlerRoot.cer` file and click **Open**. Tick the **Trust this CA to identify websites** checkbox and press **Ok**. Firefox will now trust HTTPS server certificates generated by Fiddler.

Opera
In Opera, click **Tools > Preferences**. Click the **Advanced** tab, and click **Security** in the list. Click **Manage Certificates**. Click the **Authorities** tab and click the **Import...** button. Select the `FiddlerRoot.cer` file and click **Open**. Click the **Install** button and click the **Ok** button to confirm that you want to trust the certificate. Opera will now trust HTTPS server certificates generated by Fiddler.

Cross-machine scenarios
If you have configured Fiddler to proxy HTTPS traffic from other computers, those other computers must be manually configured to trust the root certificate from the Fiddler server machine. You can enable this trust by downloading the root certificate from the `http://FiddlerMachineName:8888/` page, then using the manual `certmgr.msc` steps to trust that root certificate.

One important reminder: Each Fiddler root certificate is generated uniquely *per-machine*. If a client PC has previously generated a Fiddler root certificate, that root certificate will interfere when proxying traffic through Fiddler running on a different machine. That's because the root certificates will not match (they'll have the same Subject CN but different public keys). This mismatch will cause fatal errors when establishing HTTPS connections-- even if the client has been configured to trust both root certificates. To avoid this problem, first remove all existing Fiddler root certificates from the client before trusting the new root certificate downloaded from the Fiddler server machine.

HTTPS and Devices

Windows Phone

In order for a Windows Phone device to trust the FiddlerRoot certificate, you must install the certificate onto the phone. To do so, open *http://FiddlerMachineName:8888/* from the device, and download the root certificate. Tap to open the `FiddlerRoot.cer` file, and when prompted by the **Install certificate?** screen, click the **Install** button.

Android and iOS

On Windows, Fiddler 4.5's default Certificate Maker is based on the `makecert.exe` command-line tool. The certificates it generates are accepted by virtually all Windows clients and most other platforms as well. However, Apple iOS devices including the iPad, iPhone, and iPod require that the root and server certificates contain additional metadata not included in `makecert.exe`-generated certificates. Some Android versions have similar requirements.

To enable Fiddler to generate certificates compatible with these devices, you have two options:

Use Windows 7+ Certificate API

On Windows 7 or later, click **Tools** > **Fiddler Options** > **HTTPS**. Click the **FiddlerDefaultCertificateProvider** link. In the screen that appears, choose **CertEnroll** from the Engine dropdown.

After making the change, untick the **Decrypt HTTPS traffic** checkbox. Click the **Remove Interception Certificates** button and accept all prompts. Restart Fiddler and retick the **Decrypt HTTPS traffic** checkbox.

Use the Bouncy Castle Certificate Maker addon

Alternatively, download the **Certificate Maker** addon from `http://fiddler2.com/r/?FiddlerCertMaker`.

This addon replaces the default certificate generation code in Fiddler with a version based on the open-source Bouncy Castle cryptography library. The plugin generates iOS-compatible certificates by default, and respects several Preferences to enable compatibility with a wide-variety of platforms.

For instance, say that a client requires that server certificates must have the `Critical` constraint applied on the `EKU`. You can configure the Certificate Maker plugin to add that constraint by using QuickExec to set the preference:

```
prefs set fiddler.certmaker.bc.ee.criticaleku True
```

The server certificates that generated by this plugin are not placed in the Windows Certificate store and are instead kept only in memory. Every time Fiddler restarts, new server certificates will be generated. (In contrast, certificates generated by the default certificate provider are individually added to the Personal certificates store as they are generated, and are only removed when you push the **Remove Interception Certificates** button.)

After configuring Fiddler to generate certificates that are compatible with your device, you must configure the device to trust Fiddler's root certificate. To do so, configure your device to use Fiddler as its proxy as described earlier in this book. Then open `http://ipv4.fiddler:8888/` from your device, and download the root certificate. Open the `FiddlerRoot.cer` file:

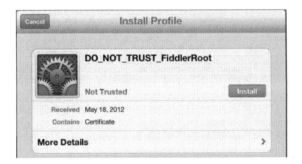

Tap the **Install** button. You'll then see a warning, which you may acknowledge by pressing the **Install** button:

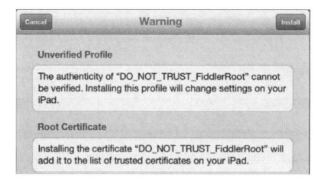

After Fiddler's root certificate is installed, your device's browser and applications should no longer complain about certificate errors when Fiddler is decrypting their traffic.

If you later decide to uninstall the root certificate from the device, open the **Settings** app, click **General**, and scroll down to **Profiles** at the bottom. Select the DO_NOT_TRUST_FiddlerRoot profile, and tap **Remove**.

Buggy HTTPS Servers

A small number of HTTPS servers implement the TLS protocol handshake incorrectly and will fail when Fiddler handshakes with them. The same connection failure will occur when a web browser connects to the server, but that failure may be silently handled by the browser automatically falling back to use an older version of the handshake protocol.

Fiddler can be configured to offer only specific protocol versions to the server in order to accommodate buggy implementations. You can use the **Enabled Protocols** link on the Tools > Fiddler Options > HTTPS tab to control which protocol versions Fiddler will use when connecting to the server.

Alternatively, you can limit the protocols on a per-request basis. Inside the OnBeforeRequest function, add code like so:

```
if (oSession.HTTPMethodIs("CONNECT") && oSession.HostnameIs("buggy.example.com"))
{
  oSession["x-OverrideSslProtocols"] = "ssl3";
}
```

By offering only SSLv3, you can accommodate servers that do not properly support extensions or other features of the TLS protocol.

Certificate Validation

When Fiddler connects to a HTTPS server, it will validate the server's certificate to ensure that the certificate is valid and contains the target site's hostname. By default, any certificate errors are presented for you to decide how to proceed:

If you choose **No**, the connection will be dropped. If you choose **Yes**, the certificate error will be ignored and the connection will be used as if it were valid. Fiddler will cache your decision until restarted. Because Fiddler generates its own certificate to secure the connection from the client, the client application will be unaware that the server's original certificate was invalid.

Certificate Pinning

A very small number of HTTPS client applications support a feature known as "Certificate Pinning" whereby the client application is hardcoded to accept only one *specific* certificate. Even if the connection uses a certificate that chains to a root that is otherwise fully-trusted by the operating system, such applications will refuse to accept an unexpected certificate.

To date, some Twitter and Dropbox apps include this feature, and Windows 8 Metro apps *may* opt-in to requiring specific certificates rather than relying upon the system's Trusted Root store. Firefox's automatic browser update feature will silently fail when Fiddler is decrypting its traffic. The Microsoft Security toolkit named EMET can enable pinning in any application for certain "high-value" sites (including Windows Live). The Chrome browser supports pinning, but it exempts locally-trusted roots like Fiddler's.

When a Certificate-Pinned application performs a HTTPS handshake through a CONNECT tunnel to Fiddler, it will examine the response's certificate and refuse to send any further requests when it discovers the Fiddler-generated certificate.

Unfortunately, there is no general-purpose workaround to resolve this; the best you can do is to exempt that application's traffic from decryption using the **HTTPS** tab or by setting the x-no-decrypt Session flag on the CONNECT tunnel. The flag will prevent Fiddler from decrypting the traffic in the tunnel and it will flow through Fiddler uninterrupted.

Use an Existing Certificate

While Fiddler is designed to automatically generate its own interception certificates, it is *possible* to configure it to use an external certificate and private key; for instance, if you host your own HTTPS server, you can configure Fiddler to use its CA-signed public certificate and private key. This mechanism allows you to bypass Certificate Pinning on sites you control, or temporarily run as a reverse proxy for a public HTTPS site.

 Warning: In general, using publicly-trusted certificates with Fiddler is a risky proposition. If your client PC has unfettered access to the private key matching a CA-signed certificate, there's a serious risk of having that key compromised by malware or other attacks.

To configure Fiddler to use a specific certificate for a target host, edit the **Main** function of your Fiddler-Script to store the certificate:

```
CertMaker.StoreCert("example.com", "C:\\temp\\cert.pfx", "TopSecretPassword");
```

This call instructs Fiddler to use the certificate and private key stored in the file `C:\temp\cert.pfx` that was protected using the password `TopSecretPassword` when a client sends a request to `https://example.com`.

FIDDLER AND FTP

Like HTTP, the File Transfer Protocol (FTP) is a TCP/IP-based protocol used for transferring files, but it predates and is not compatible with HTTP. However, the protocol remains the one exception to the rule that Fiddler can only view HTTP-based protocols. That's because when a client browser or application is configured to proxy FTP traffic using a CERN-style proxy (like Fiddler), the client will convert FTP download requests into HTTP GET requests before sending them to the proxy.

The client's expectation is that the proxy will then act as a *gateway*, converting each FTP-over-HTTP request into a FTP request that will be sent to the origin server using the FTP protocol. Only the URL and Authorization header are used in the FTP request; all other request headers are ignored.

Fiddler can deal with FTP traffic in three ways:

1. By acting as a HTTP-to-FTP gateway.

2. By chaining to an upstream CERN-style proxy server (e.g. Microsoft ISA) which will act as the HTTP-to-FTP gateway.

3. By responding to requests using the AutoResponder (or similar features).

To configure Fiddler to register as the system's FTP proxy, click **Tools** > **Fiddler Options**. On the **Connections** tab, tick the **Capture FTP requests** option and restart Fiddler.

If Fiddler receives a FTP request which is not sent to an upstream gateway proxy and which is not handled by an AutoResponder rule, it will attempt to connect to the server using the FTP protocol. Fiddler will reformat the FTP server's response as an HTTP response and return it to the client. There are several limitations when acting as a HTTP-to-FTP gateway; for instance, some of the Session's Timers will not be set. Streaming of FTP responses is not supported-- the complete FTP response will be buffered before being converted and returned to the client.

FIDDLER AND WEB AUTHENTICATION

Most public websites use HTML Forms for authentication—they prompt the client for a username and password. If the credentials supplied are valid, the client gets a login cookie that is sent for all subsequent requests. Fiddler can easily view, modify, and submit such cookies.

However, HTTP and HTTPS offer two native mechanisms for authenticating a client:

- HTTP Authentication
- HTTPS Client Certificates

Fiddler can be used with servers using either form of authentication.

HTTP Authentication

With HTTP Authentication, the client makes a HTTP request and the server responds with a HTTP/401 or HTTP/407 response demanding credentials. HTTP/401s are sent by web servers that require authentication, while HTTP/407s are sent by proxy servers.

There are four common authentication schemes in use in HTTP:

- Basic
- Digest
- NTLM
- Negotiate

In **Basic** authentication (RFC 2617) the client supplies the username and password in the Authorization request header. The client's credentials are simply base64-encoded and are trivially decoded by Fiddler's Auth Inspector. The Basic authentication scheme is primitive and obviously unsafe to use over unencrypted HTTP connections.

In **Digest** authentication, also described in RFC 2617, the server presents a challenge to the client using the WWW-Authenticate response header. The client combines the challenge data and its knowledge of the user's password to compute a message digest that proves to the server that it knows the password. This authentication scheme is stronger than Basic but is rather uncommon, owing to limited server support and various client bugs.

The **NTLM** authentication scheme is rarely used on the public Internet but is commonly used on Windows-based Intranets. When the server presents a HTTP/401 to the client, the client reissues the request indicating that it supports NTLM, then the server provides a challenge. The client uses the challenge and the credentials to generate the reply to the challenge, and the server returns the resource if the challenge was answered successfully. This pattern means that when NTLM authentication occurs, the client receives two HTTP/401 challenges before the resource is finally returned with a HTTP/200.

Unlike Basic and Digest, the NTLM scheme is not generally per-request. Instead NTLM is *per-connection*, meaning that a single authentication proof will be used to authorize all subsequent requests on the same connection. That's why you'll often see a flurry of HTTP/401s when first loading an Intranet site, then don't see any subsequent authentication challenges on later page loads.

The **Negotiate** authentication scheme (sometimes called Integrated Windows Authentication) is a "wrapper" protocol that uses either NTLM or the Kerberos protocol under the covers. At the HTTP layer, Negotiate generally behaves much like NTLM, requiring between one and three roundtrips per connection.

When NTLM or Negotiate is used through a proxy, client applications require the proxy to add a Proxy-Support: Session-Based-Authentication response header. This header indicates that the proxy understands that authenticated connections must not be shared between different clients. Fiddler adds this header automatically.

Automatic Authentication in Fiddler

Fiddler is able to automatically authenticate to servers that use the Digest, NTLM and Negotiate protocols. When Fiddler automatically authenticates, the client that issued the request will not see the interim HTTP/401 or HTTP/407 responses. That's because Fiddler itself consumes these responses, answers the server's challenges, and returns data to the client only after authentication is complete.

Enable the **Rules** > **Automatically Authenticate** menu option to instruct Fiddler to automatically respond to server or gateway proxy authentication challenges. Alternatively, set the X-AutoAuth property on the Session to a plaintext credential string. If you use a value of (default), then Fiddler will use the credentials of the Windows logon user account in which Fiddler is running:

```
static function OnBeforeRequest(oSession: Session)
{
  // To use the current Fiddler user's credentials:
  if (oSession.HostnameIs("ServerThatDemandsCreds")) {
    oSession["x-AutoAuth"] = "(default)";
  }

  // or, to use explicit credentials...
  if (oSession.HostnameIs("ServerUsingChannelBinding")) {
    oSession["x-AutoAuth"] = "austin\\ericlaw:MyP@$$w0rd";
  }

  //...
```

 Warning: If Fiddler is configured to accept requests from other devices or user-accounts, using (default) introduces a security vulnerability. That's because those requests will be authenticated using the credentials of the account in which Fiddler is running.

If the **Automatically Authenticate** box is ticked on the Composer's **Options** subtab, requests from the Composer automatically set the `x-AutoAuth` flag to the value of the `fiddler.composer.AutoAuthCreds` Preference.

For scenarios that require HTTP Basic authentication, you can simply generate the required `username:password` string, base64-encoding it using the TextWizard. Take the base64-encoded credential string and add it as the value of an `Authorization` or `Proxy-Authorization` request header. The header can be added to outbound requests using the Filters tab, FiddlerScript, or the Composer's **Request Headers** box.

Authentication Problems

Because Fiddler acts as a proxy and offers powerful capabilities like HTTPS decryption, sometimes authentication scenarios are impacted when Fiddler is running. Three common Authentication issues relate to Channel-Binding Tokens, WinHTTP credential release, and Loopback authentication protections. Each will be described in turn.

Channel-Binding

One shortcoming of the NTLM authentication scheme is that it can fall victim to "pass-through" attacks. In such an attack, the client is lured to a malicious site which presents an authentication challenge that was originally generated by a victim server. The client dutifully responds to the authentication challenge, and the malicious site uses that challenge-response to authenticate to the victim server. This attack permits the attacker to steal data from the victim server using the unwitting client's credentials.

To address this problem, the concept of Channel-Binding was introduced. Channel-Binding binds the authentication challenge-response to the underlying connection so that it cannot be reused on another connection. Typically this works by binding the credentials to the current HTTPS connection. Channel-Binding is enabled via the **Extended Protection** option in IIS.

Channel-Binding presents a problem for Fiddler because the client binds its credentials to its connection *to Fiddler*, such that when Fiddler forwards those credentials to the actual server, the server rejects them. To resolve this problem, you can configure Fiddler to *itself* authenticate to the server, taking the client out of the loop. Because Fiddler itself generates the challenge-response, using the Channel-Binding information matching its own connection to the server, the credentials will be accepted. To configure Fiddler to authenticate on the client's behalf, see the "Automatic Authentication in Fiddler" section above.

WinHTTP Credential Release Policy

The WinHTTP network stack does not support the concept of security zones, which means that it sometimes will refuse to respond to authentication challenges when a proxy like Fiddler is involved. This problem sometimes appears when attempting to download documents from SharePoint sites using the Microsoft

Office client applications. You can resolve this problem by configuring Fiddler to authenticate on the client's behalf. Alternatively, see `http://support.microsoft.com/kb/956943` to learn how to modify the `AuthForwardServerList` in the registry.

Loopback Protection

Windows also attempts to protect the user against "loopback authentication" attacks. In these attacks, a client thinks that it is authenticating to a remote server but it is really authenticating back to the local computer. Such attacks usually attempt to elevate privilege from a low-privilege process to a higher-privilege local process. When Windows encounters an unexpected attempt to authenticate to the local machine, the authentication request will be blocked.

To disable loopback protection, set the flag `DisableLoopbackCheck=1` as described at: `http://support.microsoft.com/kb/926642`.

HTTPS Client Certificates

In addition to the HTML Forms-based and HTTP Authentication protocols, a third authentication type is used for high-security sites. HTTPS Client Certificates are a very strong form of authentication used in some high-stakes scenarios like banking and document-signing. When using Client Certificate authentication, the client sends a certificate to the server to cryptographically prove the identity of the user.

One of the key design goals of Client Certificate authentication is to prevent network intermediaries (like Fiddler) from abusing the client's credentials. Even if the client application sent its certificate to Fiddler, Fiddler cannot successfully reuse that certificate to respond to the server's demand, because the client never provides Fiddler with its private key.

To resolve this limitation, you can supply any necessary client certificates and private keys directly for Fiddler to use when handshaking with the server. By default, if a server prompts the client for a certificate, Fiddler will look inside the `%USERPROFILE%\Documents\Fiddler2\` folder for a file named `ClientCertificate.cer` and will use that certificate when responding to the server's certificate demand.

In some cases, you may want to use a different client certificate for each secure connection. To do so, specify the location of the certificate using the `https-Client-Certificate` property on the `CONNECT` tunnel to the secure server. For instance, you can write code like this:

```
static function OnBeforeRequest(oSession: Session)
{
  if (oSession.HTTPMethodIs("CONNECT")) {
    if (oSession.HostnameIs("exampleA")) {
      oSession["https-Client-Certificate"] = "C:\\certs\\CertA.cer";
    }
    else if (oSession.HostnameIs("exampleB")) {
      oSession["https-Client-Certificate"] = "C:\\test\\CertB.cer";
    }
  }
}
```

```
//...
```

The `.CER` file does not contain the private key associated with the certificate's public key. Instead, the `.CER` file merely acts as reference to Windows' Personal Certificates store. The Windows certificate store holds the private key associated with the certificate and releases it only as needed. Client certificates stored on a Smartcard will automatically appear within the Personal store (see `certmgr.msc`) when the Smartcard is inserted:

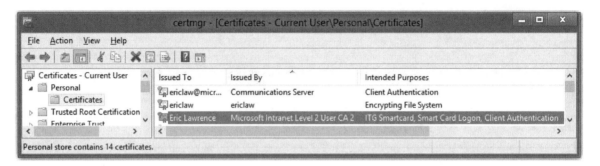

When the Smartcard is inserted, you may export a `.CER` file from `certmgr.msc` and use it just like any other client certificate. Note that your Smartcard must remain inserted for Fiddler to use its private key.

If the desired certificate isn't yet installed in the Personal Certificates store (e.g. you only have a .pfx file) you must first import it into the certificate store, then export a `.CER` file. After your certificate is installed, simply right-click the certificate and choose **All Tasks > Export...**. Save the `.CER` file to either the default `ClientCertificate.cer` location or the location you specify in the `https-Client-Certificate` flag.

Inspectors

OVERVIEW

Fiddler's Inspectors are used to display the request and response for the selected Session in the Web Sessions list. Inspectors appear in three places: On the **Inspectors tab** in the main Fiddler window, in standalone **Inspect Session** windows (opened using the Web Sessions context menu), and in the AutoResponder's **Edit Response** window.

On the Inspectors tab, the Request Inspectors are shown in a panel at the top, and the Response Inspectors are shown at the bottom. You can switch between Inspectors by clicking on the desired Inspector's name (e.g. HexView).

When you first double-click or press the Enter key on a Session in the Web Sessions list, the Inspectors tab will become active. Each request or response inspector will be polled to ask it how applicable it is to inspecting the selected request and response. For instance, the ImageView Inspector returns a high "score" for image/* types while returning a low score for textual types. In contrast, the TextView Inspector returns a high score for textual types and a low score for binary formats.

Whichever inspectors return the highest score for the Session will become active. To force Fiddler to always activate a particular Request Inspector, set the `fiddler.ui.inspectors.request.alwaysuse` preference to the title of the Inspector's tab. To force Fiddler to always activate a specific Response Inspector, set the `fiddler.ui.inspectors.response.alwaysuse` preference to the title of the Inspector's tab.

A thin blue line splits the top and bottom panels; you can use the mouse to move the line and resize the panels. Double-clicking the line maximizes the Response Inspectors panel.

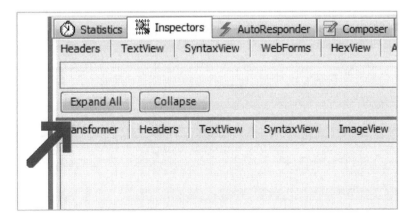

To get even more display area, the Inspectors tab can be extracted from the main window, either by clicking the Tearoff button in the toolbar or by typing the `tearoff` command in the QuickExec box. Closing the Inspectors window will return them to their default position on the main window.

Right-clicking on an individual request or response inspector's tab will show a menu containing two options: **Inspector Properties** and **Hide Inspector**. The first shows information provided by the Inspector about itself, while the second will remove the inspector from the Inspectors tab. To restore a hidden Inspector later, edit the `fiddler.inspectors.hidelist` Preference and restart, or hold the SHIFT key while starting Fiddler.

By default, the Inspectors are readonly when inspecting a Session, unless the Session is currently paused at a breakpoint. Additionally, the Inspectors will permit editing if the Session is in an Unlocked state, which can be activated by using the command on the Edit menu. Most Inspectors will display with a specific background color while in readonly mode, and a different color (typically white) when editing is permitted. The default readonly color is light-blue but it can be changed using the **Tools** > **Fiddler Options** > **Appearance** tab.

Building new Inspectors to add to Fiddler is straightforward, and step-by-step instructions are provided later in this book. The Fiddler community has developed several powerful Inspectors for data formats including WCF Binary, Fast Infoset, and EAS XML; you can find those Inspectors at `http://fiddler2.com/addons`.

The remainder of this chapter will describe the Inspectors I've built, most of which are installed by Fiddler itself.

AUTH

Type	Request & Response
Allows Editing	No

Fiddler's Auth Inspector interprets the contents of the Authorization- and Authentication-related headers on requests and responses. Typically, these headers can be found on HTTP/401 and HTTP/407 responses that demand credentials, and the subsequent requests that provide the requested credentials.

For instance, if you enable the "Require Proxy Authentication" rule in the Rules menu, Fiddler will return a HTTP/407 response demanding that the user supply credentials for each request. This demand is made by the Proxy-Authenticate header, which the Auth Response Inspector displays:

```
Auth

Proxy-Authenticate Header is present: Basic realm="FiddlerProxy"

No WWW-Authenticate Header is present.
```

After the user enters the name *UserName* and the password *SecretKey* in the browser's Authentication dialog, the browser's subsequent requests supply a Proxy-Authorization header with the user's credentials. Since the authentication scheme in use in this scenario is HTTP Basic, the credentials are encoded using base64 encoding. The Auth Request Inspector decodes the string automatically and displays it in plaintext:

```
Auth

Proxy-Authorization Header is present: Basic VXNlck5hbWU6U2VjcmVOS2V5
Decoded Username:Password= UserName:SecretKey

No Authorization Header is present.
```

Most websites will use a stronger form of authentication– HTTP Digest or the Windows NTLM or Negotiate schemes. The latter are especially popular on Windows networks.

Fiddler' Auth inspector knows how to parse NTLM blobs and will show you the information contained within those blobs, like so:

```
-[NTLM Type3: Authentication]-----------------------------
Provider: NTLMSSP
Type: 3
OS Version: 6.3:9600
Flags:    0xa2888205
    Unicode supported in security buffer.
    Request server's authentication realm included in Type2 reply.
    NTLM authentication. Negotiate Always Sign. Negotiate NTLM2 Key.
```

```
      Target Information block provided for use in calculation of the
         NTLMv2 response.
      Supports 56-bit encryption. Supports 128-bit encryption.
   lmresp_Offset: 134; lmresp_Length: 24; lmresp_Length2: 24
   ntresp_Offset: 158; ntresp_Length: 396; ntresp_Length2: 396
   Domain_Offset: 88; Domain_Length: 14; Domain_Length2: 14
   User_Offset: 102; User_Length: 14; User_Length2: 14
   Host_Offset: 116; Host_Length: 18; Host_Length2: 18
   msg_len: 554
   Domain: AUSTIN
   User: ericlaw
   Host: ERICLAWT8
   lm_resp: 00 00 00 00 00 00 00 00 00 00 00 00 00 00 00 00 00 00 00 00 00 00 00 00
   nt_resp: 42 40 AE AB 3E D7 7F 02 B5 F9 76 D7 C9 5E 6B 82 01 01 00 00 00 00 00 00
            05 96 B2 D4 01 23 CD C1 D3 D9 8A 33 47 87 40 3D 00 00 00 00 02 00 52 ...
```

The Auth Inspector cannot currently parse Kerberos authentication messages, but will show the decoded bytes of the challenge and response.

CACHING

Type	Response only
Allows Editing	No

The Caching Response Inspector examines the HTTP response headers to determine whether the selected response is cacheable under the rules of HTTP, and if so, for how long. It consults the response headers `Cache-Control`, `Expires`, `Pragma`, `Vary`, `ETag`, `Age`, and `Last-Modified` in its evaluation of the response.

Some browsers (including Internet Explorer) support the specification of caching information in HTML documents using `META HTTP-EQUIV` tags. The Caching Inspector scans responses that have a HTML `Content-Type` and will display any `HTTP-EQUIV` or `PRAGMA` directives found in the markup. (You should avoid using such directives, as they are not consistently supported and implementations have many bugs).

For responses which do not explicitly specify their cacheability or freshness lifetime, the Caching Inspector will compute the "heuristic freshness lifetime" using the `Last-Modified` header and the algorithm suggested in Section 4.2.2 of RFC 7234.

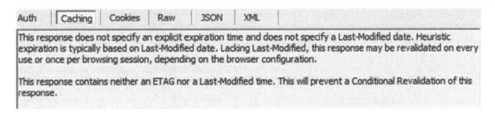

You can learn more about how browsers utilize caches at `http://fiddler2.com/r/?httpperf`.

COOKIES

Type	Request & Response
Allows Editing	No

The Cookies Inspector displays the contents of any outbound `Cookie` and `Cookie2` request headers and any inbound `Set-Cookie`, `Set-Cookie2`, and `P3P` response headers. Note that the `Cookie2` and `Set-Cookie2` headers are uncommon and not supported by Internet Explorer and some other browsers.

The display of the cookies is basic (you can see the same information in the Headers Inspector). This Inspector's value primarily consists of examining the `P3P` response header, if present, to determine whether the cookie is likely to be stored. P3P (Platform for Privacy Preferences) is a standard whereby the server can communicate to the client how it will be using the cookies that accompany the `P3P` header; P3P is implemented in IE6 through IE11, but is slated to be dropped in IE12 / Codename "Spartan".

```
Set-Cookie: ASPSESSIONIDCCBTDCRD=CIFKIKJDFMJFFODAJPFMFKGN; path=/
P3P: CP="ALL IND DSP COR ADM CONo CUR CUSo IVAo IVDo PSA PSD TAI TELo
         OUR SAMo CNT COM INT NAV ONL PHY PRE PUR UNI"
```

The tokens in the `P3P` header's `CP` (Compact Policy) string are interpreted by the Inspector and their meaning is listed:

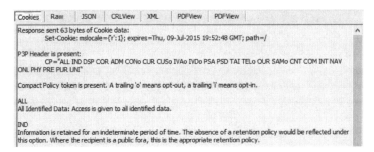

The Inspector will further evaluate the string to determine whether the cookie is deemed "acceptable" by the default privacy policy used by Internet Explorer. It's worth mentioning that some sites (Facebook and Google, as of this writing) send invalid P3P statements to circumvent the browser's privacy features. Under the rules of P3P, unknown tokens (like those sent by such sites) are deliberately ignored.

The Cookies Request Inspector displays the size of the outbound `Cookie` header, helping identify over-sized cookies to eliminate or shrink to improve the network performance.

The Cookies Response Inspector flags common problems. For instance, Internet Explorer will refuse to set a cookie for any server whose hostname contains an underscore character, and the Inspector will warn you if it encounters this condition.

HEADERS

Type	Request & Response
Allows Editing	Yes

Every HTTP request begins with plaintext headers that describe what resource or operation is sought by the client. The first line (the "Request Line") of the request contains three values, the HTTP Method (e.g. "GET" or "POST"), the URL path which is being requested (e.g. "/index.htm"), and the HTTP version (e.g. "HTTP/1.1"). Following the Request Line are one or more lines containing name-value pairs of metadata about the request and the client, such as the User-Agent and Accept-Language.

Similarly, every HTTP response begins with plaintext headers that describe the result of the request. The first line of the response (the "Status Line") contains the HTTP version (e.g. "HTTP/1.1"), the response status code (e.g. "200") and the response status text (e.g. "OK"). Following the Status Line are one or more lines containing name-value pairs of metadata about the response and the server, such as the length of the response file, its Content-Type, and information about how the response may be cached.

The Headers Inspector allows you to view the HTTP headers of the request and the response, showing the name-value pairs in a treeview below the Request Line or Status Line. The name-value pairs of headers are grouped based on their function and then sorted alphabetically by name. Groupings are simply for your ease of reading, and are not sent on the network. For Request headers, the groups include [Cache, Client, Entity, Transport, Cookies/Login, Miscellaneous]. For Response headers, the groups include [Entity, Transport, Cookies/Login, Security, Miscellaneous].

By default, the contents of the Headers Inspector are read-only and cannot be edited. While in readonly mode, the background color of the treeview and the Raw Headers box will display using the readonly color (light-blue). When you select a Web Session paused at a breakpoint, or when you select the **Unlock for Editing** option on the Edit menu, the Headers Inspector enters Edit mode. While in Edit mode, the background color is the default window color (white), and the contents of the headers may be edited.

Click the **Raw** hyperlink at the top-right of the Inspector to display the plaintext of the headers as they are sent on the network. Click the **Header Definitions** link to view a help topic describing common HTTP headers and their use.

Due to limitations in the Windows treeview control, only the first 260 characters of the header's name and value are shown. To view headers which exceed this length, select the header and press Enter or F2, or right-click the header and choose **View Header**. The Header Viewer window will open in read-only mode and allow you to inspect the full name and value. The length (in characters) of the value will be displayed in the title bar of the window.

While the Inspector is in readonly mode, any `Cookie` request headers are broken out into name-value pairs for easier reading. While in Edit mode, any `Cookie` header is shown as a single line, as it will be sent on the wire.

Context Menu

Right-click on the list of Headers to show a menu with the following options:

View Header	Open the Header Viewer window for the selected header.
Edit Header	(*Shown only in Edit mode*) Open the Header Editor window for the selected header.
Copy Header	Copy the entire selected header to the clipboard.
Copy Value only	Copy the selected header's Value to the clipboard.
Send to TextWizard	Send the selected header's Value to the TextWizard to permit decoding of encoded text.
Add Header	In Edit mode, create a new blank header.
Remove Header	In Edit mode, remove the selected header.
Paste Headers	In Edit mode, attempt to add new headers based on the information on the clipboard.
Lookup Header	Open a web page with information about the selected HTTP header.

Keyboard Shortcuts

After selecting a Session in the Web Sessions list, you can press CTRL+H to activate the Request and Response Header Inspectors. Within the Inspector, the following hotkeys are available:

CTRL+C	Copy the selected header to the clipboard.
CTRL+SHIFT+C	Copy the selected header's value to the clipboard.
F2 or Enter	Open the Header Viewer or Header Editor window for the selected header.
CTRL+V	In Edit mode, attempt to add one or more new headers based on the text on the clipboard.
Insert	In Edit mode, create a new blank header.
Delete	In Edit mode, remove the selected header.

Editing

When the Inspector is in Edit mode, you can make changes to the headers before they are sent to the server or the client. You can directly change the contents of the Request or Status Line by editing the text in the box at the top of the Inspector. To edit an individual name-value header, select it and press F2 or hit Enter and the Header Editor window will appear. To add a new Header, press the Insert key; a new header will appear and the Header Editor will automatically open.

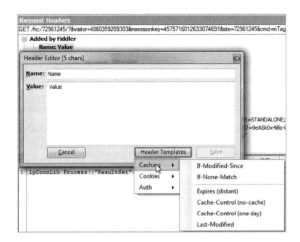

You may update the name and value of the new header using the boxes, or you may click the **Header Templates** button at the bottom of the window to choose from commonly-used headers.

If you prefer to edit the entire set of headers at once, click the **Raw** link at the top-right of the Inspector.

HexView

Type	Request & Response
Allows Editing	Yes

The HexView Inspector allows you to view the request and response headers and body using a hexadecimal edit box. This capability is most useful when inspecting binary content.

The Inspector contains a HexEdit control organized into three vertical columns. In the left column, in light grey, is the hexadecimal address for the adjacent line of bytes. In the center column are the hexadecimal representations of the individual bytes. The right column redisplays those bytes, interpreted as ASCII text. If the HexView is configured to show the headers, the request headers will be shown using in blue text and response headers will be shown in green. The body bytes are shown in black.

At the bottom of the Inspector is a status bar containing three panels. The first panel shows the current cursor position within the bytes in decimal form and hexadecimal form. If the Inspector is configured to show the header bytes, the offset will automatically reset to zero when the cursor enters the body bytes.

If one or more bytes are selected in the control, the middle panel displays the length of the current byte selection.

The right panel indicates the current mode: **Readonly**, **Overwrite**, or **Insert**. The Inspector is in readonly mode except when the Session is paused at a breakpoint or is Unlocked for Editing. In Edit mode, you may press the `Insert` key to toggle between overwriting bytes and inserting new bytes.

The HexView Inspector's context menu offers the following items:

Insert File Here…	In Edit mode, insert the bytes of a selected file at the current cursor position.	
Copy submenu	Copy	Copy selected bytes to the clipboard as both binary and interpreted as a string.
	Copy as Base64	Copy selected bytes, formatted as a Base64-encoded string.
	Copy as 0x##	Copy selected bytes, formatted as a C# array declaration.
Select Bytes…	Prompt for a number of bytes to select, then select that number of bytes starting at the current cursor position. Enter a leading $ character if you wish to specify the number of bytes in hexadecimal format; this is useful if you wish to examine HTTP Chunked Encoding blocks, as the length of each block is specified as a hexadecimal number.	
Save Selected Bytes…	When one or more bytes are selected, save the selected bytes to a file.	

Goto Offset…	Move the cursor to a specified byte position. Enter a leading + or – symbol to specify a relative offset from the current cursor position instead of an absolute position. Enter a leading $ character if you wish to specify the number of bytes in hexadecimal format.
Find Bytes…	Search for a specific sequence of bytes. The search begins at the current cursor position. Press F3 to continue the search after each match.
Find String…	Search for a specific sequence of UTF-8 characters. The search begins at the current cursor position. Press F3 to continue the search after each match.
Show Headers	Check to display header bytes. When unchecked, only the body bytes will be shown.
Show Offsets	Check to display file offsets in the first column of the display.
Set Bytes per Line…	Specify the number of bytes to show on each line of the display. Enter 0 to instruct the HexView to automatically choose the number of bytes based on the available width (a minimum of four bytes per line will be shown).

IMAGEVIEW

Type	Response
Allows Editing	Yes
Platform	Best on Windows; limited on Mono

The ImageView Inspector allows you to view the response as an image. The Inspector can display most common web image formats, including JPEGs, PNGs, and GIFs, as well as less common formats including cursors, WebP, JPEG-XR, bitmaps, EMF/WMF, and TIFF. The Inspector does not support display of SVG graphics; if IE9 or later is installed, SVG responses can be viewed using the WebView Inspector.

The text panel at left shows information about the currently selected image, including its size in bytes, pixel dimensions, and file format. At the bottom of the panel is a dropdown that allows you to control how the image is scaled:

- **Autoshrink** – Images larger than the display area are scaled down.

- **Scale to fit** – Images larger than the display area are scaled down, and images smaller than the display area are scaled up to fill the area.

- **No scaling** – Images are shown at their native dimensions.

Middle-clicking on the image will silently copy the image to your Desktop folder. Double-clicking on the image will open a full-screen view. In full-screen view, the following functions are available:

Key or Mouse action	Function
Enter or Z	Toggle Zoom between Full-Screen and Actual Size
H	Flip the image horizontally
V	Flip the image vertically
R	Rotate the image clockwise by 90 degrees.
Mousewheel up	Zoom to Full-Screen
Mousewheel down	Show Actual Size
Escape	Exit the full-screen viewer

To more rapidly view a large number of image responses, use the Gallery extension.

The Inspector's context menu allows you to copy the image to the clipboard as a bitmap or as a DataURI, a text format which can be embedded in HTML or stylesheets and displayed in modern browsers (IE8+). The **Save to Desktop** option saves the image file to your Desktop folder using the current time as the basis for the filename. The **Set Workspace Color**… option allows you to change the background color (normally light blue) which can provide useful contrast when examining small or transparent images.

Metadata Display

For many formats, the image may include metadata like comments, copyright information, or animation information. Commonly, embedded data includes "bloat" like Adobe editing data or image thumbnails, which are never used by browsers and simply waste the bandwidth for both the client and the server.

A surprising number of photos, mostly taken with smartphones, include the GPS coordinates of the camera. When the ImageView loads a geo-tagged photo, the GPSInfo is displayed and a **Find on Map…** link appears. When clicked, the location is mapped using Bing Maps:

If you prefer to use Google Maps, you can simply set a preference. In the QuickExec box, enter:

```
prefs set fiddler.inspectors.images.MapURI http://maps.google.com/?q={0}
```

ImageView Tools

The Inspector's context-menu is extensible so Image-related tools can be invoked from its **Tools** sub-menu. When invoked, the image will be stored to a temporary file and sent to the target application for deeper analysis, optimization, or other processing:

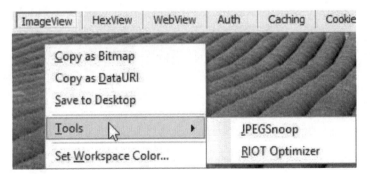

To populate the **Tools** submenu, create a registry key named `ImagesMenuExt` and under it add a subkey naming your tool. Provide `Command`, and `Parameters` keys to specify how to launch the tool. The `{in}` token within the Parameters field will be replaced with the path to the temporary file created when the tool is invoked.

You may specify a Types entry to limit the image types for which the tool is offered; list multiple types with a semicolon between each, or omit the entry entirely to offer the tool for all image types.

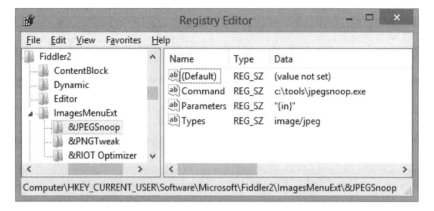

PNGDistill Image Tool

By default, Fiddler installs one Image Tool, called **PNGDistill**. This tool, offered for PNG and ICO files (icon files may contain embedded PNGs), optimizes the filesize of the image. The tool works by stripping metadata sections unrelated to image display (e.g. Adobe editing metadata) and by recompressing the data stream using the Zopfli compression engine.

If you wish to run PNGDistill against an entire local folder of images, you can do so from the command prompt:

```
for /f "delims=|" %f in ('dir /b *.png') do pngdistill "%f" replace
```

This script runs PNGDistill on every image in the current folder, replacing any image for which the distillation process saved bytes. You can then update the images on your server with the optimized images.

JSON

Type	Request & Response
Allows Editing	No

The JSON Inspector interprets the selected request or response body as a JavaScript Object Notation (JSON) formatted string, showing a treeview of the JSON object's nodes. If the body cannot be interpreted as JSON, the treeview will remain empty. The JSON Inspector is able to render the data even if the request or response is compressed or has Chunked encoding applied; you do not need to remove the encoding to display the content. If the JSON data is malformed (if for instance, the name component of a name/value pair is unquoted) the JSON Inspector will show a warning in the footer.

Many responses delivered with the JSON Content-Type are not really JSON. Instead, they're JSONP, a JavaScript file consisting of a single function call with a string argument containing JSON. The JSON Inspector is able to handle many types of JSONP by ignoring the leading function call and trailing parenthesis and semicolon.

The JSON Inspector can also render the "Binary JSON" format (http://bsonspec.org/). When rendering BSON, the top node of the tree will show BSON instead of JSON:

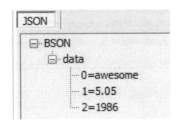

The context menu offers just two commands. Click **Copy** to copy the selected node to the clipboard (or press CTRL+C). Click **Send to TextWizard** to send the selected node's content to the TextWizard window for encoding or decoding.

The **Expand All** button in the footer expands all nodes of the tree, while the **Collapse** button collapses all nodes. The JSON tree will be automatically expanded if the body contains less than 2000 nodes; for performance reasons, you must manually expand the tree for larger JSON documents.

RAW

Type	Request & Response
Allows Editing	Yes

The Raw Inspector allows you to view the complete request and response, including headers and bodies, as text. The term "raw" is a bit of a misnomer, because Fiddler is still interpreting the bytes of the request and response; you should use the HexView Inspector to examine the bytes of non-textual traffic. If you need a truly raw view of network traffic, use a packet sniffer like Microsoft Network Monitor (NetMon) or Wireshark.

Most of the Inspector is a large text area that displays headers and the body interpreted as text using the character set detected using the headers, the byte-order-marker, or an embedded META tag declaration. Pressing CTRL+G in the text area allows you to move the cursor to a specific line number. When right-clicking, the text area's context menu offers standard Cut, Copy and Paste options. The menu also offers an option to send the currently selected text to the TextWizard tool. There are two checkboxes on the menu to control the Word Wrap and AutoTruncate display features.

Along the bottom of the Inspector is a bar that offers additional features. First is a search box that allows you to select matching text within the content. The search text is case-insensitive and does not support regular expressions. Pressing the Up or Down arrow keys in the search box will scroll the text area above (to allow you to view search results in context). Matches are selected as you type, and the box will turn green if a match was found or red if no further matches were found. Pressing Enter or F3 will select the next match. Pressing CTRL+Enter will highlight all matches in the content.

The **View in Notepad** button saves the text to a temporary file and opens a text editor to view the file. The editor launched can be set using the Tools > Fiddler Options > Tools tab.

The Inspector replaces any null bytes with the Unicode replacement character (�) and as such can be used to view binary response bodies, although the HexView remains more suitable for that task. Because displaying large binary bodies in the textbox can require large amounts of CPU time and memory, the Inspector is configured to automatically truncate the display of large responses. The threshold at which truncation occurs is controlled by the Content-Type and four preferences:

- `fiddler.inspectors.request.raw.truncatebinaryat`
- `fiddler.inspectors.request.raw.truncatetextat`
- `fiddler.inspectors.response.raw.truncatebinaryat`
- `fiddler.inspectors.response.raw.truncatetextat`

By default, binary Content-Types are truncated at 128 bytes, and text types are truncated at 262144 bytes. Truncation can be disabled using the context menu.

PDFVIEW

Type	Response
Allows Editing	No
Platform	Windows-only; Separate download

The PDFView Inspector allows you to view Portable Document Format (PDF) response bodies. PDF is a complicated binary format and as such a custom Inspectors is required to display these responses in a useful way. Available only on Windows, the PDFView Inspector is a separate download due to its relatively large size (~3mb).

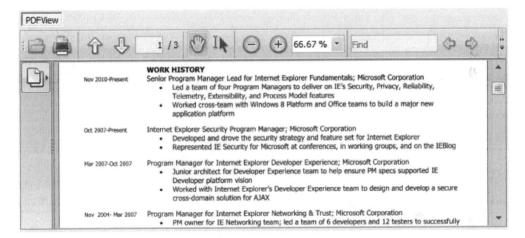

The Inspector is built using Telerik's RadPdfViewer and does not require you to have any third-party PDF-viewer applications installed. The toolbar at the top of the Inspector exposes a full command set, so you can navigate, search, and print the document as well as copy text from it, zoom in/out, etc.

SYNTAXVIEW

Type	Request & Response
Allows Editing	Yes
Platform	Windows-only; Separate download

The SyntaxView Inspector allows you to view request and response body text highlighted according to type-specific rules. This is a very useful feature when reading HTML, XML, CSS, and JavaScript. The Inspector uses the `Content-Type` header when deciding which highlighting rules to apply.

The SyntaxView Inspector is one of the most useful Inspectors available for Fiddler. It isn't included in the default install package only for size reasons. To ensure that Fiddler updates are as compact as possible, the SyntaxView extension is available as a separate download from http://fiddler2.com/r/?SYNTAXVIEWINSTALL.

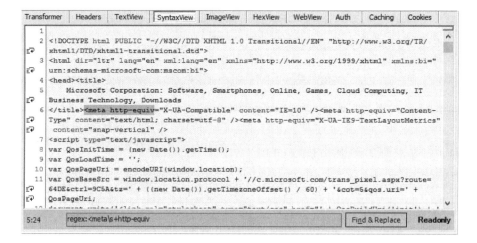

The bar along the bottom of the Inspector exposes additional information and functionality. First is a display of the current caret position in **Line:Column** format. Next is the QuickFind box which enables inline search. Next is a button which launches advanced Find and Replace functionality. At the far right of the bar is text indicating whether the Inspector is in **Readonly** or **Edit** mode.

The QuickFind box supports the use of Regular Expressions; simply prefix your search string with the text REGEX: and the remainder of the string will be interpreted as a regular expression.

In addition to the standard Cut, Copy, Paste, Undo, and Redo commands, the SyntaxView's Context Menu offers the following features:

Format CSS	Attempt to format the document as a cascading stylesheet.
Format XML	Attempt to parse the document as XML. If successful, the text is reformatted as an indented XML treeview.
Format Script/JSON	Attempt to parse the document as JavaScript/JSON.
Send to TextWizard	Send the selected text to the TextWizard window for encoding or decoding.
Find & Replace…	Open a Find and Replace dialog that offers a variety of search and replacement options.
Word Wrap	This checkbox toggles whether text is word-wrapped. Note: word-wrapping huge lines (like an ASPNET ViewState string) can require significant CPU time.
Editor Options…	Open an options window containing dozens of advanced text display options. Note: Changes made in this dialog are not currently persisted and are lost when Fiddler restarts.

The three **Format** commands are available even when the Inspector is in readonly mode, but the reformatting is only permanently applied in Edit mode.

TextView

Type	Request & Response
Allows Editing	Yes

The TextView Inspector allows you to view the request and response bodies as text. The Inspector truncates its display at the first null byte it finds, and as such is unsuitable for displaying binary content.

Most of the Inspector is a large text area that displays the body text interpreted using the character set detected using the headers, the byte-order-marker, or an embedded META tag declaration. Pressing CTRL+G in the text area allows you to move the cursor to a specific line number. When right-clicking, the text area's context menu offers standard Cut, Copy and Paste options and a checkbox to control word wrapping. The menu also offers an option to send the currently selected text to the TextWizard tool.

The bar along the bottom of the Inspector offers additional information and features. The first box shows the current caret position in **Line:Column** format. The next box shows the current character offset within the content in **Offset/Total** format. The third box shows the character count of the current text selection, if any.

Next is a search box that allows you to select matching text within the content. The search text is case-insensitive and does not support regular expressions. Pressing the Up or Down arrow keys in the search box will scroll the text area above (to allow you to view search results in context). Matches are selected as you type, and the box will turn green if a match was found or red if no further matches were found. Pressing Enter or F3 will select the next match. Pressing CTRL+Enter will highlight all matches in the content.

The **View in Notepad** button saves the text to a temporary file and opens a text editor to view the file. The editor launched can be set using the Tools > Fiddler Options > Tools tab.

The **...** button at the right end of the bar saves the content to a temporary file and shows Windows' **Open With** prompt to allow you to select an application to load the file.

TRANSFORMER

Type	Response only
Allows Editing	Always

Background on HTTP Encodings

The HTTP specification defines a number of response encoding methods that can be used to improve performance.

- **Compression** algorithms like DEFLATE can be applied to HTTP bodies to shrink the number of bytes that must be transferred over the network. Text-based Content-Types like HTML, script, and CSS shrink by 80% or more when compressed.

- **Chunked Transfer-Encoding** allows transmission of a body without knowing its length ahead of time. Ordinarily, the body's size is sent as a Content-Length header before the content. However, pre-calculating a body's size could require a great deal of time and memory, particularly if the body is being generated by running a database query or other operation.

  Without Chunked Transfer-Encoding, a server returning a response of indeterminate size would be forced to send a Connection: close header and close the connection when the response is complete. Such closures break the HTTP Keep-Alive mechanism and introduce a performance bottleneck.

  Chunking works by sending one or more chunks of data, each preceded by a *chunk length* value specified as a hexadecimal number. A chunk length of 0 signals the end of the body. For instance, here's a response which has been chunked:

```
HTTP/1.1 200 OK
Content-Type: text/plain
Transfer-Encoding: chunked

2b
This is a response which has been delivered
21
using HTTP Chunked encoding. To r
38
educe overhead, the chunks should be larger than those in
0c
 this exampl
18
e; 2kb is a common size.
0
```

Add and Remove Encodings using the Transformer

Encodings can make it difficult to inspect entity bodies. The Transformer Inspector allows you to add or remove HTTP-based encodings from the response. At the top of the Transformer tab, the body's current size is listed; keep an eye on this number as you add or remove encodings.

```
Transformer

Response body: 53,987 bytes.

☐ Chunked Transfer-Encoding                              Help...

  HTTP Compression
    ● No Compression
    ○ GZIP Encoding            ☐ Use Zopfli to GZIP/DEFLATE
    ○ DEFLATE Encoding
    ○ BZIP2 Encoding
```

The **Chunked Transfer-Encoding** checkbox adds or removes Chunked Transfer-Encoding from the response. Toggling this checkbox applies or removes the encoding, then adds or removes the `Transfer-Encoding` and `Content-Length` response headers. After enabling chunking, the HTTP Compression box is disabled. To make changes to compression, you must first remove chunking, then adjust HTTP compression.

The radio buttons in the **HTTP Compression** box allow you to compress or decompress the body:

- **No compression**: The body is not compressed.

- **GZIP**: The body is compressed using `GZIP`. This encoding uses `DEFLATE` internally, but with slightly different binary formatting.

- **DEFLATE**: The body is compressed using the `DEFLATE` (RFC1951) algorithm.

- **BZIP2**: The body is compressed using the `BZIP2` algorithm. `BZIP2` typically provides better compression than `GZIP` or `DEFLATE` at the cost of additional CPU time. This format was briefly supported by the Google Chrome browser but is currently not supported by any mainstream browser or server. It exists in Fiddler for comparison purposes and to enable testing to determine how clients handle unknown encodings.

Selecting a radio button applies or removes the compression from the body, then adds, updates, or removes the `Content-Encoding` header and adjusts the `Content-Length` header.

Check the **Use Zopfli to GZIP/DEFLATE** checkbox to use Google's Zopfli compressor to compress content instead of the default compressor. The Zopfli compressor takes much longer to compress content (around 100 times as long) but it achieves higher compression than most other compressors. Zopfli-compressed content is compatible with all clients and decompresses just as quickly. You should use Zopfli to compress large static assets like script libraries and stylesheets.

Use the Transformer Inspector to determine the effectiveness of HTTP compression when applied to your content—for most textual types, compression reductions of around 80% are common. When content is compressed using GZIP, its original size is recorded in the compressed data, and Fiddler will display this information and the compression ratio at the bottom of the Inspector:

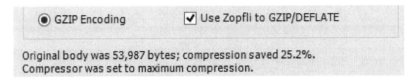

Unlike most Inspectors, the Transformer allows you to modify readonly responses without unlocking them first. This capability allows you to more simply remove encodings on Sessions for easy inspection.

Presently, the Transformer Inspector is available for responses only. Use of HTTP encodings for requests is presently rare, and not supported by most clients and servers.

Other Ways to Remove Encodings

Because most of Fiddler's Inspectors do not function well with encoded content, when an encoded Session is selected, a yellow bar will appear above the list of Inspectors. Clicking the bar will immediately remove all encodings from the request or response.

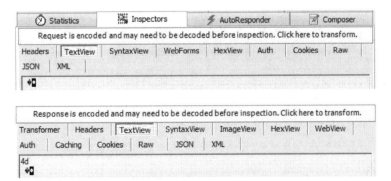

To remove encodings from both the request and response simultaneously, right-click the Session in the Web Sessions list and choose **Decode Selected Sessions** from the context menu. Enable the **Decode** option in the toolbar to automatically remove all encodings as Fiddler reads requests from the client and responses from the server.

WEBFORMS

Type	Request only
Allows Editing	Yes

The WebForms Request Inspector parses the request's query string and body for any HTML form-data. If a form is found, it is parsed and the name/value pairs are displayed in the grid view. For instance, the following request:

```
POST /sandbox/FileForm.asp?Query=1 HTTP/1.1
Content-Type: application/x-www-form-urlencoded
Host: www.fiddler2.com
Content-Length: 54

2=Data%3e123&fileentry2=a%2etxt&_charset_=windows-1252
```

...is displayed as follows:

Headers	TextView	SyntaxView	WebForms	HexView	Auth

QueryString

Name	Value
Query	1

Body

Name	Value
2	Data>123
fileentry2	a.txt
charset	windows-1252

This Inspector works best with `application/x-www-form-urlencoded` data used by most simple web forms. Support for `multipart/form-data` forms, commonly used for file uploads, is limited to display only. To modify a file upload, use the HexView Inspector instead.

WEBVIEW

Type	Response only
Allows Editing	No
Platform	Windows-only

The WebView Response Inspector allows you to view responses in a web browser control, which provides a quick preview of how a given response may appear in a browser. The web browser control is configured to prevent additional downloads when rendering the response to prevent muddling your Web Sessions list-- this means that most images, styles, and objects will be missing from the displayed content. Additionally, scripting and navigation are blocked, providing a read-only preview of HTML pages.

Beyond HTML, the WebView Inspector is able to render several additional media types. With IE8 installed, the Inspector can render any binary image (png, jpg, gif, etc) smaller than 24kb[1]. When IE9 is present, the Inspector can display images up to 1.5gb in size. Additionally, it can display SVG documents and will generate preview pages for WOFF, TTF, and EOT font files, MP3 audio files, and h264 video files. For instance, inspecting a WOFF file will generate the following display:

When previewing an audio or video file, an "AutoPlay" checkbox appears at the top-right of the tab. When this box is ticked, media files will automatically begin playback when loaded. When unticked, the media will be loaded but will not begin playing until the play button is clicked inside the preview.

---

[1] This limit exists because the Inspector uses a Data URI to render the image, and IE8's Data URI length limit is 32kb, which is equal to 24kb of binary.

XML

Type	Request & Response
Allows Editing	No

The XML Inspector interprets the selected request or response body as an Extensible Markup Language (XML) document, showing a treeview of the XML document's nodes. If the body cannot be interpreted as XML, the treeview will remain empty.

Each XML element is represented as a node in the tree, and the attributes of the element are displayed in square brackets after the element's name.

The XML Inspector is able to render the data even if the request or response is compressed or has HTTP Chunked Encoding applied; you do not need to remove the encoding to display the content.

The context menu offers just two commands. Click **Copy** to copy the selected node to the clipboard (or press CTRL+C). Click **Send to TextWizard** to send the selected node's content to the TextWizard window for encoding or decoding.

The **Expand All** button in the footer will expand all nodes of the tree, while the **Collapse** button will collapse all nodes of the tree. The XML tree will be automatically expanded if the body contains less than 2000 nodes; for performance reasons, you will have to manually expand the tree for larger documents.

Extensions

OVERVIEW

Fiddler's rich extensibility model enables developers to go beyond Inspectors to add powerful new features via easily-installed extensions.

Popular 3rd Party Extensions

Independent developers have built many Fiddler extensions, some of which are listed in the directory at http://fiddler2.com/addons. At the time of this writing, the most popular 3rd-party extensions enhance Fiddler's ability to test the performance and security characteristics of web applications.

Performance Add-ons

On its own, Fiddler can be used for many important performance-analysis and optimization tasks, but several extensions add even more power.

- **neXpert Performance Report Generator** – Written by a Microsoft Online Services testing team, neXpert will evaluate your websites' adherence to performance best-practices, generating a report which flags problems and recommends solutions. License: Freeware.

- **StresStimulus** – This load-testing extension permits you to record and run load-test scenarios against your website to evaluate its ability to scale to handle large numbers of simultaneous users. License: Free trial.

Security Add-ons

Many Security testing goals can be accomplished with Fiddler, and Web Security experts have built several powerful add-ons that enable even novices to discover and resolve security issues.

- **Watcher** – Developed by the Casaba Security team, Watcher is a "passive security auditor" which observes a browser's interactions with your site. The tool scans requests and responses, flagging potential security vulnerabilities. This powerful tool is used by professional security penetration testers to evaluate major sites. License: Open Source.

- **x5s** – Another add-on from Casaba Security, x5s evaluates your website's vulnerability to cross-site scripting bugs caused by character-set related issues. License: Open Source.

- **Content Security Policy Generator** – Generating a Content Security Policy (CSP) that protects your site from XSS attacks can be tricky, but this Fiddler extension makes it easy. License: Open Source.

- **intruder21** – Enables fuzz-testing of your web applications. After you identify target requests in Fiddler, this extension generates fuzzed payloads and launches those payloads against your site. License: Freeware.

- **Ammonite** – Detects common website vulnerabilities including SQL injection, OS command injection, cross-site scripting, file inclusion, and buffer overflows. License: Free trial.

Extensions I've Built

The remainder of this chapter describes the most useful extensions that I have developed, all of which are available for free download from `http://fiddler2.com/addons`.

Some of the extensions will be useful for most users of Fiddler and aren't built into the tool simply for download size reasons. Other extensions are only useful for narrow scenarios, and providing their functionality via the add-on model allows me to prevent "bloat" in Fiddler—and ensure that Fiddler's add-on model is powerful enough to meet the needs of the development community.

Source code for many of these extensions is available so that they may serve as examples for developers who wish to extend Fiddler to better meet their own needs.

JavaScript Formatter

When the JavaScript Formatter is installed, you can right-click on any Session with a JavaScript response and choose **Make JavaScript Pretty**. This command reformats (or "beautifies") JavaScript to significantly improve its readability if it had been "crunched" or "minified". For instance, the following line of script:

```
1  /* Copyright (C) 2012 Microsoft Corporation */(function(){var b=window,e=
   b.jQuery,f=b.Debug,g=b.wLive={Core:{},Controls:{}},a=b.$Config;a.
   handlerBaseUrl=a.handlerBaseUrl||"";if(!a.sd){var d=document.domain,c=d.
   split(".");a.sd=c.length===1?"":"."+c[c.length-2]+".com"}a.mkt=a.mkt||"
   na";a.prop=a.prop||"X";if(typeof window.SymRealWinOpen!=="undefined")
   window.open=window.SymRealWinOpen}}();(function(){var a=window.e=a.
```

...is reformatted for readability:

```
1  /* Copyright (C) 2012 Microsoft Corporation */
2  (function() {
3      var b = window, e = b.jQuery, f = b.Debug, g = b.wLive = {
4          Core: {}, Controls: {}
5      },
6      a = b.$Config;
7      a.handlerBaseUrl = a.handlerBaseUrl || "";
8      if (!a.sd) {
9          var d = document.domain, c = d.split(".");
10         a.sd = c.length === 1 ? "" : "." + c[c.length - 2] + ".com"
11     }
12     a.mkt = a.mkt || "na";
13     a.prop = a.prop || "X";
14     if (typeof window.SymRealWinOpen !== "undefined")
15         window.open = window.SymRealWinOpen
16 })();
```

To enable automatic reformatting of all script responses, enable the **Make JavaScript Pretty** option on Fiddler's Rules menu. When JavaScript is reformatted during download, the client will only see the reformatted form, which can be helpful when you are using the browser's script debugging tools.

You can manually control whether the JavaScript formatter runs on a response using the X-Format-JS Session flag. When this flag is set to a value of 0, false, or no, the extension will not format the response body, even if the **Make JavaScript Pretty** option is enabled on the Rules menu. Any other value will cause the JavaScript response body to be formatted, even if the **Make JavaScript Pretty** option is *not* enabled on the Rules menu.

This extension is not compatible with a very small number of responses, for which the reformatting process may introduce corruption. That problem arises in two scenarios: first, when a response is sent with a JavaScript MIME type but it's not actually JavaScript (seen on some Google properties). Second, the reformatting process may cause problems if the (very obscure) JavaScript line-continuation feature is used. Line continuation allows script developers to end a line with a backslash and the JavaScript engine will automatically concatenate that line with the following. The JavaScript Formatter's parser is not yet aware of this feature and will not format such lines properly.

GALLERY

The Gallery extension is designed to display any images that have been found in the selected Sessions. This extension is useful when you wish to interact with a large number of images, or wish to quickly select a Session based on the image it returned.

The extension has only a few options, displayed across the top of its tab:

By default, each image is shown as a 150x150 pixel thumbnail, and images smaller than 10kb in size are ignored. Click the **Filter sessions** link to select the Sessions for which images appear, unselecting any Sessions which do not represent images or whose thumbnails were removed from the view. Click the **Help** link to get a quick summary of the extension's features.

Hover over a thumbnail to show the Session ID, URL, dimensions, and image format in a balloon tip.

Middle-click a thumbnail to remove the image from the Gallery. Right-click a thumbnail to switch away from the Gallery and inspect the chosen image's Session using the Inspectors. Hold Shift while right-clicking or double-clicking and Inspectors will instead open in a popup window.

Full-Screen View

Double-click on a thumbnail to enter the full-screen image viewer mode. If the image's Session has a Comment set, this comment is shown as a caption at the bottom of the screen.

While in full-screen mode, use the mouse or keyboard to control the view:

- To exit full screen mode, middle-click or press the Escape key.

- To advance to the next image, left-click, hit Spacebar, hit the Right arrow key, or hit Page Down. To go back to the previous image, right-click, hit Shift+Spacebar, hit the Left arrow key, or hit Page Up.
  To play a sound as the picture advances, set the fiddler.sounds.Gallery.SlideShowAdvance preference to the filename of the desired .wav audio file.

- To toggle the Zoom level (Actual Size, or Stretch-to-Fit), press the Z key, Enter, or use the mouse wheel. If the image is shown Actual Size and is larger than the screen, you can use the mouse to pan around the image.

- To start an automatically-advancing slideshow, press any number key 1 to 9, representing the number of seconds to linger on each image. Press the 0 key to cancel the slideshow's automatic advancement. By combining the slideshow with the Comment-displayed-as-caption behavior, you can use Fiddler as a basic photo presentation tool.

- Various options are available to temporarily change the appearance of an image: Press H to flip the displayed image horizontally, or V to flip the image vertically. Hit R to rotate the image by 90 degrees clockwise. Press I to invert the image's colors. Press S to apply a Sepia tone, and G to convert the image to grayscale. Press C to swap the green and blue colors in the image. Press E to convert the image to grayscale except for any Red pixels; this is a slow operation and may take several seconds for large images. Press U to undo all of the manipulations made to the display of the image.

- Press the T key to tile the current image as the background for the full-screen view.

- Press the Delete key to remove the image from the Gallery and advance to the next image.

Press the P key in full-screen mode to enter a "Picture Pile" submode, in which all of the images will be rendered in turn atop one another, as if you'd just emptied a shoebox full of photos.

SHOW IMAGE BLOAT

When you're trying to squeeze every last millisecond of performance from your website, ensuring that it uses the network as efficiently as possible is critical. Most sites spend most of their load time waiting for the network, so sending fewer bytes is one great way to ensure that your pages load as quickly as possible.

For many webpages, images account for the largest number of bytes transferred. You should ensure that you send as few images as needed, and that each image is configured to cache appropriately if it will ever be reused. Beyond those simple steps, you should also ensure that your images are encoded as efficiently as possible.

You can use Fiddler's **Bytes/Pixel** Custom Column to find unoptimized images. All of the popular raster web image formats utilize compression internally, and for all practical purposes, 32-bits-per-pixel is sufficient for perfect visual fidelity. Thus, any image using over 4 bytes per pixel should immediately be considered suspect. There are four common scenarios for seeing high numbers of bytes-per-pixel:

1. The image is an animated image (so the pixel count is misleading)
2. The image was saved in a poor format (e.g. a large photo saved as a lossless PNG)
3. The image was poorly compressed (e.g. low compression settings)
4. The image contains a significant amount of non-image data

Of these, issue #4 appears to be extremely prevalent. Image-editing products like Photoshop often store editing data within images. The expectation is that the graphic designer will use the editor's "Save for Web" feature to export an image stripped of all of the unnecessary data, but all too often this step is skipped and a bloated image is instead published to the live website.

While the Bytes/Pixel Custom Column is a powerful way to find suspicious images, the **Show Image Bloat** extension offers a fun visual way to find images bloated with metadata. To use the extension, simply tick the **Rules > Show Image Bloat** menu item.

The extension scans GIF, JPEG and PNG image files for unnecessary embedded metadata. If waste is found, the image will be obscured with a "brick wall" whose height is based on the wasted percentage of the file's size.

For instance, when loading NASA's homepage, this 43kb JPEG image:

…is rewritten to show that nearly 23kb of the file's size is due to bloat:

If you examine the original image using the ImageView Inspector, you can see that it contains an unnecessary thumbnail over 8kb in size, and over 14kb of Adobe Photoshop metadata. The designer didn't use the "Save for Web" feature in Photoshop to remove bloat, so the image is over twice as big as it needs to be.

When you browse with the Show Image Bloat extension enabled, each image will be filled from the bottom based on the percentage of the file which consists of unnecessary bloat; an image with 2% overhead will show a small line at the bottom, while a product logo containing 90% bloat will be nearly completely obscured by the fill. When the extension rewrites an image containing more than 2% bloat, the Web Sessions list will contain two entries—one for the rewritten image, and one for the original response:

#	Host	URL	Comments
🖼	www.nasa.gov	/sites/default/files/styles/36…	ImageBloat rendering showing 22,981/43,081 bytes (53.3%)
🖼	www.nasa.gov	/sites/default/files/styles/36…	Original server response for Session #497

Select the original response and use the ImageView Inspector to understand the source of the wasted bytes.

If you'd like to use a different fill color for the "bricks", enter the following command in the QuickExec box:

```
prefs set fiddler.ui.Colors.ImageBloat #FF4500
```

…where the final parameter is a hex color value or color name.

CONTENT BLOCKER

The Content Blocker extension enables you to easily block selected content from download by returning a HTTP/404 response to the client. This functionality allows you to test your web applications' behavior if content is blocked by an ad-blocker or the Tracking Protection feature found in IE8 and later.

To install the extension, you must download it from the Fiddler website and copy the DLL into your \Documents\Fiddler2\Scripts folder. After installing the extension, a new **ContentBlock** menu will appear on the Fiddler main menu.

The **ContentBlock** menu offers several simple options:

Enabled	Tick this option to enable blocking.
Block Paths	Tick this option to block requests whose URL path contains the text /ad
Edit Blocked Hosts	Click to open a new window and edit the list of hosts from which content will be blocked. The list consists of fully-qualified hostnames and is delimited by semicolons. You may use wildcards, e.g. *.adserver.com;*-ads.com.
Always Block Flash	Tick this option to block Adobe Flash content regardless of its origin.
Block X-Domain Flash	Tick this option to block Adobe Flash content if it originates from a different site than the requesting page. The Referer header is consulted in making this determination.
Short-circuit Redirects	Tick this option and Fiddler watches for outbound requests that contain a HTTP or HTTPS URL in a querystring parameter. If found, Fiddler will cancel the original request and return a HTTP/307 response to the URL found in the query string. This option is useful for bypassing "logging" redirector pages.
Hide Blocked Sessions	Tick this option to hide blocked Sessions from the Web Sessions list.

You can easily add a host to the list of blocked hosts by right-clicking a Session in the Web Sessions list and choosing **Block this Host** from the context menu.

This extension was developed as an example of how to use the Fiddler extension model (its source is included in the download) and as such it offers some redundant functionality that can be found in other parts of Fiddler.

Traffic Differ

The Traffic Differ extension aims to help you easily determine how two sets of captured traffic are different. This can be useful if, for instance, you have one SAZ file captured by a customer that encountered a problem on your site and another SAZ file captured which represents the "working" case.

The Traffic Differ enables you to load these two SAZ files and then compare the Sessions within them as a whole. Alternatively, you can drag and drop Sessions from the current Web Sessions list to either of the Session lists and use those Sessions for comparison.

Two side-by-side Session lists show each Session's status code, URL, response size, and a hash of the response body.

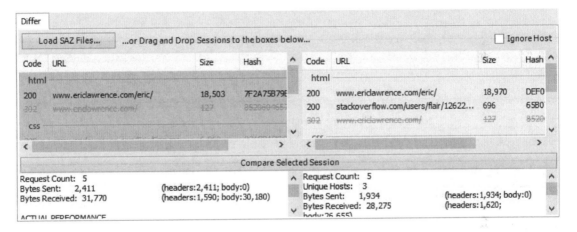

Check the **Ignore Host** checkbox to treat all requests as if they originated from a single host (useful when comparing a capture from a Test server against one from a Live server, for instance.)

To compare any two individual Sessions between the two captures, select one Session in each list and then click the **Compare Selected Session** button. The file comparison tool will launch and compare the request and response headers and body text.

FiddlerScript Editors

The Syntax Highlighting extensions package adds a new **FiddlerScript** tab to the main Fiddler UI and also provides a standalone **Fiddler ScriptEditor** application offering similar functionality. It also includes the SyntaxView Inspectors, described in the Inspectors chapter.

FiddlerScript Tab

The FiddlerScript tab allows you to easily view and update your FiddlerScript rules directly in the Fiddler UI. Across the top of the tab are a few UI controls:

Save Script	Save changes made to the script
Go to dropdown	This dropdown lists key methods in the FiddlerScript. Select a method from the list to scroll to it. Choose the ***FiddlerScript Reference** option to open the FiddlerScript reference web page. Hidden feature: Double-click the Go to text label itself to collapse the script source blocks to definitions.
Find... box	Search the script for the specified text.
ClassView	Toggle the visibility of the ClassView sidebar.

Below these controls is a syntax-aware source code editor containing the current text of your FiddlerScript. The editor supports context-sensitive code completion and will show available properties, fields and methods in a popup window as you type:

Code lines that you've changed will show a yellow bar in the left margin:

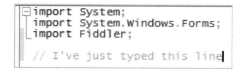

...until you save your changes using the **Save Script** button.

If Fiddler encounters a script error when compiling your script, the FiddlerScript tab will activate and scroll to show the error.

ClassView Sidebar

The ClassView sidebar allows you to explore the key objects, properties, and methods available to your script. Note that the ClassView does not expose *all* available functionality, only the functionality that is most commonly used by scripts.

Click an item in the treeview to show the description of that item at the top of the sidebar. Press CTRL+C to copy the selected item's name to the clipboard, useful to easily insert it in your script.

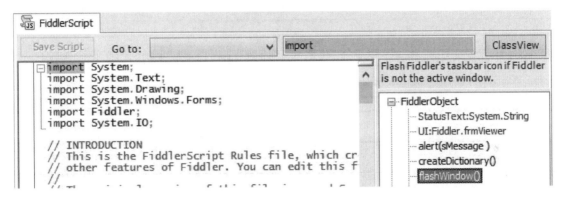

The sidebar's items are color-coded depending on their type:

Color	Type
Black	Method
Blue	Property
Green	Field
Purple	Event

Fiddler ScriptEditor

The Fiddler ScriptEditor program opens when you click **Rules** > **Customize Rules** or hit CTRL+R in Fiddler. You can also launch the Fiddler ScriptEditor from anywhere in Windows by tapping Windows+R and typing fse in the Windows Run prompt.

The standalone ScriptEditor offers the same general functionality as the FiddlerScript tab, with the convenience of running in its own window. Unlike the FiddlerScript tab, however, the standalone application is not notified of script compilation errors and will not notify you of any problems that Fiddler encounters when compiling your script.

The **Go** menu offers commands to navigate quickly to important methods in the FiddlerScript, and to scroll to a specific line.

The **Insert** menu offers a number of pre-built snippets that you can add to your script. To use them, place the cursor where you'd like the snippet added, then click the menu item representing the desired snippet.

For instance, place the cursor just inside the Handlers class' opening brace:

```
class Handlers
{
        |
```

Then click **Insert > Context Menu Item**:

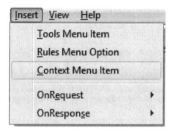

The Editor will insert a template `ContextAction` block which will add a new menu item to the Web Sessions context menu:

```
class Handlers
{
    // Create a new item on the right-click menu of the Session List.
    public static ContextAction("&UNTITLED")
    function DoUNTITLED(oSessions: Fiddler.Session[]){
        for (var x = 0; x < oSessions.Length; x++){
            // Write your code here
        }
    }
}
```

The **View** menu offers options to adjust the display of the source code, including changing the font size, showing line numbers, and expanding and collapsing method blocks. It also includes the toggle which shows and hides the ClassView Explorer sidebar.

AnyWHERE

Most modern browsers support HTML5 Geolocation, a feature that allows JavaScript to determine the user's real-world location. Most browsers implement this functionality by querying the operating system for a list of nearby Wi-Fi access points, then submitting that list to a webservice which maps the nearby access points to a longitude/latitude pair. The webservice provides that value to the browser, which then returns it to JavaScript.

Fiddler's AnyWHERE extension allows you to trivially spoof the responses to geolocation webservice queries, enabling you to "trick" the browser into thinking you're somewhere you are not. The window allows you to type in your current location, or select a location from a list of worldwide points-of-interest:

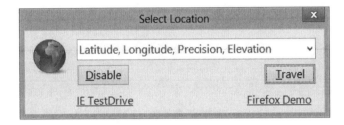

Because browser geolocation webservice queries travel over HTTPS, you must enable HTTPS decryption for this add-on to operate. This extension supports IE9+, FF4, Chrome, and Opera, but it will not work if the browser's geolocation feature is not based on webservice lookups. For instance, when IE10 is running on a Windows 8 device that includes GPS hardware, Windows will use that hardware rather than calling a webservice to determine the location.

Source code for this extension is provided in the download package.

Store, Import, and Export Traffic

SESSION ARCHIVE ZIP (SAZ) FILES

Fiddler's default save format is the Session Archive Zip (SAZ) file. SAZ files are simply Zip archives that are constructed in a particular way that Fiddler understands. By renaming a .SAZ file to .ZIP, you can use Windows Explorer or WinZip to explore the SAZ file to see how it works under the covers.

The SAZ format is Fiddler's "lossless" format—it contains all of the headers and bodies for each Session that Fiddler captured, along with metadata including comments, color markers, and timing information. Because it contains all of the traffic, a SAZ file may grow quite large, especially if it contains images, sounds or video responses. In contrast, HTML, script, and CSS files tend to compress by 80% or more. It is possible to store SAZ files with gigabytes of data and tens of thousands of Sessions, but because such files are unwieldy to load or transfer, you will generally want to use Fiddler's filtering features to minimize the amount of data stored in any given SAZ.

You can later reload a SAZ file into Fiddler to view the Sessions contained within; these Sessions will be colored with a light green background color for easy identification. One thing Fiddler *won't* restore in Sessions loaded from a SAZ file is Session ID; when a SAZ is loaded, each Session gets a new ID starting at the current index. Before sharing a SAZ file with someone else, use the **Comments** button or **Edit > Mark** menu to tag any Sessions of interest.

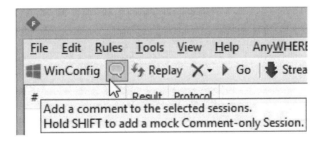

If Fiddler reloads a Session which does not already have a comment, it will automatically add a comment containing the *original* Session's ID:

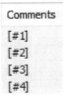

Fiddler's AutoResponder is also able to import a SAZ file and replay the responses contained within to mimic the original traffic flow; this is useful when attempting to locally reproduce problems captured in remote environments.

Protecting SAZ Files

SAZ files contain all captured web traffic, which often includes sensitive information like usernames, passwords, cookies, and account information. Therefore, you should only share SAZ files with trusted people or organizations.

If a SAZ file must be stored in an unprotected location or transferred over an insecure connection, you can help keep it private by encrypting the contents before saving. To do so, select **Password-Protected SAZ** in the **Save as type** dropdown on the Save Session Archive prompt.

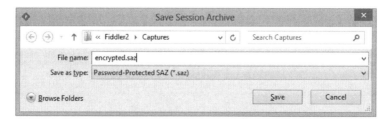

After choosing to save in encrypted format, a password will be requested:

The text at the bottom-left of the password prompt shows the length of the typed password and a checksum string.

Password-Protected SAZ files are encrypted using 128-bit AES encryption, a strong form of encryption that is also used for HTTPS traffic and by government and military organizations. Of course, to keep the file private, your password must be kept secret. If the file is being shared with someone else, you must privately communicate the password to the other person. Don't forget your password—there's no practical way to reopen your SAZ file without it.

To configure Fiddler to use 256-bit AES instead of 128bit, set the preference `fiddler.saz.AES.Use256Bit` to `true`; this is overkill for most situations. Alternatively, set the legacy `bUseAESForSAZ` property on the `CONFIG` object to `false` to configure Fiddler to use the legacy PKZIP obfuscation scheme, which is very fast but provides much weaker protection of the file's contents.

FIDDLERCAP

SAZ files have proven so useful in capturing and reproducing problems with web applications that I soon found that many web developers were requesting SAZ captures from novice PC users. In the hope of making that a more practical request, I built **FiddlerCap**. FiddlerCap is a lightweight tool designed to allow non-technical users to capture SAZ files for later analysis by experts using the full Fiddler debugger.

FiddlerCap offers a simplified user-interface and streamlined workflow for capturing web traffic; unlike Fiddler itself, it cannot modify traffic and has no extensibility mechanisms. Like Fiddler, you can use FiddlerCap to collect web traffic from any application developed using any technology. FiddlerCap is built atop the FiddlerCore library and uses a FiddlerCore proxy instance running on port 8889 to capture web traffic.

Install FiddlerCap by visiting `http://fiddlercap.com`, a simple page which provides simple step-by-step instructions on how to use the tool to capture web traffic. By default, FiddlerCap installs to a folder on your desktop and it does not require Administrative permissions. To simplify worldwide use, FiddlerCap has been localized to Spanish, French, Italian, Japanese, Portuguese, and Russian.

When the install completes, the tool automatically opens. The window is divided into three groups: **Capture**, **Capture Options**, and **Tools**.

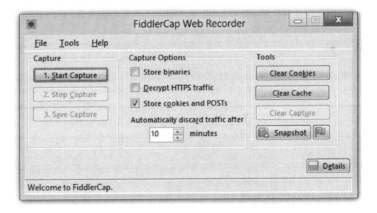

The ![Details] button at the bottom right of the FiddlerCap window will expand the window to show a simple Session list of the captured traffic. Sessions' content cannot be inspected, but individual Sessions may be removed by selecting them and pressing the `Delete` key.

Capture Box

The Capture box offers the minimum set of controls needed to collect a capture. Press the **Start Capture** button to begin capturing web traffic. A new browser window will open for you to reproduce the problem, although FiddlerCap will capture traffic from any process that respects the system proxy setting—not just that single browser window. The FiddlerHook extension for Firefox is not available for FiddlerCap; if Firefox's network traffic isn't automatically captured, open the browser's **Tools** > **Options** > **Advanced** > **Network** > **Connection Settings** screen and select the **Use System Proxy Settings** option.

After the problem has been reproduced, click the **Stop Capture** button to end the capture of traffic. Lastly, click the **Save Capture** button to select where to save the .SAZ file. By default, the SAZ file will be saved on the desktop. To encrypt the SAZ file with a password, select the **Password-Protected SAZ** option in the **Save as type** dropdown:

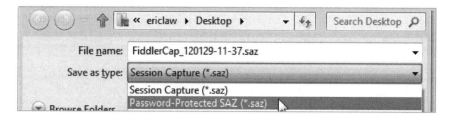

Capture Options Box

The Capture Options box controls the options used in capturing.

The **Store binaries** checkbox (unticked by default) controls whether binary response bodies (e.g. images, audio, video, and application/octet-stream downloads) will be stored in the capture. Omitting these bodies (storing only their headers) can dramatically shrink the size of the final SAZ file, although obviously if the problem being reproduced depends on the content of such downloads, you should enable the Store binaries option.

The **Decrypt HTTPS traffic** checkbox (unticked by default) controls whether or not HTTPS traffic will be decrypted by FiddlerCap. When you check this box, an explanatory message is shown:

```
---------------------------
A note about HTTPS Decryption
---------------------------
HTTPS decryption will enable your debugging buddy to see the raw traffic sent
via the HTTPS protocol.

This feature works by decrypting SSL traffic and reencrypting it using a
locally generated certificate. FiddlerCap will generate this certificate
and remove it when you close this tool.

You may choose to temporarily install this certificate in the Trusted store
to avoid warnings from your browser or client application.
---------------------------
```

After this note is dismissed, a Windows Security prompt is presented to allow you to trust FiddlerCap's root certificate:

Close FiddlerCap to automatically delete all of the certificates it generated during the capture; you will be prompted for permission to delete the root certificate from the Trusted Certificates store.

The **Store cookies and POSTs** option (checked by default) controls whether FiddlerCap will store POST request bodies and the HTTP headers Cookie, Set-Cookie, Set-Cookie2, Authorization, and Proxy-Authorization. Disabling this option can slightly shrink the capture and somewhat reduces the amount of privacy-impacting information stored in the SAZ file. Even when this option is disabled, however, captures may contain other sensitive information and thus they should only be shared with trusted parties.

The **Automatically discard traffic after # minutes** option allows you to control how many minutes of traffic are saved in the SAZ file. This option is most useful when trying to capture a problem that only happens intermittently. You can leave FiddlerCap running in the background and it will periodically expire older traffic to reduce the size of the capture and the amount of memory used. When you encounter the problem you are trying to capture, you can save just the last few minutes' worth of traffic to the archive.

Tools Box

The Tools box offers options that may be useful in reproducing a problem. The **Clear Cookies** button will purge all persistent cookies for Internet Explorer and other applications that are based on WinINET. The **Clear Cache** button will purge all cached files from the Internet Explorer / WinINET cache to help ensure that all responses are seen by FiddlerCap instead of possibly being pulled from the local cache.

The **Clear Capture** button is enabled only while FiddlerCap is capturing; it immediately clears all previously captured Sessions from the capture.

The **Snapshot** button will take a screenshot of the monitor FiddlerCap is running on and add it to the capture as a JPEG-formatted image. It will be stored in a new Session whose URL contains the current timestamp in the format `http://localhost/Screenshot_h-mm-ss.jpg`.

Click the Flag button  to add a comment to the capture:

The comment text will be stored as the HTTP response body of a new Session with a URL of http://USERCOMMENT/MARKER.

FIDDLER'S VIEWER MODE

Ordinarily, only one instance of Fiddler may be started at a time; attempting to launch a new instance of Fiddler while it's already open will simply reactivate the existing Fiddler instance. However, it is sometimes useful to open additional instances of Fiddler to view SAZ files or compose requests, independent of the existing Fiddler instance.

To achieve those goals, Fiddler supports opening additional **Viewer** instances by passing the `-viewer` command line argument, or by clicking the **New Viewer** option on Fiddler's File menu. You may also right-click on a SAZ file in Windows Explorer and choose **Open in Viewer** from the context menu:

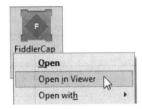

Viewer Mode instances can be identified by the Viewer Mode icon in the status bar: 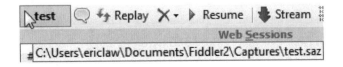 and by the text at the front of the toolbar. When no SAZ file is loaded, the text shows **FiddlerViewer:**

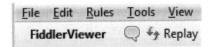

You can name this Viewer instance by clicking on the text and entering a new title:

If you load a SAZ file into the instance, the text will change to the name of the SAZ file, with a tooltip showing the full path to the file:

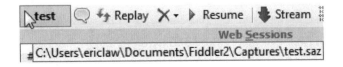

Fiddler Viewer instances cannot capture traffic, and most configuration changes made in Viewer mode (e.g. hiding the toolbar or reordering columns in the Web Sessions list) will be discarded when the instance is closed.

IMPORT AND EXPORT SESSIONS

Beyond the native SAZ format, Fiddler offers a rich set of Importers and Exporters (known collectively as "Transcoders") that allow it to share captured network traffic with other tools. In addition to the Transcoders bundled with Fiddler, an extensibility mechanism permits support of additional formats to be added by other developers.

Fiddler's Import and Export functionality can be found on the File menu. The **Import Sessions…** command will allow you to load Sessions from other formats, while the **Export Sessions** submenu allows you to export either all Sessions or only the Sessions selected in the Web Sessions list.

Import Formats

Fiddler includes five built-in Importers:

1. Folder Tree
2. HTTPArchive
3. Internet Explorer's F12 NetXML
4. Packet Capture
5. TestStudio LoadTest

Point the **Folder Tree** Importer at a folder containing one or more SAZ files and it will import each of the files in that folder and its children. The Importer will cache any passwords you supply and reuse them when opening subsequent files; this feature is useful when reloading a large number of files protected by a small number of reused passwords.

HTTPArchive format (HAR; http://groups.google.com/group/http-archive-specification) is a lossy JSON-based format which is exported by many tools including Firebug, Chrome's Developer tools, and HTTPWatch. Versions 1.1 and 1.2 of the format are supported.

F12 **NetXML** format is a very similar format exported by the Internet Explorer 9 to 11's Developer Tools' Network tab. The format is actually just an HTTPArchive file encoded using XML instead of JSON[2]. Fiddler is the only popular tool to read the NetXML Format; you can use Fiddler to load NetXML and save it to a more common format like HAR.

Note that both HAR and NetXML are lossy formats, so some data will be missing (in particular, larger binary bodies like images may not be present).

The **Packet Capture** importer finds web traffic stored in Wireshark PCAP format or Microsoft Network Monitor CAP files. Fiddler will parse the raw TCP/IP data and create new Sessions based on any HTTP traffic found within. Only HTTP traffic is visible; HTTPS traffic is encrypted so Fiddler can only display any encrypted tunnels but not the encrypted Sessions sent over those connections.

TestStudio LoadTest format is used by Telerik's TestStudio LoadTest product. This format contains HTTP and HTTPS requests that were captured for replay by the TestStudio testing agent. Import a `.tstest` file to see the request steps that make up the Load Test.

After choosing a format to Import from, you will be prompted to select the file to import. The selected file will be parsed and the traffic will be added to the Web Sessions list.

Build Your Own

Support for additional Import formats can be added by any developer, as shown in the section "Build Import and Export Transcoders" later in this book.

Export Formats

Fiddler includes a broad set of Exporters that allow it to export traffic for use in other tools or applications. The remainder of this chapter describes the export formats supported by Fiddler itself.

cURL Script

cURL (`http://curl.haxx.se/`) is a popular command line tool used to make HTTP and HTTPS requests. Fiddler's cURL Script exporter will export a batch script that invokes cURL for each request to replicate the sequence of Sessions as captured by Fiddler.

HTML5 AppCache Manifest

HTML5 introduced the concept of an Application Cache, which allows a web developer to provide a manifest of pages that should be cached to permit offline use. The manifest specifies which resources the browser should download into the AppCache and which resources should always be retrieved from the network.

---

[2] This was not an intentional difference on Microsoft's part: the original HTTPArchive format spec defined the format using XML syntax. Only a small comment at the top of the specification noted that JSON should be used instead.

Manifests are simply text files and you can create them with your text editor of choice. However, this process can be tedious and begs for an automated solution. Fiddler's HTML5 AppCache Manifest Exporter makes the process of generating a manifest a straightforward exercise:

1. Clear your browser cache.

2. Start Fiddler.

3. Load your website in the browser.

4. In Fiddler, click **File** > **Export Sessions** > **All Sessions**….

5. In the Select Format window, pick **HTML5 AppCache Manifest**.

6. Click **Next**. In the **Adjust AppCache Manifest** window, check any resources that you wish to exclude from the CACHE section of the manifest; those will be added to the NETWORK section of the manifest:

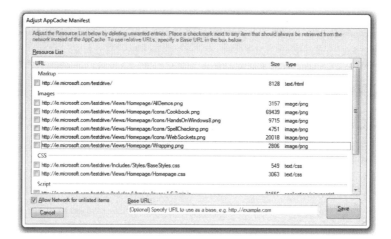

7. If you'd like, use the text box at the bottom to specify a **Base URL** if the resource URLs should be relative to the manifest. For instance, in the example above, I will place the manifest in the folder http://ie.microsoft.com/testdrive, so I will use that as the Base URL.

8. Click the **Save** button to generate and display the manifest in your text editor:

```
IETestDrive.appcache - Notepad
File  Edit  Format  View  Help
CACHE MANIFEST
# Generated: 9/14/2011 6:36:33 PM

# Deploy so that URLs are relative to: http://ie.microsoft.com/testdrive

CACHE:
/
/Includes/Libraries/jquery-1.6.2.min.js
/Includes/Script/BrowserInfo.js
/Includes/Script/TestDriveCommon.js
/Includes/Styles/BaseStyles.css
/views/Homepage/AllDemos.png
/views/Homepage/Homepage.css
/views/Homepage/Homepage.js
/views/Homepage/Icons/Cookbook.png
/views/Homepage/Icons/HandsOnWindows8.png
/views/Homepage/Icons/Spellchecking.png
/views/Homepage/Icons/webSockets.png
/views/Homepage/Wrapping.png

NETWORK:
*
```

9. If you're happy with the manifest, save it to your web server in the appropriate location. Ensure that your web server is configured to return the manifest file type with `Content-Type: text/cache-manifest`

10. In your web page, ensure that your page will run in Standards mode (e.g. using the HTML5 doctype) and add a `manifest` attribute on the `HTML` element pointing to your application's manifest.

```
<!DOCTYPE html>
<html manifest="app.manifest" >
<head>
```

Keep in mind that when the browser is using AppCached content, those resources will be reused from the cache and not pulled from the network (until the cache is expired). Because the content is cached locally, you will not see requests to re-download that content in Fiddler. If you wish to use Fiddler to modify such content, you will need to clear your browser's cache so that the browser is forced to re-download the content from the network on next use.

HTTPArchive v1.1 and v1.2

The HTTPArchive format is a JSON format that contains Web Sessions' headers, some bodies, and timing information. The primary difference between versions 1.1 and 1.2 of the format is that the newer version permits the inclusion of small binary bodies.

By default, Fiddler will store text bodies up to 1MB in length and binary bodies up to 32768 bytes in length; these values can be changed by setting the appropriate preferences:

```
fiddler.importexport.HTTPArchiveJSON.MaxTextBodyLength
fiddler.importexport.HTTPArchiveJSON.MaxBinaryBodyLength
```

If a body is too long, it will not be stored in the file and instead a comment will be added to the Session noting the omission.

MeddlerScript

Meddler (`http://webdbg.com/Meddler/`) is a simple HTTP/HTTPS response-generation tool which I developed to allow building of tiny, self-contained reproductions of HTTP traffic. Meddler is essentially a "scripted socket" which allows very low-level manipulation of sockets, a capability useful for debugging browsers or other clients. The hip kids now use Node.js for this purpose.

When you export Web Sessions to MeddlerScript, the result is an `.ms` file that can be loaded into Meddler to "play back" that traffic. Conceptually, this is very similar to using Fiddler's AutoResponder tab to play back previously captured traffic from a SAZ file, but Meddler scripts can be easier to automate and they permit low-level tweaks (e.g. *"Wait 300ms between sending the headers and the first byte of the body, then write the body in 2048 byte chunks each 10 seconds apart"*) that cannot be easily replicated using Fiddler itself.

Unless you're building a browser or other HTTP client, exporting MeddlerScript probably will not be very useful for you.

Raw Files

The Raw Files Exporter allows you to store individual response bodies to files on disk. This can be tremendously useful when dumping media content. For instance, say you've browsed around a photography website and collected a bunch of photos in the Web Sessions list. You can use filters and other features in Fiddler to select only the photos of interest (e.g. JPEG files over 20k). You can then select **File** > **Export Sessions** > **Selected Sessions** and choose **Raw Files** in the **Select Export Format** box.

The **File Exporter** window allows you to configure the export process.

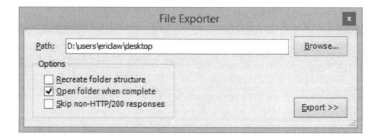

The **Path** box allows you to select the base path under which a new folder will be created. The new folder will be named \Dump-*MonthDay-Hour-Minute-Second*\.

The **Options** box contains three checkboxes. **Recreate Folder Structure** will create subfolders for each resource based on the hostname and path of the file. Use this to mimic a site's hierarchy on your local disk. The **Open folder when complete** option will open Windows Explorer to display the root folder into which files were exported when the export has completed. The **Skip non-HTTP/200 responses** option ignores any Sessions except those with a HTTP/200 status code.

Click the **Export >>** button to begin the export.

Beyond dumping media files, the **Raw Files** Exporter allows you to easily mirror a captured website to your disk. You can then drag/drop the contents of the folder to the AutoResponder tab, and Fiddler will then play back that local content mirror based on inbound requests. This practice can be very convenient for debugging a website when you want to use other tools (e.g. Expression Web or Visual Studio) to edit HTML content locally.

Visual Studio WebTest

Generating a Visual Studio `.WebTest` file allows you to use the Visual Studio Web Test product to reissue previously captured requests for functional-testing and load-testing purposes. Visual Studio Web Test is included in some editions of Visual Studio 2008 and later.

WCAT Script

As explained on the tool's website:

> Web Capacity Analysis Tool (WCAT) is a lightweight HTTP load generation tool designed to measure the performance of a web server within a controlled environment. WCAT can simulate thousands of concurrent users making requests to a single web site or multiple web sites. The WCAT engine uses a simple script to define the set of HTTP requests to be played back to the web server.

Fiddler's WCAT Exporter allows you to easily generate request-generation scripts for WCAT to replay against your servers to verify their ability to handle load.

You can download the 32bit or 64bit WCAT installer from http://fiddler2.com/r/?WCAT.

Build Your Own

Support for additional Export formats can be added by any developer, as shown in the section "Build Import and Export Transcoders" later in this book.

FiddlerScript

Extend Fiddler with FiddlerScript

The earliest versions of Fiddler had no extensibility model at all; the features I coded were all that users had available. It didn't take long to recognize that I would never be able to keep up with the myriad feature requests coming in from Fiddler users who were using the tool to solve a huge variety of problems.

One of the biggest early limitations was that Fiddler only offered one filter (Hide Images) and thus it was easy to get overwhelmed by the sheer volume of traffic flowing through the tool. I had planned to build a filtering interface full of dropdown fields and textboxes which would allow users to filter traffic based on boolean criteria that I would make available. There were two obvious problems with this approach: first, it would require that I do a lot of tedious UI development, and second, I knew that most users wouldn't be happy with it. Advanced users find it very cumbersome to build complicated queries using UI controls, and novice users would be easily confused when trying to build complicated queries that involved nested AND, OR, and NOT operators.

Fortunately, laziness often leads to better engineering. I remember thinking one night: *"It's so easy for me to build complicated filter expressions inside Fiddler's code itself. If only users could just write code to do filtering."* Happily, this thought led to a *"eureka"* moment– the recollection that the .NET Framework makes it very easy to integrate a script engine into an application, and exposing the application's object model to that script engine is easy. With a few dozen lines of code added in late 2003, Fiddler got infinitely more powerful.

Even as Fiddler was modernized over the last twelve years, including the introduction of Fiddler extensions and many built-in filtering capabilities, the FiddlerScript engine has remained an indispensable component of Fiddler. By mastering FiddlerScript, you will get much more out of Fiddler.

Note: When running on Linux or Mac atop the Mono Framework, FiddlerScript is based on C# rather than JScript.NET, as the latter language is not available on that platform. Mono FiddlerScript's C# syntax is slightly different than that of JScript.NET, but the supported features and scenarios are nearly identical across platforms.

About FiddlerScript

As each Session flows through Fiddler, methods in the `CustomRules.js` script file are run, enabling you to hide, flag, or modify Sessions based on criteria of arbitrary complexity. Your rules script can be modified and recompiled dynamically at runtime without restarting Fiddler. This book does not provide a comprehensive reference to the JScript.NET language upon which FiddlerScript is based. If you plan to code especially powerful or complicated FiddlerScript, you should consider finding a copy of Microsoft JScript.NET Programming. That book presents a comprehensive view of the language, including useful information I haven't seen anywhere else. (I discovered it in 2012, ten years after its only printing. In one of those "small world" coincidences, it was authored by Justin Rogers, a colleague from the Internet Explorer team.)

JavaScript is a language familiar to most Fiddler users, and JScript.NET isn't syntactically much different than the C# language beloved by most .NET programmers. There are two differences that JavaScript developers moving to JScript.NET should be aware of:

1. JScript.NET supports a C#-like mechanism for declaring classes that contain fields, properties and methods. Fiddler integrates your script by calling methods on a `static class` named `Handlers`, described below.

2. When declaring a variable, you may (and should) declare that variable's type. Type definitions improve the performance of the generated code and allow the compiler to flag errors at compile time instead of runtime.

To set the type of a variable, just specify the type after the variable name and before any initial value, like so:

```
var sMyString: String = "StringValue";
var bMyBool: boolean = false;
var iMyInt: int = 42;
```

For ease of development, the FiddlerScript engine will automatically call specially-named functions in your script when events of interest occur. However, less-interesting events do not get this special treatment and you must directly attach handlers for such events. To supply an event handler in script, call the hidden `add_EventName` method generated by the compiler for each event. For instance, to handle the `OnClearCache` event, use the following code:

```
// Inside your main function, call the hidden add_ method
// using the format Object.add_EventName(handlerFunction)
FiddlerApplication.add_OnClearCache(catchClearCache);

// Implement the event handler
static function catchClearCache(sender, args:CacheClearEventArgs) {
  MessageBox.Show("User cleared the cache.");
}
```

If you do attach any event handlers in this way, you should use the *remove_EventName* method to remove the event handler in your script's `OnRetire` function.

Over the years, a variety of powerful features were added to FiddlerScript, including the ability to extend the Fiddler UI and accept automation commands from the `ExecAction.exe` command line tool. Some features of Fiddler (for instance, UserAgent spoofing and performance simulations) are built in Fiddler-Script because users often want to customize these features slightly. By implementing such features in the easily-updated script, Fiddler enables users to customize the tool to their exact needs.

Edit FiddlerScript

To see the current FiddlerScript loaded in Fiddler, choose **Customize Rules** on Fiddler's **Rules** menu. The configured script editor will launch and show the script. By default, Notepad will be used as the script editing program, but you can adjust this preference using the **Tools** > **Fiddler Options** > **Tools** tab. If you plan to do any non-trivial modifications to the FiddlerScript, I highly recommend that you install the Fiddler ScriptEditor, a syntax-highlighting editor that can either run standalone or on a tab within Fiddler itself. When installed, the Fiddler ScriptEditor will set itself as the default script editor.

Update FiddlerScript at Runtime

When you save the `CustomRules.js` file, Fiddler will play a sound while reloading the source code and attempting to recompile it. If compilation succeeds, the new script will be used for all subsequent Sessions. If compilation fails, you'll be shown an error message and no script will run until the error is corrected and the script is recompiled.

The compiler's error message will show the offending line and attempt to explain the nature of the error:

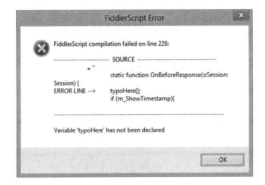

Keep in mind that each time your script is recompiled, the previously-running script is retired. The values of variables or properties in the script are reset to their default values every time the script is reloaded. If you need to preserve a variable's value from the old script instance to the new one, you should use a Preference to load and store the value. See the `BindPref` attribute (page 212) for more information.

Reset to the Default FiddlerScript

Don't worry about "breaking" your script—if you make a mistake and corrupt the script to the point where you don't know how to fix it, simply delete the `CustomRules.js` file from the `%USERPROFILE%\Documents \Fiddler2\Scripts` folder. The next time Fiddler is started, your `CustomRules.js` file will be recreated by copying the `SampleRules.js` file from the Fiddler application folder.

One important consequence of updating your `CustomRules.js` file is that when you install new versions of Fiddler, your old rules file will be preserved. Any new or updated rules stored in the new version of the `SampleRules.js` file will not be loaded unless you delete your `CustomRules.js` file or copy the updated content from the sample script.

FiddlerScript Functions

When FiddlerScript is compiled, Fiddler obtains references to several key static functions, all of which are found on a class named Handlers. Each of these functions and their use is described in this section.

Session Handling Functions

As each Session is processed, the Fiddler invokes specially-named functions in your FiddlerScript. If your script contains the named function, it will be invoked with one argument-- a reference to the current Session. Each function should be declared as a **public static function**.

These functions are called on the Session's background handler thread, not the UI thread, and thus you should avoid making any UI calls from within these functions.

OnPeekAtRequestHeaders

The OnPeekAtRequestHeaders function runs as soon as the request headers have been read from the client. This function generally runs before the request body has been read, so avoid manipulating the Session's requestBodyBytes array to avoid causing a null-reference exception.

In practice this function is rarely useful, because until the complete request has been read, there's not a lot your script can do. There are exceptions: for instance, you might set the ui-hide flag based on oSession.LocalProcess, or you might set oRequest.BufferRequest = false to stream the request to the server.

OnBeforeRequest

The OnBeforeRequest function executes after the client's complete request has been read and before the request is sent to the server. This function gives you the opportunity to modify the request's headers or body before the server sees it.

OnPeekAtResponseHeaders

The OnPeekAtResponseHeaders function runs as soon as the response headers have been read from the server. This function generally runs before the response body has been read, so avoid manipulating the Session's responseBodyBytes array to avoid causing a null-reference exception.

One of the best uses of this function is to examine the response headers to determine whether the response should be streamed or buffered as it is read from the server. If the response should be buffered so that its body may be modified by the OnBeforeResponse function, set oSession.bBufferResponse=true inside this function.

OnWebSocketMessage

The OnWebSocketMessage function is called when a request or response message is received on a WebSocket connection. You can use this method to alter the contents of the message or prevent it from being transmitted.

OnBeforeResponse

The OnBeforeResponse function *typically* executes after the server's full response has been read and before the response is sent to the client. This function gives you the opportunity to modify the response's headers or body before the client browser sees it.

However, when a Session has buffering disabled, the OnBeforeResponse function is called *after* the response has already been streamed to the client. Hence, if you modify the previously-streamed response in this function, only Fiddler will see the modified response—the client already received the unmodified original.

OnReturningError

The OnReturningError function executes in the event that a Fiddler-generated error message (for instance, "DNS Lookup Failed") is returned to the client. This handler provides the opportunity to customize the message that the client application sees. For instance, you could show a more friendly error page, log the error in a database, flag the error in the Web Sessions list, or undertake other actions.

OnDone

The OnDone function executes after the response has been returned to the client or the Session is otherwise completed. This event is suitable for updating statistical information, archiving the Session to a database, and similar operations. Note that this event runs after the last regular update to the Session's entry in the Web Sessions list, so if you make any changes to its display, you'll need to call the Session's RefreshUI method.

General Functions

FiddlerScript includes a number of functions which run based on events in Fiddler itself, and not in response to any given Session. Each function should be declared as a public static function.

Main

This function runs immediately after the script is successfully compiled. It provides an opportunity to attach event handlers, reload variables in the script from the Preferences system, or perform other one-time initialization.

OnRetire

This function runs immediately before the script is unloaded, either because Fiddler is closing or because a new script is being loaded. It provides an opportunity to detach event handlers you've added, log the value of script variables in persistent storage, or perform other cleanup.

OnBoot

This function runs only when Fiddler first boots. If this function's script is changed at runtime, the new code will not execute until the next time you start Fiddler.

OnShutdown

This function runs when Fiddler is shutting down. In practice, there's rarely a need to put any code in this function.

OnAttach

This function runs after Fiddler registers as the system proxy. By default this will happen when Fiddler starts up, and if the user toggles capturing off and back on using the status bar button, the F12 key, or the **File** > **Capture Traffic** menu toggle.

OnDetach

This function runs after Fiddler has unregistered as the system proxy and the default proxy is restored. By default this will happen when Fiddler shuts down, and if the user ever disables capturing using the status bar button, the F12 key, or the **File** > **Capture Traffic** menu toggle.

OnExecAction(sParams: string[])

This function runs when the user enters a command in the QuickExec box beneath the Web Sessions list, or if a command is sent to Fiddler from the `ExecAction.exe` command line program. The single parameter passed into the function is an array of `strings` which are tokenized from the supplied command. For instance, for the command `LOG PARAM1 "AND ONE MORE"`, the array contains three strings, "LOG", "PARAM1" and "AND ONE MORE".

The `OnExecAction` function is called after all extensions which implement the `IHandleExecAction` interface have the opportunity to handle (and optionally cancel) the command.

The default implementation of this function inside the `SampleRules.js` file shows how you can use it to set script variables, run functions, or otherwise control Fiddler's behavior.

FIDDLERSCRIPT AND AUTOMATION TOOLS

Fiddler was designed primarily for interactive use, where you directly use the Fiddler user-interface to perform whatever debugging tasks you'd like to accomplish. However, Fiddler includes a limited set of features to support automated use.

Quiet Mode

First is the `-quiet` command line argument. When Fiddler is activated with this switch, the main Fiddler window is automatically minimized to the System Tray. Fiddler will automatically suppress most of its prompts and alerts when running in quiet mode; for instance, no Certificate Warnings or HTTP Errors will pop up message boxes in this mode. The `CONFIG.QuietMode` property can be respected by extensions or FiddlerScript to accommodate the quiet mode of operation.

Driving Fiddler from Batch Scripts

Of course, running Fiddler silently isn't usually enough to accomplish most automation goals—you also will need to enable your test harness or script to drive Fiddler. Depending on your framework, you might use UI Automation to drive Fiddler's existing interface directly, but there's a more robust and reliable option available. As we saw previously, the `OnExecAction` function in FiddlerScript is run whenever the user enters a command in the QuickExec box. However, that's not the only way to invoke script commands—you can also use the `ExecAction.exe` command line tool installed by Fiddler.

For instance, if you wanted to invoke the `dump` command to save all of the Sessions in the Web Sessions list to a SAZ file, you can simply run:

```
"%PROGRAMFILES%\Fiddler2\ExecAction.exe" dump
```

The utility will pass the `dump` command into Fiddler's extensions and FiddlerScript, and the default handler in the FiddlerScript file will perform the specified action. If you need to pass multiple parameters into the tool, you can do so by quoting the arguments:

```
"%PROGRAMFILES%\Fiddler2\ExecAction.exe" "select text/html"
```

You may use the backslash character to escape quotation marks if you need them in your command:

```
ExecAction.exe "prefs set \"MyExt.UI.Title\" \"A Quoted Value\""
```

If you pass an incorrect number of arguments to the utility (zero or more than one), it will display help text and set the `ERRORLEVEL` to 1. If the utility cannot find the Fiddler window, it will display a message indicating that Fiddler could not be found and set the `ERRORLEVEL` to 2.

Driving Fiddler from Native or .NET Code

Under the covers, the ExecAction utility is extremely simple. If your test harness is written in C++ or any .NET language, you can easily pass messages directly to Fiddler without relying upon ExecAction.exe. Simply determine the main Fiddler window's handle, and then call SendMessage to pass a WM_COPYDATA structure containing the desired command's text.

Using C++, the barebones logic is as follows:

```
#include "stdafx.h"
int _tmain(int argc, _TCHAR* argv[])
{
  // Note: Fiddler uses a hidden window with this title
  HWND hWndControl = FindWindow(NULL, L"Fiddler - HTTP Debugging Proxy");

  if (NULL == hWndControl)
  {
    printf("ERROR: Fiddler window was not found.\n");
    return 2;
  }

  tagCOPYDATASTRUCT oCDS;

  oCDS.dwData = 61181; // Use 61180 for ANSI; 61181 for Unicode
  oCDS.cbData = lstrlen(argv[1]) * sizeof(WCHAR);
  oCDS.lpData = argv[1];

  SendMessage(hWndControl, WM_COPYDATA, NULL, (WPARAM) wParam, (LPARAM) &oCDS);
  return 0;
}
```

If you're using .NET code, first you must define some functions and constants for PInvoke:

```
internal const int WM_COPYDATA = 0x4A;

[DllImport("user32.dll", EntryPoint = "SendMessage")]
internal static extern IntPtr SendWMCopyMessage(IntPtr hWnd, int Msg,
  IntPtr wParam, ref SendDataStruct lParam);

[DllImport("user32.dll")]
internal static extern IntPtr FindWindow(string lpClassName, string lpWindowName);

[StructLayout(LayoutKind.Sequential, CharSet=CharSet.Unicode)]
internal struct SendDataStruct
{
  public IntPtr dwData;
  public int cbData;
  public string strData;
}
```

Then, simply use these methods to send the command string to the Fiddler window:

```
SendDataStruct oStruct = new SendDataStruct();
oStruct.dwData = (IntPtr) 61181;
oStruct.strData = "TheString";
oStruct.cbData = Encoding.Unicode.GetBytes(oStruct.strData).Length;
IntPtr hWnd = FindWindow(null, "Fiddler - HTTP Debugging Proxy");
SendWMCopyMessage(hWnd, WM_COPYDATA, IntPtr.Zero, ref oStruct);
```

You can use this technique to perform lightweight and ad-hoc automation of Fiddler. For more complicated jobs, you should prefer to build a custom tool based on the FiddlerCore class library described in the final chapter of this book.

EXTEND FIDDLER'S UI - MENUS

When Fiddler compiles your script, it looks for attributed methods that are used to create new commands in the Fiddler user-interface. You can add new items to the **Rules** menu, **Tools** menu, and **Web Sessions** context menu, as well as adding new top-level menus of your own.

Extend the Tools Menu

You can add new items to the Tools menu by adding a `ToolsAction` attribute to a method of the **Handlers** class. The attribute specifies the text of the item to show on the **Tools** menu, and it immediately precedes the method that will be run if the user clicks on the menu item. For instance, the following block, when placed inside your `Handlers` class, will add an item titled **Launch Opera** to the Tools menu:

```
// Launch Opera
ToolsAction("Launch Opera")
public static function DoLaunchOpera() {
  System.Diagnostics.Process.Start("opera.exe", String.Empty);
}
```

You may optionally specify a second string argument on the `ToolsAction` attribute to place your command inside a submenu. The signature of your method may optionally specify a single parameter which will receive an array of the Sessions currently selected in the Web Sessions list when the menu item is invoked.

```
// Launch Opera to the URL of the first selected session
ToolsAction("Opera to &URL", "Launch")
public static function DoLaunchOperaToURL(oS: Session[]) {
  if (oS.Length > 0) {
      System.Diagnostics.Process.Start("opera.exe", oS[0].fullUrl);
  }
}
```

If the user clicks on your menu when no items are selected, the `oS` array will have a `Length` property value of 0.

To specify an accelerator key for your menu item, include an ampersand (&) in its name. The &U in the previous example creates the following menu item with the U key as an accelerator:

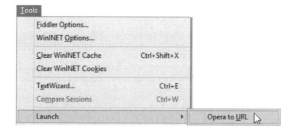

Extend the Web Sessions Context Menu

You may similarly extend the Web Sessions context menu by adding a **ContextAction** attribute to a method of the **Handlers** class. The new context menu items created by your script are added to the top of the context menu. To place your commands inside a submenu, specify a second parameter in the ContextAction attribute:

```
ContextAction("Selected Sessions", "Decode")
public static function DoRemoveEncoding(oS: Session[]) {
  for (var x=0; x < oS.Length; x++) {
     oS[x].utilDecodeRequest();
     oS[x].utilDecodeResponse();
  }
}
```

Because both ContextAction and ToolsAction attributes apply to the same method signature, you can apply both to a single method to expose the functionality on both the Tools menu and the Web Sessions context menu:

```
ContextAction("Opera", "Revisit In")
ToolsAction("Opera to &URL", "Launch")
public static function VisitInOpera(oS: Session[]) {
   if (oS.Length > 0) System.Diagnostics.Process.Start("opera.exe", oS[0].fullUrl);
}
```

Extend the Rules Menu

Your script may add new entries to the Rules menu, but they will work somewhat differently than the items added to the Tools menu and Web Sessions context menu. Instead of annotating a function, you must instead annotate a variable (field) of the **Handlers** class using a RulesOption attribute. For instance, to add the **Hide 304s** menu item, the following script is used:

```
RulesOption("Hide 304s")
public static var m_Hide304s: boolean = false;
```

Two types of variables may be bound to Rules menu items: booleans, and strings.

Note: The default value of the field is used to set the initial state of the menu item when the script is compiled. After that initial setting, the binding between the UI and the field is one-directional. That means that when the user clicks a field-bound menu item, the value of the bound boolean or string is changed, but if the script itself changes the variable's value, no change is made to the menu item's state.

Boolean-bound Rules

When Fiddler encounters a boolean variable in the script that is annotated with a RulesOption attribute, a menu item will be created using the text provided. The menu item's checked state will set the value of the boolean.

In the prior example, the boolean's value is false, so the menu item will be unchecked by default. When the user clicks the menu item, it will become checked and Fiddler will change the value of the bound m_Hide304s variable to true. Every time your script is recompiled, the default values of your boolean variables are restored, and the checkmarks on the Rules menu are updated accordingly.

Simply declaring the attributed m_Hide304s variable doesn't yet do anything useful—the variable simply tracks the state of the menu item. The *functionality* of the rule is provided by a block of code added to the OnBeforeResponse method found later in the script:

```
if (m_Hide304s && (304 == oSession.responseCode)) {

    oSession["ui-hide"] = "true";

    // Note: This block could be placed in the OnPeekAtResponseHeaders method,
    // since it does not depend upon the availability of the response body.
}
```

This block first checks to see if the rule is enabled and, if so, checks that the server returned a HTTP/304. If so, the block sets the ui-hide flag on the Session, which causes it to be hidden from the Web Sessions list.

You can also use different forms of the RulesOption attribute to create submenus of options. To do so, provide the name of the submenu as the second parameter of the attribute. For instance, the following three fields create a Performance submenu that exposes the three options:

```
RulesOption("Simulate &Modem Speeds", "Per&formance")
public static var m_SimulateModem: boolean = false;

RulesOption("&Disable Caching", "Per&formance")
public static var m_DisableCaching: boolean = false;

RulesOption("&Show Time-to-Last-Byte", "Per&formance")
public static var m_ShowTTLB: boolean = false;
```

If you would like some of the items on your submenu to be mutually exclusive (showing as a radio group instead of a set of checkboxes), you can set a third boolean parameter to true, and you can add a splitter after a menu item by setting yet a fourth boolean parameter to true.

To create this menu:

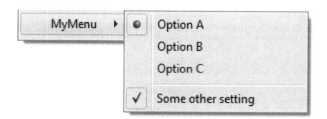

Add the following script:

```
RulesOption("Option A", "MyMenu", true)
public static var m_OptionA: boolean = true;

RulesOption("Option B", "MyMenu", true)
public static var m_OptionB: boolean = false;

RulesOption("Option C", "MyMenu", true, true)  // Splitter after option
public static var m_OptionC: boolean = false;

RulesOption("Some other setting", "MyMenu", false)
public static var m_OtherSetting: boolean = true;
```

String-bound Rules

When Fiddler encounters a string in the script that is annotated with a RulesString attribute, a new submenu item will be created. The first parameter to the RulesString constructor is a string containing the submenu's name, while the second parameter is a boolean indicating whether an item labeled **Disabled** should be added to the submenu.

Possible values for the string's value are provided by adding one or more RulesStringValue attributes to the same variable; each attribute specifies two strings: the MenuItem's text and the value to which the variable should be set. Each RulesStringValue adds a new mutually-exclusive menu item on the submenu. When the user selects one of the menu items, the variable will be updated to the value of the selected item and all other menu items on the menu will be unchecked.

For instance, this script:

```
RulesString("MyStringRule", true)
RulesStringValue("MyMenuText1", "MyValue1")
RulesStringValue("MyMenuText2", "MyValue2")
RulesStringValue("MyMenuText3", "MyValue3")
public static var m_StringRule: String = String.Empty;
```

…creates the following menu:

By default, the menu's items will be sorted alphabetically by the MenuItem's text. In some cases, you may wish to specify a different order. To do so, use the RulesStringValue overload that accepts an integer ordering parameter. For instance, you can create a menu that looks like this:

...using this script:

```
RulesString("MyStringRule", true)
RulesStringValue(1, "First Item", "one")
RulesStringValue(2, "Second Item", "two", true)
RulesStringValue(3, "Third Item", "three")
RulesStringValue(4, "Fourth Item", "four")
RulesStringValue(5, "Ask me...", "%CUSTOM%")
public static var m_StringRule: String = "two";
```

This example also shows how to set one of the entries as the default (see the last parameter on the "Second Item" RulesStringValue). Also, note the magic value %CUSTOM% used for the "Ask me…" menu item. When clicked, the user will be prompted to enter a value for the variable:

When the prompt is shown, the current value of the string variable will be presented for the user to modify.

Fiddler's **Rules > User-Agents** feature is implemented using a string variable named sUA bound to a RulesString submenu. Code in the OnBeforeRequest method checks whether the bound variable is set; if so, the request's User-Agent header is overwritten:

```
if (null != sUA) {
  oSession.oRequest["User-Agent"] = sUA;
}
```

Binding Script variables to Preferences

Because recompiling your FiddlerScript reinitializes all of its variables, you may want to use the **BindPref** attribute to preserve the value of a variable:

```
BindPref("fiddlerscript.ephemeral.bpResponseURI")
public static var bpResponseURI:String = null;
```

Fiddler will automatically reload the variable's value from a preference when FiddlerScript loads, and will automatically update the preference value when FiddlerScript unloads (either because Fiddler is closing or because you've made a change to the script and it is automatically recompiling).

If your preference name contains the text ephemeral, the value will be discarded when Fiddler exits; otherwise, the value will be restored the next time Fiddler starts.

Creating New Top-Level Menus

Using FiddlerScript, you can also easily add new top-level menus to expose custom commands. To do so, add a method with a QuickLinkMenu attribute to specify the name of the top-level menu. Then, add one or more QuickLinkItem attributes that specify the text of a menu item and a string to pass into the method if the user selects the specified item.

For instance, the following text will add a new **Links** menu containing two items:

```
QuickLinkMenu("&Links")
QuickLinkItem("IE GeoLoc TestDrive",
  "http://ie.microsoft.com/testdrive/HTML5/Geolocation/Default.html")
QuickLinkItem("FiddlerCore", "http://fiddler.wikidot.com/fiddlercore")
public static function DoLinksMenu(sText: String, sAction: String)
{
  Utilities.LaunchHyperlink(sAction);
}
```

When the user clicks on the FiddlerCore item, the DoLinksMenu function will run, passing in the URL associated with that menu item in the second parameter to the function. Items in the menu are sorted alphabetically by their menu text.

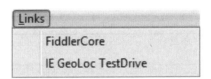

Of course, you're not limited to creating menus of links. You can create a Browser Launch menu that will allow you to launch the browser of your choice to the URL of the first selected Session:

```
QuickLinkMenu("&Browse")
QuickLinkItem("&IE", "iexplore.exe")
QuickLinkItem("&Firefox", "firefox.exe")
QuickLinkItem("&Opera", "Opera.exe")
QuickLinkItem("&Chrome", "Chrome.exe")
public static function DoBrowsersMenu(sText: String, sAction: String)
{
  var oS = FiddlerApplication.UI.GetSelectedSessions();
  var sURL = String.Empty;
```

```
    if (oS.Length > 0) { sURL = oS[0].fullUrl; }

    System.Diagnostics.Process.Start(sAction, sURL);
}
```

Similarly, you could use a switch() statement to dispatch command invocations for handling by other functions.

EXTEND FIDDLER'S UI - ADDING TABS

While most major UI extensions are built in C#, you can add simple UI tabs very easily using FiddlerScript.

For example, say that you've decided that `http://httpstatusdogs.com` is the coolest site on the Internet, and you want to enhance Fiddler with this meme. Doing so is super-simple with FiddlerScript.

At the very top of the script file, add the line:

```
import System.Text;
```

Then, move the cursor to just inside the Handlers class. There, add the following code:

```
public BindUITab("HTTPStatusDogs", true)
static function ShowStatusDogs(arrSess: Session[]):String
{
   if (arrSess.Length < 1) return "<html>Please select one or more Sessions.</html>";

   var oSB: System.Text.StringBuilder = new System.Text.StringBuilder();
   oSB.Append("<html><head>");
   oSB.Append("<style>iframe { width: '100%'; height: 600px; frameBorder:0 }</style>");
   oSB.Append("</head><body>");
   for (var i:int = 0; i<arrSess.Length; i++)
   {
     oSB.AppendFormat(
        "<iframe frameBorder=0 scrolling='no'
src='http://httpstatusdogs.com/{0}'></iframe>",
        arrSess[i].responseCode);
   }
   oSB.Append("</body></html>");
   return oSB.ToString();
}
```

When you save the script, it will automatically recompile and a new "HTTPStatusDogs" tab will appear; when you activate it, the image for each Selected Session's HTTP response code will be shown in the tab.

The "magic" that makes this work is invoked by the `BindUITab` attribute atop the function declaration:

```
public BindUITab("HTTPStatusDogs", true)
static function ShowStatusDogs(arrSess: Session[]):String
```

The presence of this attribute informs Fiddler that the following function will provide data to be rendered to a new tab, whose name is provided by the first parameter, `"HTTPStatusDogs"`. The second parameter, `true`, indicates that the string returned by the function should be rendered as HTML in a web browser view. To easily debug your HTML, change that true to `false`, and Fiddler will instead show the returned string as plain text in a textbox.

Extend Fiddler's UI - Adding Columns to the Web Sessions List

Where possible, you should prefer to use Fiddler's built-in Customize Columns feature to add new columns to the Web Sessions list. However, in cases where that feature isn't flexible enough, FiddlerScript can be used to add new columns, either by specifying an attribute or by making a method call.

Binding Columns using Attributes

The `BindUIColumn` attribute is used to create a new column in the Web Sessions list and bind to it a function that computes the text for that column. The function must accept a `Session` object as a parameter, and return a `string` as its result.

The following script adds a new column to the Web Sessions list that shows the request method for each Session:

```
BindUIColumn("Method", 60)
public static function FillMethodColumn(oS: Session) : String {
  if ((oS.oRequest != null) && (oS.oRequest.headers != null))
  {
    return oS.oRequest.headers.HTTPMethod;
  }
  return String.Empty;
}
```

After saving the script, a new **Method** column is added to the UI and values are added to the column for each subsequent Session:

#	Method	Protocol	Host
1	CONNECT	HTTP	Tunnel to
2	GET	HTTPS	fiddler2.com
5	GET	HTTP	www.telerik.com
43	OPTIONS	HTTPS	api.dec.sitefinity...
44	POST	HTTPS	api.dec.sitefinity...

Your function must be robust against being called before the data it relies upon is ready. For instance, if you were to add a column that counts the number of times the word `fuzzle` appears in the HTTP response, your method should immediately return an empty string every time it is called until the `responseBodyBytes` array is created after the response is read from the server. Otherwise, the method will throw a Null Reference Exception every time it is called before the server response is completed.

Because your function will run multiple times for each Session as the Session proceeds from one state to the next, you should ensure that it runs as quickly as possible. One strategy to minimize the work of this function is to cache values using a new flag on the Session object. Obviously, the benefit of caching a computed value will increase as the complexity of the computation of that value increases. For instance, if the calculation involves converting the responseBodyBytes array to plaintext and searching that text for a string, this can be a very expensive operation which will greatly benefit from caching its result.

The following is an example which converts a non-binary response body to a string and then searches it for the word "fuzzle", caching the result of the search in a flag on the Session object:

```
BindUIColumn("HasFuzzle", 60)
public static function FillFuzzleColumn(oS: Session) {

  // Check the cache and return the value if we already computed it
  if (oS.oFlags.ContainsKey("HasFuzzle")) {
    return oS.oFlags["HasFuzzle"];
  }

  // Exit if we don't yet have a response
  if (!oS.bHasResponse) {
    return String.Empty;
  }

  // Avoid looking inside binary content
  if (Utilities.IsBinaryMIME(oS.oResponse.MIMEType)) {
    oS.oFlags["HasFuzzle"] = "n/a";
    return "n/a";
  }

  var s = oS.GetResponseBodyAsString();
  var i = -1;

  if (s.Length > 0) {
    i = s.IndexOf("fuzzle", StringComparison.OrdinalIgnoreCase);
    if (i >= 0) {
      oS.oFlags["HasFuzzle"] = "Yes!";
      return "Yes!";
    }
  }

  oS.oFlags["HasFuzzle"] = "Nope";
  return "Nope";
}
```

This example first checks the cache for a previously computed value, and if one is found, it is immediately returned. Next, the example validates that the data it needs for the calculation is available. If not, it returns an empty string. Next, it checks to see whether the response body is advertising a binary Content-Type; if so, it caches an "n/a" result and returns it. Finally, it converts the response body to a string and hunts for the target word. It caches and returns the result of the search.

The complete set of `BindUIColumn` constructors includes versions that allow you to indicate that the column's contents should be sorted as integers, and to specify the column's width and its relative display ordering amongst the other columns.

```
public BindUIColumn(string sTitle)
public BindUIColumn(string sTitle, bool bSortNumerically)
public BindUIColumn(string sTitle, int iWidth)
public BindUIColumn(string sTitle, int iWidth, int iDisplayOrder)
public BindUIColumn(string sTitle, int iWidth,
                    int iDisplayOrder, bool bSortColumnNumerically)
```

Binding Columns using AddBoundColumn

In addition to adding columns by annotating a function with the `BindUIColumn` attribute, you can also add a column directly by calling the `AddBoundColumn` method on the Web Sessions listview. Various overloads of the function define the title of the column, its width, its relative display ordering amongst the other columns, its sort behavior, and a flag or function to which the column will be bound.

The call:

```
FiddlerObject.UI.lvSessions.AddBoundColumn("ClientPort", 50, "X-CLIENTPORT");
```

…adds a new column with the title **ClientPort** and a default width of 50 pixels. The contents of the column are bound to the value of each Session's `X-ClientPort` flag, which will be empty if the flag does not exist. The third parameter allows you to specify either a Session Flag name, or the name of a request or response header using the `@request` or `@response` prefixes. For instance:

```
FiddlerObject.UI.lvSessions.AddBoundColumn("Server", 50, "@response.Server");
```

…creates a column with the title **Server**, displaying the contents of the response's `Server` header, if present.

Similarly,

```
FiddlerObject.UI.lvSessions.AddBoundColumn("Reason", 50, "@request.X-Download-
Initiator");
```

…creates a column with the title **Reason**, displaying the request's `X-Download-Initiator` header's value, if present. You can configure IE9+ to emit this header on each request; it provides a terse explanation of why a given request was made. For instance, it will indicate if the request was caused by navigation, an `IMG` tag's download, etc. See `http://fiddler2.com/r/?InitiatorHeader` to download configuration scripts that enable and disable sending of this header.

You may also call `AddBoundColumn` and provide a callback function's name, along with a boolean indicating that the column's values should be interpreted and sorted as numbers. For instance:

```
// Callback function that returns the "Time to first byte" value
```

```
static function getTTLB(oS: Session): String
{
  var iMS = Math.round((oS.Timers.ServerDoneResponse
                      - oS.Timers.FiddlerBeginRequest).TotalMilliseconds);
  if (iMS > 0) return iMS.ToString();
  return 0;
}

FiddlerObject.UI.lvSessions.AddBoundColumn("TTLB", 0, 50, true, getTTLB);
```

The true parameter indicates that the column's values are numeric, while the 0 parameter indicates that this should be inserted as the first column displayed in the Web Sessions list. Note that the display order parameter is *relative*, not absolute, so calling:

```
FiddlerObject.UI.lvSessions.AddBoundColumn("4", 0, 50, func4);
FiddlerObject.UI.lvSessions.AddBoundColumn("3", 0, 40, func3);
FiddlerObject.UI.lvSessions.AddBoundColumn("2", 0, 30, func2);
FiddlerObject.UI.lvSessions.AddBoundColumn("1", 0, 20, func1);
```

…will result in four new columns of increasing width, titled 1, 2, 3, and 4, in that order from left to right.

If you'd like to change a column's width or ordering within the Web Sessions list, you can use the SetColumnOrderAndWidth method. The method takes three parameters: the title of the column to adjust, the new position, and the new width. The latter two parameters may be set to -1 to leave the order or width unchanged.

For instance, to move the Protocol column to the far left of the Web Sessions list without changing its width, call:

```
FiddlerApplication.UI.lvSessions.SetColumnOrderAndWidth("Protocol", 0, -1);
```

Again, keep in mind that column ordering behaves as an insertion operation. So, if you call:

```
FiddlerApplication.UI.lvSessions.SetColumnOrderAndWidth("#",        0, -1);
FiddlerApplication.UI.lvSessions.SetColumnOrderAndWidth("Result",   1, -1);
FiddlerApplication.UI.lvSessions.SetColumnOrderAndWidth("Protocol", 0, -1);
FiddlerApplication.UI.lvSessions.SetColumnOrderAndWidth("Host",     0, -1);
```

The final ordering is [Host, Protocol, #, Result], because the Host column was inserted at index 0, pushing the Result and Protocol columns rightward.

FIDDLEROBJECT FUNCTIONS

The FiddlerScript engine itself provides a number of simple utility functions and properties that you may use to accomplish common tasks. These methods and properties are exposed by the `FiddlerObject` object and include:

FiddlerObject.ReloadScript()

Immediately reload the script file from disk and recompile it, resetting any unbound variables to their default values.

FiddlerObject.StatusText

This property allows you to set the text on Fiddler's status bar. It may safely be set from any thread, as it will internally call `BeginInvoke` on the UI thread if set from a background thread. The default FiddlerScript file sets the status bar text when the script is first compiled:

```
static function Main() {
  var today: Date = new Date();
  FiddlerObject.StatusText = " CustomRules.js was loaded at: " + today;
}
```

The `OnExecAction` handler in the default script uses the `StatusText` property to communicate the results of commands to the user.

FiddlerObject.log(sTextToLog)

Log text to Fiddler's event log. The first character of the provided text may be an exclamation mark, underscore, or forward slash to cause the Log tab to format the text in bold, underlined, or italic text respectively.

The following example:

```
static function OnPeekAtResponseHeaders(oSession: Session) {
  FiddlerObject.log("_Underlined\t#" + oSession.id.ToString());
  FiddlerObject.log("!Bolded\t" + oSession.fullUrl);
  FiddlerObject.log("/Italicized\t" + oSession.oResponse.MIMEType);
}
```

…yields the following output:

FiddlerObject.playSound(sSoundFilename)

Load and play the specified `.wav` audio file. This can be useful if your script needs to draw the user's attention to an exceptional event. Be sure to escape slashes in the path to the file, for instance:
`FiddlerObject.playSound("C:\\Windows\\Media\\ding.wav");`

FiddlerObject.flashWindow()

Flash the Fiddler window's entry in the Windows task bar to help draw the user's attention.

FiddlerObject.alert(sMessage)

Display the provided message in a message box with the title "FiddlerScript."

FiddlerObject.prompt(sMessage)

This method and its overloads:

```
FiddlerObject.prompt(sMessage, sDefaultValue)
FiddlerObject.prompt(sMessage, sDefaultValue, sTitle)
```

…allow you to prompt the user for a string using the prompt message provided in the first parameter. The second and third overloads allow you to optionally specify a default value and the title of the prompt dialog box.

For instance, this line will prompt the user for a HTML tag name:

```
var sTagName: String =
    FiddlerObject.prompt("Enter a HTML tag name", "<br />", "Specify Tag");
```

When the prompt is displayed, Fiddler will flash its window's entry in the Windows task bar to help draw the user's attention. If the user presses Cancel on the prompt, the supplied default value (or `String.Empty`) will be returned.

FiddlerObject.createDictionary()

Create a simple `Dictionary<string, object>` object suitable for passing to the `DoImport` and `DoExport` methods on the `FiddlerApplication` object. This method is necessary because the JScript.NET language does not expose any other way to create a generic `Dictionary<>` object.

The following example generates a HAR file on the desktop containing all of the captured Sessions:

```
var oSessions = FiddlerApplication.UI.GetAllSessions();
```

```
var oExportOptions = FiddlerObject.createDictionary();
oExportOptions.Add("Filename", "C:\\users\\ericlaw\\desktop\\out1.har");
// oExportOptions.Add("MaxTextBodyLength", 0);    // Set if desired
// oExportOptions.Add("MaxBinaryBodyLength", 0);  // Set if desired
FiddlerApplication.DoExport("HTTPArchive v1.2", oSessions, oExportOptions, null);
```

FiddlerObject.WatchPreference(sPrefBranch, oFunc)

Invoke this method, passing a string prefix and callback function, to be notified when any change occurs within the specified branch of Preferences.

```
static function Main() {
   FiddlerObject.WatchPreference("fiddler.script", ObservePrefChange);
}

static function ObservePrefChange(oSender: Object, oPCEA: PrefChangeEventArgs) {
   var sMsg: String = oPCEA.PrefName + " changed to " + oPCEA.ValueString;
   MessageBox.Show(sMsg, "A pref was changed");
}
```

This method exists because, if your FiddlerScript were to call `FiddlerApplication.Prefs.AddWatcher` directly, the entire script engine would be leaked each time the script is recompiled. That leak would occur because the callback event could not be garbage-collected due to the outstanding reference held by the Preferences object.

IMPORT ASSEMBLIES

The .NET Framework offers a huge library of functionality that you can take advantage of in your Fiddler-Script. For instance, you can use the classes in System.Data to log traffic to a database, or use classes in the System.IO namespace to write files to disk.

To reference an assembly that is installed in the system's Global Assembly Cache, simply add the appropriate namespace to the list of #import statements at the top of your script:

```
import System;
import System.Windows.Forms;
import Fiddler;
import System.IO;
```

Then use the classes as needed:

```
static function OnBeforeResponse(oSession: Session)
{
    File.WriteAllBytes("C:\\temp\\Session"+oSession.id.ToString()+".dat",
        oSession.responseBodyBytes);
}
```

You can also use methods in your own assembly DLLs even if those assemblies are not loaded into the global assembly cache. There are two ways to enable FiddlerScript to find the assembly.

The first is to add the Assembly's full path inside **Tools > Fiddler Options > Extensions**:

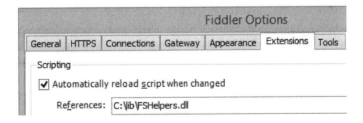

Alternatively, you may use a Preference to specify the default library path used to find assemblies. Set the Preference fiddler.script.LibPath to the fully-qualified path that contains your DLLs. For instance, type the following in the QuickExec box:

```
prefs set fiddler.script.LibPath "C:\src\Library DLLs\"
```

…and when your FiddlerScript is next compiled, Fiddler will look for referenced assemblies in the Library DLLs folder.

EXAMPLE SCRIPTS

While you can use FiddlerScript to build nearly any type of functionality, in most cases you will use script to modify either the request or response. This section contains a few examples to get you started.

Request Scripts

Place these snippets inside the OnBeforeRequest function so that they run before the request is sent to the server.

Add (or Overwrite) a Request Header

Modify request headers easily using the indexer property on the oRequest object:

```
oSession.oRequest["HeaderName"] = "New value";
```

This will add the specified header, or overwrite the first existing header named HeaderName.

To add the Session's ID to the outbound request headers so that they will be captured in the server's logs, use the line:

```
oSession.oRequest["X-Fiddler-SessionID"] = oSession.id.ToString();
```

Remove Request Headers

Remove all headers of a specified name:

```
oSession.oResponse.headers.Remove("Cookie");
```

Flag Requests that Send Cookies

Session flags can be set based on request headers:

```
if (oSession.oRequest.headers.Exists("Cookie"))
{
  oSession["ui-color"]="red";
  oSession["ui-customcolumn"] = oSession.oRequest["Cookie"];
}
```

Rewrite a Request from HTTP to HTTPS

Modify the UriScheme property for requests to change the protocol used:

```
if (!oSession.isHTTPS && !oSession.HTTPMethodIs("CONNECT") &&
    oSession.HostnameIs("myServer"))
{
  oSession.oRequest.headers.UriScheme = "https";
}
```

Swap the Host Header

When Fiddler gets a request whose URL doesn't match its Host header, the original Host value is stored in the Session flag X-Original-Host and the URL's Host is stored in the X-URI-Host flag. Then, by default, the Host value is replaced with the host parsed from the URL. The following script reverses behavior by routing the request to the host specified by the original Host header.

```
if (oSession.BitFlags & SessionFlags.ProtocolViolationInRequest) {
  var sOverride = oSession["X-Original-Host"];
  if (!String.IsNullOrEmpty(sOverride)) {
    oSession["X-overrideHost"] = sOverride;
    oSession["ui-backcolor"] = "yellow";
  }
}
```

Drop a Connection

FiddlerScript can drop the client's connection, like the AutoResponder Actions *drop and *reset.

```
if (oSession.uriContains("DropIt") && (null != oS.oRequest.pipeClient)) {

  // Use this to close the connection using TCP/IP RST
  oS.oRequest.pipeClient.EndWithRST();

  // or use this to close the connection using TCP/IP FIN
  // oS.oRequest.pipeClient.End();

  // So that the UI shows what we did, create a placeholder
  // response for display purposes:
  if (this.state < SessionStates.SendingRequest) {
    oS.utilCreateResponseAndBypassServer();
  }

  oS.oResponse.headers.HTTPResponseCode = 0;
  oS.oResponse.headers.HTTPResponseStatus = "0 Connection dropped by script";
  oS.responseBodyBytes = new byte[0];
  oS.state = SessionStates.Aborted;
  return;
}
```

Prevent Response Streaming

To ensure that the server's response is buffered to permit tampering, you must set the Session object's bBufferResponse field *before* the response is read from the server; do so inside the OnBeforeRequest or PeekAtResponseHeaders handlers:

```
if (oSession.HostnameIs("myServer") && oSession.uriContains(".aspx"))
{
  oSession.bBufferResponse = true;
}
```

Response Scripts

You can modify responses just as easily. If your code only needs to access the response's headers, use the `OnPeekAtResponse` headers function. If you need access to the response body, place your code inside the `OnBeforeResponse` function. There, the script will run after the response body is read from the server but before the response is returned to the client. That is, unless buffering is disabled, in which case the function will run after the response has been streamed to the client, hiding any modifications you make to the body from the client.

Hide Sessions that Returned Images

You can set the `ui-hide` flag to hide traffic from the Web Sessions list:

```
if (oSession.oResponse.MIMEType.Contains("image")) {
  oSession["ui-hide"] = "Script hiding images";
}
```

Flag Redirections

Examine the `responseCode` property to identify redirects:

```
if ((oSession.responseCode > 299) && (oSession.responseCode < 400)) {
  oSession["ui-customcolumn"] = oSession.oResponse["Location"];
  oSession["ui-bold"] = "redirect";
}
```

Replace Text in Script, CSS, and HTML

Change any CSS vendor-prefixes from `-Moz-` and `-WebKit-` to `-MS-`:

```
if (!Utilities.IsBinaryMIME(oSession.oResponse.MIMEType)) {
  oSession.utilDecodeResponse();
  oSession.utilReplaceInResponse("-moz-", "-ms-");
  oSession.utilReplaceInResponse("-webkit-", "-ms-");
}
```

Remove All DIV Elements

Use regular expressions to modify the response body:

```
if (oSession.oResponse.MIMEType.Contains("html")) {
  var oBody = oSession.GetResponseBodyAsString();

  // Replace all content of DIV tags with an empty string.
  // WARNING: Doesn't work well with nested DIVs.
  var oRegEx = /<div[^>]*>(.*?)<\/div>/gi;
  oBody = oBody.replace(oRegEx, "");

  // Set the response body to the div-less string
  oSession.utilSetResponseBody(oBody);
}
```

Other Scripts

Not all scripts must interact with Sessions as they are processed; some add commands and options to the Fiddler UI itself.

Add a Systemwide Hotkey

Fiddler can register hotkeys that are available everywhere in Windows and invoke the code of your choice. Inside your `Main` function, add:

```
UI.RegisterCustomHotkey(HotkeyModifiers.Windows, Keys.G, "screenshot");
```

...to bind the `Windows+G` key combination to the `screenshot` command inside the `OnQuickExec` function:

```
case "screenshot":
    UI.actCaptureScreenshot(false);
    return true;
```

Certificate Info Custom Column

You may want to identify servers whose HTTPS certificates use the SHA-1 hash algorithm or weak RSA keys; Fiddler doesn't have a built-in Custom Column provider that exposes this data. Inside your Handlers class, add the following block:

```
public static BindUIColumn("CertInfo")
function ShowCertHash(oS: Session): String
{
    return oS.oFlags["X-Cert-Info"];
}
```

The CertInfo column will show the `X-Cert-Info` flag, which we must create inside the `OnPeekAtResponseHeaders` function:

```
if (oSession.isHTTPS) {
    try {
      var oC: System.Security.Cryptography.X509Certificates.X509Certificate2 = null;
      if ((null == oSession.oResponse) || (null == oSession.oResponse.pipeServer) ||
          !(oC = oSession.oResponse.pipeServer.ServerCertificate))
              oSession["X-Cert-Info"] = "No Path to cert";
      else
      {
        var sKey = "?";
        try {
          sKey = oC.PublicKey.Key.KeySize.ToString() + "bits";
        }
        catch(e) { // because .NET Throws on non-RSA/DSA keys like ECC
          sKey = oC.GetKeyAlgorithm();
          if (sKey == "1.2.840.10045.2.1") sKey = "ECC";
        }
```

```
          oSession["X-Cert-Info"] = ("Key:" + sKey + " Hash:"
            + oC.SignatureAlgorithm.FriendlyName);
        }
      }
    catch (e) { oSession["X-Cert-Info"] = "JSErr" + e.message;}
  }
```

Similarly, perhaps you wish to show a WebSocket's individual messages as entries inside the Web Sessions list:

```
static function OnWebSocketMessage(oMsg: WebSocketMessage) {
  if (oMsg.PayloadLength < 1) return;

  var oRQH: HTTPRequestHeaders = new HTTPRequestHeaders(
                             "/" + (oMsg.IsOutbound ? "WS-SEND":"WS-RECEIVE")
                         + "#" + oMsg.ID.ToString(), ['Host: WEBSOCKET']);
  var oRPH: HTTPResponseHeaders = new HTTPResponseHeaders(200,
                         ['Content-Type: application/websocket-binary']);

  UI.AddMockSession(oRQH, null, oRPH,
                   oMsg.PayloadAsBytes()).oFlags["ui-indent"]="1";
}
```

Generate Mock Sessions

You may wish to use Fiddler to store and display data that was not captured from the network. For instance, the following function adds a **Paste JSON** command to the Tools menu. When clicked, it copies text from your clipboard into Fiddler as a new well-formed Web Session, ready for display by the JSON Inspector:

```
public static ToolsAction("Paste JSON")
function doJSON()
{
    var oRQH: HTTPRequestHeaders = new HTTPRequestHeaders(
                             "/clipboard.json", ['Host: localhost']);
    var oRPH: HTTPResponseHeaders = new HTTPResponseHeaders(200,
                 ['Content-Type: application/json; charset=UTF-8', 'Custom: 1234']);

    var oS: Fiddler.Session =
        UI.AddMockSession(oRQH, null, oRPH,
          System.Text.Encoding.UTF8.GetBytes(Clipboard.GetText()));

    oS.oFlags["x-Builder-Inspect"] = "true";
    oS.oFlags["x-unlocked"] = "true";
}
```

Show Response Hash

The GetResponseBodyHash function computes the MD5, SHA1, or SHA256 hash of an unchunked and decompressed copy of the response body; this can be used to verify download integrity, for instance.

```
public static ContextAction("Show Hashes")
function doHash(arrSess: Session[])
```

```
{
    for (var i: int=0; i<arrSess.Length; i++)
    {
        FiddlerObject.alert(
            "_MD5_\n"+arrSess[i].GetResponseBodyHash("md5") + "\n\n" +
            "_SHA1_\n"+arrSess[i].GetResponseBodyHash("sha1") + "\n\n" +
            "_SHA256_\n"+arrSess[i].GetResponseBodyHash("sha256") + "\n");
    }
}
```

Similarly, you can use the hash to query common antivirus engines to check whether a given download is considered "infected":

```
public static ContextAction("VirusTotal")
function doVTCheck(arrSess: Session[])
{
    for (var i: int=0; i<arrSess.Length; i++)
    {
        var oS = arrSess[i];
        if (oS.bHasResponse)
        {
            Utilities.LaunchHyperlink(String.Format(
                "https://www.virustotal.com/en/file/{0}/analysis/",
                oS.GetResponseBodyHash("sha256").Replace("-","")));
        }
    }
}
```

Combine Partial Responses

A HTTP/206 is a "partial" response returned for a request made with the Range request header. The CombinePartialResponses method accepts two or more Sessions and attempts to generate a Session with a complete response body based on the partial responses.

```
public static ContextAction("Combine206s")
function doCombine(arrSess: Session[])
{
    var s: Fiddler.Session = Utilities.CombinePartialResponses(arrSess);
    if (s != null) {
        for (var i = 0; i < arrSess.Length; i++)
        {
            arrSess[i]["ui-strikeout"] = "used";
        }
        UI.RefreshRange(arrSess);
        s["ui-backcolor"] = "Aquamarine";
        MessageBox.Show("Done");
    }
}
```

To use this command, select all of the partial responses in the Web Sessions list, and choose **Combine206s** command from the list's context menu.

Remove Many Headers at Once

Before saving a SAZ file, you may wish to "clean up" multiple Sessions by removing data from them; for instance, you may wish to remove Authentication-related headers from a SAZ file you plan to share with someone else. The RemoveRange method provides a quick way to remove many HTTP headers in one call:

```
public static ContextAction("Clean")
function doClean(arrSess: Session[])
{
    for (var i: int=0; i<arrSess.Length; i++)
    {
        // Strip any background color overrides
        arrSess[i].oFlags.Remove("ui-backcolor");

        arrSess[i].utilDecodeResponse();

        var oRH = arrSess[i].oRequest.headers;
        oRH.RemoveRange(["Cookie", "DNT", "User-Agent", "Accept", "UA-CPU",
                         "Accept-Language", "Accept-Encoding", "Pragma",
                         "Connection", "X-Download-Initiator"]);

        oRH = arrSess[i].oResponse.headers;

        oRH.RemoveRange(["x-amz-meta-idata", "X-Amz-Cf-Id", "Vary", "Cloudflare",
                         "X-Powered-By", "X-ASPNET-Version", "x-amz-id-2",
                         "x-amz-request-id", "Last-Modified", "x-amz-version-id",
                         "Accept-Ranges", "ETag", "Pragma", "Connection", "Server",
                         "Cache-Control", "Date", "X-Cache", "Expires",
                         "Age", "Via", "X-Varnish", "Access-Control-Allow-Origin",
                         "X-Content-Type-Options", "X-Frame-Options",
                         "X-XSS-Protection","Keep-Alive", "Set-Cookie"]);
    }
    MessageBox.Show("Done cleanup");
}
```

Override MIME Types

A server may send an invalid MIME type, making it less convenient to use Fiddler's Inspectors to examine the response. You can use the following to manually update the MIME type on a group of Sessions:

```
public static ContextAction("Set MIME...")
function dosetmime(oS: Session[]) {
    var s = FiddlerObject.prompt(
                        "Enter the Content-Type value", "image/jpeg", "Set MIME");
    for (var i: int=0; i<oS.Length; i++)
    {
        oS[i].oResponse["Content-Type"] = s;
    }
}
```

Hide Traffic based on Process Name

The following script creates a **ShowOnly** submenu on the Rules menu that allows you to easily display captured traffic from only a single executable:

```
RulesString("ShowOnly", true)
BindPref("fiddlerscript.rules.ProcessFilter")
RulesStringValue(0,"Chrome", "chrome")
RulesStringValue(1,"FireFox", "firefox")
RulesStringValue(2,"IE", "iexplore")
RulesStringValue(3,"&Custom...", "%CUSTOM%")
public static var sOnlyProc: String = null;
```

Add the following to the OnPeekAtRequestHeaders function:

```
if (!String.IsNullOrEmpty(sOnlyProc)) {
  var s = oSession.LocalProcess;
  if (!s.StartsWith(sOnlyProc, StringComparison.OrdinalIgnoreCase)) {
    oSession["ui-hide"] = "Rules>ShowOnly";
  }
}
```

Add a Color Picker to the Tools Menu

The following script adds a **Tools** > **Utilities** submenu with a ColorPicker command:

```
public static ToolsAction("ColorPicker", "Utilities")
function doColorPicker()
{
    var oCD = new ColorDialog();
    oCD.Color = Utilities.ParseColor("Blue");
    oCD.FullOpen = true;
    if (DialogResult.OK == oCD.ShowDialog())
    {
        FiddlerApplication.Log.LogFormat("Selected color: #{0:x2}{1:x2}{2:x2}",
            oCD.Color.R, oCD.Color.G, oCD.Color.B)
        UI.ActivateView("Log");
    }
    oCD.Dispose();
}
```

More Examples

You can find more FiddlerScript sample code:

- In the SampleRules.js file installed with Fiddler

- At http://fiddler2.com/r/?FiddlerScriptCookbook

Extend Fiddler with .NET Code

Extend Fiddler with .NET

While FiddlerScript provides a simple and lightweight means of enhancing Fiddler, extending Fiddler with .NET assemblies offers significantly more power and an improved debugging experience. That's especially true if you plan to distribute your logic to other users.

Extending Fiddler with .NET enables you to build your extension in any .NET language (C# and VB.NET are the most common choices) and take advantage of the powerful IntelliSense and debugging features of Visual Studio. If your extension limits itself to the classes in the v2.0 Framework, it should work properly on every Fiddler user's system. While both FiddlerScript and .NET extensions may use any of the classes in the .NET Framework, it can be cumbersome to use many Framework classes from FiddlerScript. Compiled .NET extensions typically exhibit significantly faster load-time and run-time performance as compared to building equivalent functionality in FiddlerScript, because the latter must be recompiled each time Fiddler starts.

Extensions can be installed to users' machines without the hassle of manual modifications of the user's FiddlerScript source file, and can be uninstalled using the system's Control Panel. Each extension's assembly declares the minimum version of Fiddler with which it is compatible, and users will be prompted to update if an extension requiring a later Fiddler version is encountered. This versioning feature helps prevent problems where code that works great on your computer fails spectacularly on another user's machine because they're clinging to an outdated version of Fiddler.

Project Requirements and Settings

Writing extensions for Fiddler requires Visual Studio .NET 2005 or later, or the free .NET Framework v2 command-line compilers.

Fiddler2 loads only .NET Common Language Runtime (CLR) v2.0 assemblies; assemblies that target the v1.1 or v4.0 CLR will not be loaded. Fiddler itself requires only that the user have .NET Framework **2.0 SP1** installed. Your extension *may* target the .NET Framework 3.5 (which includes LINQ and other useful features) since that framework also runs on the v2.0 CLR. However, if it takes such a dependency, *your* installer must ensure that the user has the required Framework version installed, or the user will encounter "Class not found" exceptions as your extension loads.

You should also ensure your project targets **AnyCPU** to ensure that Fiddler loads it when running on a 64bit system.

Debugging Extensions

To avoid annoying end-users with warnings that they cannot do anything about, Fiddler silently handles a variety of problems when it loads and calls into extensions. However, these warnings can be extremely useful to extension developers, pointing out problems that prevent extensions from functioning properly.

Extension developers should set the `fiddler.debug.extensions.showerrors` preference to `true` ensure that exceptions and other extension-related errors are not silently caught. Additionally, they should set the `fiddler.debug.extensions.verbose` preference to `true` to spew logging information and warnings to Fiddler's Log tab.

Best Practices for Extensions

On the Internet Explorer team, we found that over 75% of browser crashes and nearly all major performance problems are caused by buggy browser extensions. Fortunately, extension quality in the Fiddler ecosystem is much better, but it's still the case that an extension can cause Fiddler to crash or perform more slowly. I'm relying on you to help ensure that users have a great experience when your extension is running inside Fiddler.

The simplest way to minimize your extension's performance impact is to ensure that it does not run when it's not being used. There are two key strategies for doing that: offer an enable switch, and use a delay-load pattern.

Best Practice: Use an Enable Switch

With very few exceptions, users should not be forced to uninstall your extension to disable it-- most users will only want your extension to run at certain times. Extensions should offer an **Enable** switch; when that switch is off, the extension should do as little work as possible. For instance, inside the ContentBlock extension, each method that handles a Session first checks to see whether blocking is enabled:

```
public void AutoTamperRequestBefore(Session oSession)
{
  // Return immediately if no rule is enabled
  if (!bBlockerEnabled) return;
  // ...
```

This best practice is followed by Fiddler itself—the AutoResponder and Filters tabs have enabling checkboxes at their top and only process Sessions when enabled.

Best Practice: Use Delay Load

Extensions and Inspectors are loaded as Fiddler starts up, so your code can directly impact the time that Fiddler takes to load. Because some users will restart Fiddler dozens of times per day, load time is a very important factor in their experience with the tool.

In many cases, a user may not use your Inspector or Extension at all within a given debugging session. For instance, perhaps the user installed your Silverlight-troubleshooter Inspector for one project, but then gets pulled away to go help with a HR system that uses only JavaScript and no Silverlight at all. If your Inspector uses a lot of memory and takes a long time to load, the user will be paying a penalty for having it installed even when it's not used. To avoid that problem, use the Delay Load pattern, in which expensive operations are only undertaken if needed. This pattern can be effectively applied to both Inspectors and other types of extensions.

For instance, the **FiddlerScript** tab uses a syntax-highlighting component to display the source of your script file; this component requires hundreds of millions of cycles and several megabytes of memory to load. If this component loads every time Fiddler starts, these cycles and memory would be wasted if the user doesn't interact with the tab. To mitigate this problem, the FiddlerScript tab only creates the syntax-highlighting component when the user first activates the extension's tab.

The OnLoad handler for the extension creates its tab, adds a "Loading…" label to it, and adds a handler to the SelectedIndexChanged event to detect when its tab is being activated.

```
public void OnLoad()
{
  myPage = new TabPage("FiddlerScript");
  myPage.ImageIndex = (int)Fiddler.SessionIcons.Script;
  this.lblLoading = new System.Windows.Forms.Label();
  this.lblLoading.Text = "Loading...";
  myPage.Controls.Add(lblLoading);
  FiddlerApplication.UI.tabsViews.TabPages.Add(myPage);

  TabControlEventHandler evtTCEH = null;
  evtTCEH = delegate(object s, TabControlEventArgs e) {
    if (e.TabPage == myTabPage)
    {
      // Create heavyweight components used to display UI
      EnsureReady();

      // Remove the unneeded event handler.
      FiddlerApplication.UI.tabsViews.Selected -= evtTCEH;
    }
  };

  // Subscribe to tab-change events
  FiddlerApplication.UI.tabsViews.Selected += evtTCEH;
}
```

Only when the extension's tab is activated does the EnsureReady method run to create the heavyweight component, hiding the "Loading…" label:

```
private void EnsureReady()
{
  if (null != oEditor) return;     // Exit if we've already been made ready

  lblLoading.Refresh();            // Force repaint of "Loading..." label

  // Create the extension's UI (slow)
  oEditor = new RulesEditor(myPage);
  lblLoading.Visible = false;      // Remove the "Loading..." label
}
```

This pattern is also used by the SyntaxView, HexView, and WebView Inspectors, all of which depend upon components that are expensive to construct. Other extensions do not bother with the Delay Load pattern if they use only a few lightweight controls and the complexity of the Delay Load pattern isn't necessary.

Best Practice: Beware "Big Data"
The user's web traffic may include giant responses (e.g. videos or other files that are hundreds of megabytes in size) that you might not have anticipated when building your extension. Requests *can* be quite large as well, but in practice, enormous downloads are much more common than large uploads.

If your extension doesn't defend itself from "big data," your code could hang Fiddler when the user selects such a Session. There are several best practices to help prevent hangs:

- Ensure that your extension "fails fast" if it encounters a response of a type or size that it wasn't designed to handle.

- Avoid making unnecessary copies of data. In most places, Fiddler uses a "copy on write" architecture to prevent unneeded duplication of data, and your extensions should do the same.

- If your extension attempts to render data by replacing embedded `nulls` using the Unicode replacement character (`0xFFFD`, rendered as �), ensure that you limit how much data you attempt to show. Otherwise, rendering a binary file could result in massive memory use because the embedded `nulls` will not terminate the text passed to a textbox or other UI control.

Fiddler's default extensions all follow these best practices to help ensure that the debugger remains responsive even when dealing with huge responses.

Best Practice: Use the Reporter Pattern for Extensions
A common goal when building an extension is to display summary data about the Sessions currently selected in the Web Sessions list. For instance, the Statistics tab shows the timing data and size of the selected Sessions, while the Timeline tab shows the start time and duration of each selected Session. Extensions of this sort are called **Reporters** because they generate a report on the selected Sessions.

A naïve implementation of a Reporter would recalculate its data each time a Session is selected or unselected. The problem with that approach is that if the user hits CTRL+A to select all of the Sessions in the list (or CTRL+X to clear it) the Reporter will end up doing billions of redundant calculations whose results are never displayed to the user.

To avoid that problem, instead handle the `FiddlerApplication.CalculateReport` event. This event is dispatched as the user selects and unselects Sessions, but it is suppressed during certain bulk operations (like loading a SAZ file or clearing the Web Sessions list), ensuring that it is dispatched only after the bulk update is completed. The event is also suppressed when Fiddler shuts down, helping to ensure that you don't perform expensive work as Fiddler is unloading and disposing of its objects.

Your event handler implementation must have the following signature:

```
public delegate void CalculateReportHandler(Session[] _arrSessions);
```

Your event handler will be called at the appropriate intervals, and an array of the currently selected Sessions will be passed as the only parameter. You should still avoid doing any redundant work—for instance, if your tab isn't presently active, you should suppress calculations until it is activated.

The Statistics tab's CalculateReport handler looks a bit like this:

```
void UpdateStatsTab(Session[] _arrSessions)
{
    // If we're not showing the Stats tab right now, bail out.
    if (FiddlerApplication.UI.tabsViews.SelectedTab !=
        FiddlerApplication.UI.pageStatistics)
    {
        return;
    }

    try
    {
        if (_arrSessions.Length < 1)
        {
            ClearStatsTab();
            return;
        }

        Dictionary<string, long> dictResponseSizeByContentType;
        long cBytesRecv;
        string sStats = BasicAnalysis.ComputeBasicStatistics(
        _arrSessions, true, out dictResponseSizeByContentType, out cBytesRecv);

        txtReport.Text = String.Format("{0}\r\n, sStats);
    }
    catch (Exception eX)
    {
        Debug.Assert(false, eX.Message);
    }
}
```

By using the CalculateReport event, your extension can avoid performing unnecessary work, helping to keep Fiddler running fast.

INTERACT WITH FIDDLER'S OBJECTS

Most FiddlerScripts and extensions use Fiddler's object model to interact with the user-interface, Session objects, the FiddlerScript engine, and features like the TextWizard. This section outlines the properties, flags, fields, and events that your code may rely upon.

The Web Sessions List

Because the Web Sessions list is the most important component of the Fiddler user-interface, your code will often need to interact with the list's entries. Fiddler exposes methods on the `FiddlerApplication.UI` object to interact with the Web Sessions list.

Session[] GetAllSessions()

Returns an array containing all of the Sessions in the Web Sessions list. If the Web Sessions list is empty, the array's `Length` will be 0.

Session GetFirstSelectedSession()

Returns the first selected Session in the Web Sessions list, or `null` if no entries are selected.

Session[] GetSelectedSessions()

Returns an array containing all of the Sessions that are currently selected in the Web Sessions list. If no entries are selected, the array's `Length` will be 0.

Session[] GetSelectedSessions(int iMax)

Returns an array containing all of the Sessions that are currently selected in the Web Sessions list, up to the maximum number specified. If no entries are selected, the array's `Length` will be 0.

void actSelectAll()

Select all Sessions in the Web Sessions list.

void actSelectSessionsMatchingCriteria(doesSessionMatchCriteriaDelegate oDel)

This powerful method allows you to supply a delegate function (similar to a predicate delegate) that is evaluated for each Session in the Web Sessions list. For each entry, if your delegate returns `true`, the Session's entry will be selected. If it returns `false`, the Session's entry will be unselected.

For instance, say that you want to select all Sessions that use the POST request method. You can use the following code:

```
FiddlerApplication.UI.actSelectSessionsMatchingCriteria(
  delegate(Session oS)
  {
    return oS.HTTPMethodIs("POST");
  });
```

Or, if you want to select all Sessions that have a `HTTP/200` response status, use this:

```
FiddlerApplication.UI.actSelectSessionsMatchingCriteria(
  delegate(Session oS)
  {
    return (200 == oS.responseCode);
  });
```

Keep in mind that your delegate will run on incomplete Sessions as well, so ensure that you test values for `null` as appropriate.

void actRemoveSelectedSessions()
Remove all selected Sessions from the Web Sessions list.

void actRemoveUnselectedSessions()
Remove all unselected Sessions from the Web Sessions list.

bool actLoadSessionArchive(string sFilename)
Load the specified SAZ file and adds its Sessions to the Web Sessions list.

void actSaveSessionsToZip()
Save the selected Sessions to a SAZ file whose filename is provided by the user in a Save File prompt. The "Zip" part of this method's name reflects the fact that a SAZ file is merely a structured Zip archive.

void actSaveSessionsToZip(string sFilename, string sPwd)
Save the selected Sessions to a SAZ file named by the provided filename. If the password parameter is non-`null`, the SAZ file will be encrypted using the specified password.

void actSessionCopyURL()
Copy the URLs of the selected Sessions to the clipboard, one per line.

void actSessionCopySummary()
Copy to the clipboard all of the text from the Web Sessions list for each of the selected Sessions. The data is copied in both tab-delimited text and HTML formats, suitable for pasting into either documents or spreadsheets.

void actSessionCopyHeadlines()
Copy a terse listing of the selected Sessions to the clipboard. For instance, when loading my homepage, the data copied is:

```
GET http://www.ericlawrence.com/
302 Object moved to /eric/

GET http://www.ericlawrence.com/eric/
200 OK (text/html)
```

```
GET http://www.ericlawrence.com/Eric/Eric.css
200 OK (text/css)

GET http://www.fiddler2.com/Eric/images/rss.gif
200 OK (image/gif)
```

int FiddlerApplication.UI.lvSessions.SelectedCount

Return the count of selected Sessions without returning those items. This provides a quick way to get a count of selected Sessions without copying those Sessions into an array as the `GetSelectedSessions` method does. This property appears directly on the Web Sessions list object.

SimpleEventHandler FiddlerApplication.UI.lvSessions.OnSessionsAdded

This event fires whenever one or more Sessions is visibly added to Web Sessions list. By default, Fiddler queues updates to the list for a short period of time to help ensure UI responsiveness.

If you choose to provide a handler for this event, ensure that the handler does not perform any expensive computations, as doing so will block the UI thread and severely impair performance.

Session Objects

Each Web Session is represented by a `Session` object which exposes fields, properties, and methods that control how the Session is processed and record information about it.

oRequest

The `oRequest` object represents the client's request. It exposes key properties including the `headers` object containing the Request's headers. The headers themselves may be accessed by the indexers on the `oRequest` or `Session` objects:

```
oSession.oRequest["HeaderName"] == oSession.oRequest.headers["HeaderName"]
    == oSession["REQUEST", "HeaderName"];
```

The `oRequest` object's `pipeClient` field represents Fiddler's connection to the client; it is cleared after processing of the Session completes. The `BufferRequest` property can be set to `false` during the `OnPeekAtRequestHeaders` event handler to direct Fiddler to stream the request to the server.

RequestHeaders

The Session's `RequestHeaders` convenience property provides direct access to the headers of the request. Rather than returning `null` if the headers do not exist, this property returns an empty `HTTPRequestHeaders` object.

requestBodyBytes

This byte array contains the raw bytes of the client's request. Because the body may be encoded, typically the `GetRequestBodyAsString` and `utilSetRequestBody` methods are used instead of manipulating the byte array directly.

oResponse

The oResponse object represents the server's response. It exposes key properties including the headers object containing the Response's headers. The headers themselves may be accessed by the indexers on the oResponse or Session objects:

```
oSession.oResponse["HeaderName"] == oSession.oResponse.headers["HeaderName"]
    == oSession["RESPONSE", "HeaderName"];
```

The oResponse object's MIMEType property returns the MIME-type portion of the response's Content-Type header. The object's pipeServer field represents Fiddler's connection to the server; it is cleared after processing of the Session completes.

RequestHeaders

The Session's ResponseHeaders convenience property provides direct access to the headers of the response. Rather than returning null if the headers do not exist, this property returns an empty HTTPResponseHeaders object.

responseBodyBytes

This byte array contains the raw bytes of the server's response. Because the body may be encoded, typically the GetResponseBodyAsString and utilSetResponseBody methods are used instead of manipulating the byte array directly.

oFlags

This StringDictionary contains flags that describe the Session. A full list of Session flags can be found in Appendix C. You may access this collection directly, or via one of the two indexer properties exposed by the Session object.

```
oSession.oFlags["FlagName"] == oSession["FlagName"] == oSession["SESSION",
"FlagName"];
```

Note: If the requested Flag does not exist, the two-parameter indexer returns String.Empty while the other versions return null:

```
if (!oSession.oFlags.ContainsKey("SomeKey")
{
  Debug.Assert(oSession["SomeKey"] == null);
  Debug.Assert(oSession.oFlags["SomeKey"] == null);
  Debug.Assert(oSession["Session", "SomeKey"] == String.Empty);
}
```

void Abort()

Abort processing of the Session, closing both client and server connections (if any). The Session's state changes to Aborted.

void Ignore()

Ignore the Session, hiding it and suppressing parsing, decryption, and the firing of Session-processing event handlers. The Response will be streamed and neither the request nor the response will be stored.

bBufferResponse

This boolean field controls whether the response will be streamed to the client as it is read from the server.

bHasResponse

This readonly property returns `true` if the Session's `state > ReadingResponse` and `oResponse` is not `null`.

bypassGateway

This boolean field controls whether the request will be sent to the upstream gateway proxy server, if any such server is configured.

clientIP

This string records the IP address from which the request originated.

clientPort

This integer records the port from which the request originated.

bool COMETPeek()

Call this method while in the `ReadingResponse` state to update the `responseBodyBytes` array with the partially-read response.

fullUrl

This property stores the complete request URI, including protocol/scheme, in the form `http://www.host.com/filepath?query`. To retarget this request to a different URL, adjust this property before the request is sent.

PathAndQuery

This property contains the path and query string from the request URL.

port

This property contains the port to which the request is targeted.

host

This property stores the host specified in the request headers; this value may include a port number.

hostname

This property stores the hostname specified in the request headers; this value will never include a port number.

bool HostnameIs(string)

This method compares the supplied hostname to the hostname of the request, returning `true` if a case-insensitive match is found.

bool HTTPMethodIs(string)

This method compares the supplied HTTP Method name to the HTTP Method of the request, returning true if a case-insensitive match is found.

bool uriContains(string)

This method searches the request URI for the supplied string, and returns true if a case-sensitive match is found.

id

This readonly integer property returns the Session's automatically-generated identification number.

isFTP

This readonly property returns true if the Session targets the FTP protocol.

isHTTPS

This readonly property returns true if the Session targets the HTTPS protocol.

isTunnel

This readonly property returns true if the Session is a CONNECT tunnel used for HTTPS or WebSocket traffic.

LocalProcessID

This readonly integer property returns the process ID of the local process which sent the request. If the request was generated from a remote client, the property returns 0.

string LocalProcess

This readonly string property returns the process name and ID of the local process which sent the request. If the request was generated from a remote client or the process cannot be determined, the property returns String.Empty.

bool utilDecodeRequest()

Call this method to remove any HTTP compression or Chunked Encoding from the request body.

bool utilDecodeResponse()

Call this method to remove any HTTP compression or Chunked Encoding from the response body.

bool RefreshUI()

Call this method to update the information displayed in this Session's entry in the Web Sessions list.

RequestMethod

This string property contains the Request Method (e.g. POST) from the client's request.

responseCode

This integer property contains the HTTP status code from the server's response.

state

Each Session's `state` property tracks its progress through the following `SessionStates`:

SessionState	Description
`Created`	The `Session` has been created but nothing's happening yet.
`ReadingRequest`	Fiddler is reading the request from the client.
`AutoTamperRequestBefore`	Fiddler extensions that provide an `AutoTamperRequestBefore` method are processing the request.
`HandTamperRequest`	The user may manually edit the request using the Fiddler Inspectors.
`AutoTamperRequestAfter`	Fiddler extensions that provide an `AutoTamperRequestAfter` method are processing the request.
`SendingRequest`	Fiddler is sending the request to the server.
`ReadingResponse`	Fiddler is reading the response from the server.
`AutoTamperResponseBefore`	Fiddler extensions that provide an `AutoTamperResponseBefore` method are processing the response.
`HandTamperResponse`	The user may manually edit the response using the Fiddler Inspectors.
`AutoTamperResponseAfter`	Fiddler extensions that provide an `AutoTamperResponseAfter` method are processing the response.
`SendingResponse`	Fiddler is sending the response to the client.
`Done`	The Session is complete.
`Aborted`	The Session was aborted (the client disconnected before reading the response, there was a fatal error in processing, etc.)

The Session moves from one state to the next until it reaches the `Done` state; in the event of an error, the Session jumps immediately to the `Aborted` state. The Session object's `OnStateChanged` event fires any time the Session's `state` property changes.

BitFlags

Each Session's `BitFlags` property holds zero or more `SessionFlags` that supply commonly-queried state information. The `SessionFlags` enumeration includes:

SessionFlags	Description
`None`	No flags are set.
`IsHTTPS`	The request's URI has a HTTPS target.
`IsFTP`	The request's URI has a FTP target.
`Ignored`	The Session should be ignored: hide from the Web Sessions list, do not store the request or response, and do not invoke event handlers.
`ClientPipeReused`	The request was read from a previously used connection from the client.
`ServerPipeReused`	The request reused an existing connection to the server.
`RequestStreamed`	The request was transmitted to the server as soon as the headers were complete; any request body was streamed to the server as it was read from the client.

ResponseStreamed	The response was not buffered and was instead streamed to the client as it was read from the server.
RequestGeneratedByFiddler	The request was generated by Fiddler itself (e.g. from the Composer tab).
ResponseGeneratedByFiddler	The response was generated by Fiddler itself (e.g. AutoResponder or the utilCreateResponseAndBypassServer method).
LoadedFromSAZ	This previously-captured Session was reloaded from a SAZ file.
ImportedFromOtherTool	The Session was imported by a Transcoder.
SentToGateway	The request was sent to an upstream (CERN) gateway proxy.
IsBlindTunnel	This CONNECT tunnel "blindly" shuttles bytes across without decryption.
IsDecryptingTunnel	This CONNECT tunnel decrypts HTTPS traffic as it flows through.
ServedFromCache	The response was served from a client cache, bypassing Fiddler. Fiddler only "sees" this Session if other software reports it to Fiddler, because Fiddler only observes network traffic.
ProtocolViolationInRequest	There was a HTTP Protocol violation in the client's request.
ProtocolViolationInResponse	There was a HTTP Protocol violation in the server's response.
ResponseBodyDropped	The response body was not stored, e.g. because the Preference fiddler.network.streaming.ForgetStreamedData is set.
IsWebSocketTunnel	This CONNECT tunnel is used for WebSocket traffic.
SentToSOCKSGateway	The request was proxied using the SOCKS protocol.
RequestBodyDropped	The request body was not stored, e.g. because the Session's Log-Drop-Request-Body flag was set.
IsRPCTunnel	The request created an RPC-over-HTTPS tunnel.

The Session object exposes two methods to evaluate the Session's BitFlags. The isAnyFlagSet method accepts a set of flags and returns true if *any* of the specified flags are set, and false otherwise. The isFlagSet method accepts one or more flags and returns true if *all* of the specified flags are set, and false otherwise.

For example:

```
bool bHadAnyHTTPErrors =
    oSession.isAnyFlagSet(SessionFlags.ProtocolViolationInRequest
                    | SessionFlags.ProtocolViolationInResponse);

bool bReusedBothConnections =
    oSession.isFlagSet(SessionFlags.ClientPipeReused
                    | SessionFlags.ServerPipeReused);
```

Timers

Fiddler records timestamps as the Session is processed using the Session's `Timers` object. These timestamps can help shed light on performance issues in your website or application, and can be seen in the Session's Properties window or the Statistics tab.

SessionTimers	Description
`ClientConnected`	Timestamp at which the client's connection to Fiddler was first established.
`ClientBeginRequest`	Timestamp at which the request's first socket `Send()` operation was serviced by Fiddler. If this request was issued on a reused connection, this timestamp could be much later than the `ClientConnected` value.
`FiddlerGotRequestHeaders`	Timestamp at which Fiddler completed reading the headers from the client.
`ClientDoneRequest`	Timestamp at which Fiddler completed reading the entire request from the client.
`GatewayDeterminationTime`	The number of milliseconds spent determining which gateway proxy should be used to handle this request. In many cases this value will be 0, but it may be hundreds or thousands of milliseconds if a WPAD Proxy Configuration script is being used to determine the upstream proxy.
`DNSTime`	The number of milliseconds spent determining the IP address of the remote host. Due to caching of DNS records, this value is often 0 for all but the first connections to a host.
`TCPConnectTime`	The number of milliseconds spent waiting for TCP/IP connection establishment to the server.
`HTTPSHandshakeTime`	The number of milliseconds elapsed while performing the HTTPS handshake with the server. This value will be 0 if Fiddler is not configured to decrypt HTTPS traffic. If decryption is enabled, when a `CONNECT` tunnel is being used for HTTPS traffic, Fiddler will populate this value.
`ServerConnected`	Timestamp at which the TCP/IP connection to the server or upstream gateway proxy was established. If this request is being sent on a reused server connection, this timestamp could be earlier than the `ClientConnected` value.
`FiddlerBeginRequest`	Timestamp at which Fiddler began sending the request to the server. If this request is being sent on a reused server connection, this timestamp could be much later than the `ServerConnected` value.
`ServerGotRequest`	Timestamp at which Fiddler completed sending the request to the server.
`ServerBeginResponse`	Timestamp at which Fiddler read the first packet of the server's response.
`FiddlerGotResponseHeaders`	Timestamp at which Fiddler completed reading the headers from the server.
`ServerDoneResponse`	Timestamp at which Fiddler completed reading the entire response from the server.
`ClientBeginResponse`	Timestamp at which Fiddler began sending the response to the client. If buffering is disabled for the current Session, this timestamp will be earlier than the `ServerDoneResponse` timestamp.

ClientDoneResponse	Timestamp at which Fiddler completed sending the response to the client.

The `ToString()` method of the `Timers` returns all of the timer values in a comma-delimited string; pass `true` as an optional parameter to return the values as a multi-line string instead.

Note: Fiddler captures timestamps using the default system clock, which typically has a precision of 15.6 milliseconds. If a given operation takes less than 15.6ms to complete, it may appear that the operation took no time at all. Windows defaults to this (relatively) granular timer resolution for power-efficiency reasons; higher resolution timers result in greater power consumption and shorter battery life on mobile devices like notebooks and tablets.

In most cases, measurements for which finer precision is required should be accomplished via lower-level monitoring (e.g. Event Tracing for Windows, Network Monitor, etc). Having said that, Fiddler can set the system clock to a high-resolution mode with 1ms-level precision. To do so, use the **Enable high-resolution timers** checkbox on the **Tools** > **Fiddler Options** > **General** tab.

HostList Objects

Oftentimes, extensions and Fiddler features are designed to operate only against a user-supplied set of sites, either to scope their functionality or to improve performance.

A **HostList** object holds a set of such rules. The object's `ContainsHost()` method offers a high-performance way to test whether a target matches any of the rules in the list.

List entries support leading wildcards (e.g. `*.example.com`), and the special tokens `<local>`, `<nonlocal>`, and `<loopback>`. The `<local>` token matches if the queried hostname contains no dots. The `<nonlocal>` token matches if the queried hostname contains one or more dots. The `<loopback>` token matches the hostnames `localhost`, `127.0.0.1`, `localhost.`, and `::1`.

The Content Blocker extension uses a HostList object. On load, it initializes the value of the `HostList` from a preference:

```
hlBlockedHosts = new HostList();
string sList = FiddlerApplication.Prefs.GetStringPref(
                        "ext.ContentBlocker.BlockHosts", null);
if (!String.IsNullOrEmpty(sList))
{
    hlBlockedHosts.AssignFromString(sList);
}
```

Then, as each Session is processed, code in the extension's `AutoTamperRequestBefore` handler checks whether the host is on the list of targets to be blocked:

```
if (hlBlockedHosts.ContainsHost(oSession.host))
{
  // Set the ReplyWithFile Session flag so that Fiddler will return
  // the specified 1x1 GIF response rather than hitting the server
  oSession["x-replywithfile"] = "1pxtrans.dat";
}
```

HostList objects are not threadsafe; instead of updating an object, you should construct a new one, as the ContentBlocker does when adding a host to the list:

```
public bool BlockAHost(string sHost)
{
  sHost = sHost.ToLower();
  if (!hlBlockedHosts.ContainsHost(sHost))
  {
    string sNewList = String.Format("{0}; {1}", hlBlockedHosts, sHost);
    hlBlockedHosts = new HostList(sNewList);
  }
  return true;
}
```

When the extension unloads, it serializes the user's block list back to the preference:

```
FiddlerApplication.Prefs.SetStringPref(
                        "ext.ContentBlocker.BlockHosts",
                        hlBlockedHosts.ToString());
```

Sending Strings to the TextWizard

In many cases, your extension will display text that has been encoded using one of several high-level encodings. If the encoding is expected and recognized, an extension might automatically encode and decode it—for instance, the WebForms Inspector decodes form fields. In other cases, however, the encoding may not be known in advance. In such cases, it can be helpful to provide a **Send to TextWizard** command to send text to Fiddler's TextWizard window without requiring the user to copy/paste text manually. Most of the Inspectors included with Fiddler offer such a command.

To launch the TextWizard from your Extension, simply call the following API:

```
FiddlerApplication.UI.actShowTextWizard(string sDefaultInput)
```

…passing the selected text in the sDefaultInput parameter. An instance of the TextWizard will open, enabling the user to easily encode or decode the text.

Logging

Fiddler's Log tab collects logged message strings that are generated by extensions, FiddlerScript, or Fiddler itself. Fiddler logs messages including application events (e.g. when a SAZ file is saved or loaded) as well as system events (e.g. when the system's network connectivity is lost or restored). An extension can log text to the Log tab using either of the following two methods:

```
FiddlerApplication.Log.LogString(string sMsg)
FiddlerApplication.Log.LogFormat(string sFormat, params object[] args)
```

These methods may be safely called from any thread and can be called before Fiddler itself has loaded; the Log object will queue any messages and publish them when a Log listener is first attached.

If you are writing an extension or a FiddlerCore-based application and wish to receive notice of logged messages, add a handler to the `FiddlerApplication.Log.OnLogString` event. Your handler will be passed the logged string as the `LogString` property of a `LogEventArgs` object.

```
public event EventHandler<LogEventArgs> OnLogString;

public class LogEventArgs:EventArgs
{
  internal LogEventArgs(string sMsg);
  public string LogString { get; }
}
```

Keep in mind that this event will often fire from background threads, so your handler must `Invoke` or `BeginInvoke` onto the UI thread if any visual updates are required.

Fiddler's Log tab uses a very simple formatting mechanism when interpreting the strings it receives in its `OnLogString` handler:

- Strings prefixed with an underscore (_) render in an <u>underlined</u> font.

- Strings prefixed with an exclamation mark (!)render in a **bold** font.

- Strings prefixed with a forward slash (/) render in an *italic* font.

Your extension can use this simple feature to draw attention to messages based on their importance. The Log tab also supports simple macro commands:

- Logging the string @Log.Clear clears the Log tab's contents.

- Logging the string @Log.Save generates a new Session in the Web Sessions list. Its response body contains the Log tab's text.

- Logging the string @Log.Export filename saves the Log tab's text to the specified filename. Use a filename ending in .rtf to save in Rich Text Format, preserving font size and weight.

Interacting with the FiddlerScript Engine

Extensions may subscribe to events related to the compilation of FiddlerScript. The Fiddler ScriptEditor extension uses these events, for example, to capture and display script compilation errors.

The `FiddlerApplication.scriptRules` object exposes three events, two of which will fire as a script file is loaded and either compiles successfully or encounters an error:

```
public event RulesBeforeCompileHandler BeforeRulesCompile;
public event RulesAfterCompileHandler AfterRulesCompile;
public event RulesCompileFailedHandler RulesCompileFailed;
```

Because the script engine was developed before I knew how to use EventArgs properly, each event has its own custom delegate:

```
public delegate void RulesBeforeCompileHandler(string sFilename);
public delegate void RulesAfterCompileHandler();
public delegate void RulesCompileFailedHandler(string sDescription, int iLine,
                                               int iStartColumn, int iEndColumn);
```

The `BeforeRulesCompile` event fires when Fiddler is instructed to load a new script file. The event handler delegate contains one parameter, the name of the script file that is to be loaded and compiled.

The `AfterRulesCompile` event fires after Fiddler successfully compiles a script file, runs its `Main` function, and updates the Fiddler UI based on the contents of the script. The event handler delegate has no parameters.

The `RulesCompileFailed` event fires if Fiddler encounters an error when compiling the script file. The event handler delegate has four parameters: the human-readable description of the problem, the line number of the error within the script file, and the starting and ending column on that line. If you plan to handle this event, please be aware that `RulesCompileFailed` usually fires very shortly after the `BeforeRulesCompile` event. If your extension loads the new script's text in its handler for the first event, ensure that you have successfully updated your copy of the script text before attempting to mark the erroneous script content for display to the user.

Fiddler includes a lightweight Preferences system used to store users' settings and configuration choices. Accessible to FiddlerScript and extensions, the system is designed to be somewhat similar to the system used by Firefox (e.g. type about:config in Firefox to view its preferences).

Fiddler's preferences are automatically serialized to and deserialized from the registry, but you should access them only through the Preferences API.

Preference Naming

Keep the following in mind as you name your preferences:

- Preference names are case-insensitive.
- Preference names must only contain letters A-to-Z, numbers, dots, and dashes.
- Preference names must be between 1 and 255 characters in length.
- Preference names containing ephemeral are neither saved to nor loaded from the registry.
- Preference names containing internal cannot be created nor updated by extensions or script.

You should name your preferences using a logical hierarchy of the format:

```
myCompany.myExtension.Feature.SettingName
```

Careful naming makes it simpler to find your preferences and improves performance if your extension or script wants to monitor preferences for changes (more on that in a moment).

The IFiddlerPreferences Interface

Fiddler's preferences are accessed using FiddlerApplication.Prefs, an object which implements the IFiddlerPreferences interface.

```
public interface IFiddlerPreferences
{
    // Indexer
    string this[string sName] { get; set; }

    // Setters
    void SetBoolPref(string sPrefName, bool bValue);
    void SetInt32Pref(string sPrefName, Int32 iValue);
    void SetStringPref(string sPrefName, string sValue);
    void RemovePref(string sPrefName);

    // Getters
    bool GetBoolPref(string sPrefName, bool bDefault);
    string GetStringPref(string sPrefName, string sDefault);
    Int32 GetInt32Pref(string sPrefName, Int32 iDefault);
```

```
    // Methods to enable change notifications
    PreferenceBag.PrefWatcher AddWatcher(string sPrefixFilter,
                            EventHandler<PrefChangeEventArgs> pcehHandler);
    void RemoveWatcher(PreferenceBag.PrefWatcher wliToRemove);
}
```

Store and Remove Preferences

You can store preferences using the `SetStringPref`, `SetBoolPref`, and `SetInt32Pref` methods. Each accepts the name of the preference and the value to store:

```
FiddlerApplication.Prefs.SetStringPref("example.str", "Remember me!");
FiddlerApplication.Prefs.SetBoolPref("example.bool", true);
FiddlerApplication.Prefs.SetInt32Pref("example.int", 5);
```

Alternatively, you can use the default indexer to store a string directly:

```
FiddlerApplication.Prefs["example.str"] = "value";
```

Internally, all preference values are stored as strings; the bool and int methods simply cast and parse the string's value.

Call `RemovePref` or store a value of `null` to remove a preference:

```
// These three lines are equivalent
FiddlerApplication.Prefs.RemovePref("NameToRemove");
FiddlerApplication.Prefs.SetStringPref("NameToRemove", null);
FiddlerApplication.Prefs["NameToRemove"] = null;
```

Retrieve Preferences

You can retrieve preferences using the `GetStringPref`, `GetBoolPref`, and `GetIntPref` methods. Each accepts the name of the preference and a default value to return if the requested preference does not exist.

```
string sStr = FiddlerApplication.Prefs.GetStringPref("example.str", "demo");
bool bBool = FiddlerApplication.Prefs.GetBoolPref("example.bool", false);
int iNum = FiddlerApplication.Prefs.GetInt32Pref("example.int", 0);
```

Alternatively, you can use the default indexer to retrieve a string preference directly:

```
string sStr = FiddlerApplication.Prefs["example.str"];
```

If the requested preference does not exist, the indexer will return `null`.

FiddlerScript can bind a field variable to a preference; the value of the preference will be loaded when the script is compiled and the value will be stored when the FiddlerScript unloads. See the `BindPref` attribute (page 212) for more information.

Watch for Preference Changes

In many cases, it's desirable for extensions or FiddlerScript to be notified when a preference of a specified name is created, updated, or removed. To avoid the overhead of constantly polling preference values, you can instead "watch a branch" of preferences whose name contains a specified prefix. For instance, watching the `fiddler.ui.toolbar` branch will raise an event whenever any preference whose name starts with that prefix is created, removed, or has its value modified. By thoughtfully naming your preferences, you can help ensure that your code is only notified of relevant changes.

Notifications in Extensions

Extensions may subscribe to receive notifications when preferences under a given prefix change by attaching a `PrefWatcher`.

```
oWatcher = FiddlerApplication.Prefs.AddWatcher(
    string sPrefixToMatch, EventHandler<PrefChangeEventArgs> fnToNotify);
```

The event handler you supply in `fnToNotify` will be invoked for every preference change under the specified prefix. The EventArgs' `PrefName` property contains the name of the preference which has changed. The `ValueString` property contains the preference's new value, or `null` if the preference was removed. The `ValueBool` convenience property interprets the new value as a boolean.

To permit garbage-collection of objects, be sure to remove your `PrefWatcher` when it is no longer needed:

```
FiddlerApplication.Prefs.RemoveWatcher(oWatcher);
```

Notifications in FiddlerScript

To ensure that `PrefWatcher` references do not prevent garbage-collection of obsolete script engines, FiddlerScript code should call the `WatchPreference` function instead of using `AddWatcher`

```
// This callback function is called on Pref changes
// under the branch we specified.
static function FnChange(o: Object, pceA: PrefChangeEventArgs) {
  if (null != pceA) {
      MessageBox.Show(pceA.PrefName + " changed to: " + pceA.ValueString);
  }
  else {
      MessageBox.Show("Unexpected.");
  }
}

static function Main() {
  // Attach a callback to the preference change
  FiddlerObject.WatchPreference("fiddler.", FnChange);
}
```

Fiddler automatically disposes of the callback function when the FiddlerScript engine unloads on shutdown or because the script has been modified and must be recompiled.

BUILD EXTENSION INSTALLERS

You may install your extensions using any technology you like; Fiddler simply requires that the .dll appear in the correct folder to load it next time that Fiddler launches.

Fiddler and all of the extensions I've written are installed using setup programs built using the Nullsoft Scriptable Install System (NSIS). You can get this great freeware from http://nsis.sourceforge.net /Download. NSIS allows you to write a script that compiles a compressed executable file containing all of the binaries that make up your project. The resulting setup program is small and works properly across all versions of Windows.

The only significant shortcoming I've encountered with NSIS is that it does not support Unicode, so you may need to use a different technology like WIX (http://wixtoolset.org/) if your installer displays non-Latin characters (e.g. Japanese).

A full explanation of how to use NSIS is beyond the scope of this book—the tool's website offers plenty of documentation at http://nsis.sourceforge.net/Docs/. However, I'll share an example setup script you can use to get started.

```
; In a NSIS Script, the semi-colon is a comment operator
Name "MyExtension"

; TODO: Set a specific name for your installer's executable
OutFile "InstallMyExtension.exe"
; Point to an icon to use for the installer, or omit to use the default
Icon "C:\src\MyExt\MyExt.ico"
XPStyle on                      ; Enable visual-styling for a prettier UI

; Explicitly demand admin permissions because we're going to write to
; Program Files. This prevents the "Program Compatibility Assistant" dialog.
; Note, you can use "user" here if you'd like, but then you must only write
; to HKCU and per-user writable locations on disk.
RequestExecutionLevel "admin"

; Maximize compression
SetCompressor /solid lzma

BrandingText "v1.0.1.0"          ; Text shown at the bottom of the Setup window

;
; TODO: Set the install directory to the proper folder.
;
; To install to the Extensions folder, use:
InstallDir "$PROGRAMFILES\Fiddler2\Scripts\"
InstallDirRegKey HKLM "SOFTWARE\Microsoft\Fiddler2" "LMScriptPath"
```

```
; To install to the Inspectors folder, use:
;InstallDir "$PROGRAMFILES\Fiddler2\Inspectors\"
;InstallDirRegKey HKLM "SOFTWARE\Microsoft\Fiddler2" "PluginPath"

Section "Main"
SetOutPath "$INSTDIR"

SetOverwrite on
;
; The next line embeds MyExt.dll from the output folder into the installer.
; When the installer runs, the file will be extracted to $INSTDIR\MyExt.dll
;

File "C:\src\MyExt\bin\release\MyExt.dll"
;
; TODO: List any other files your extension depends upon here.
; Be sure to also add those files to the list removed by the
; uninstaller at the bottom of this script
;


;
; Write information about the extension to the Add/Remove Programs dialog
;
WriteRegStr HKLM "Software\Microsoft\Windows\CurrentVersion\Uninstall\MyExt"
"DisplayName" "My Fiddler Extension"

WriteRegStr HKLM "Software\Microsoft\Windows\CurrentVersion\Uninstall\MyExt" "Comments"
"My Extension to Fiddler"

WriteRegStr HKLM "Software\Microsoft\Windows\CurrentVersion\Uninstall\MyExt"
"Publisher" 'MyCo'

WriteRegStr HKLM "Software\Microsoft\Windows\CurrentVersion\Uninstall\MyExt"
"InstallLocation" '$INSTDIR'

WriteRegDWORD HKLM "Software\Microsoft\Windows\CurrentVersion\Uninstall\MyExt"
"NoModify" 1

WriteRegDWORD HKLM "Software\Microsoft\Windows\CurrentVersion\Uninstall\MyExt"
"NoRepair" 1

;
; TODO: Update this line with the name of your uninstaller, set below
;
WriteRegStr HKLM "Software\Microsoft\Windows\CurrentVersion\Uninstall\MyExt"
"UninstallString" '"$INSTDIR\UninstallMyExt.exe"'

;
; TODO: Update this line to set a *unique* name for your uninstaller.
; Be sure to update the UninstallString value above to match.
; Also, update "Remove the uninstaller executable" line below to match.
;
```

```
WriteUninstaller "UninstallMyExt.exe"

SectionEnd ; end of default section

; ----------------------------------------------
; Perhaps surprisingly, this string cannot appear
; within the Uninstall section itself
UninstallText "This will uninstall My Fiddler Extension from your system"

Section Uninstall

Delete "$INSTDIR\MyExt.dll"
;
; TODO: Delete the other files you installed here.
;
; Remove the uninstaller regkey
DeleteRegKey HKLM "SOFTWARE\Microsoft\Windows\CurrentVersion\Uninstall\MyExt"
Delete "$INSTDIR\UninstallMyExt.exe"        ; Remove the uninstaller .exe
SectionEnd                ; eof
```

The resulting setup program will copy your assembly into the specified folder, and also add an item to the system's Add/Remove Programs applet to allow the user to uninstall the extension later.

Save the script to a file named `InstallMyExtension.nsi`. Next, create a batch file named `BuildInstaller .bat` to run the NSIS compiler and sign the resulting setup program. If you do not have a code-signing certificate, you can omit everything after the call to `MakeNSIS.exe`:

```
@title MyExtension Builder
@cd c:\src\MyExt\
@c:\src\NSIS\MakeNSIS.EXE /V2 InstallMyExtension.nsi
@if %ERRORLEVEL%==1 goto done
@CHOICE /M "Would you like to sign?"
@:sign
@signcode -spc C:\src\mycert.spc -v C:\src\mykey.pvk -n "Fiddler Extension" -i
  "http://mysite.com/myext/" -a sha1 -t http://timestamp.digicert.com
  InstallMyExtension.exe

@if %ERRORLEVEL%==-1 goto sign
@:done
@title Command Prompt
```

Run `BuildInstaller.bat` and the NSIS compiler will compile your script into the `InstallMyExtension.exe` setup program. It will then sign that new program to prevent tampering and avoid security warnings in browsers.

> **Warning**: Windows tracks the origin files using a data stream known as the "Mark of the Web." If you don't build an installer and instead ask the user to copy your extension's .DLL from a ZIP file or network share, you may find that it fails to load in Fiddler v4. .NET v4 sees the "This file is from an untrusted location" marker and will refuse to load the file by default.

BUILD INSPECTORS

Developing custom Inspectors for Fiddler is simple-- you need only implement one class and one interface. Over the years, the Inspector model has evolved to allow for more powerful Inspectors while maintaining backward compatibility, so be aware that some of the APIs you encounter will seem a bit redundant.

There are two types of Inspectors: Request Inspectors and Response Inspectors; the former are used to view and/or modify a request, while the latter are used to view and/or modify a response. Both types of Inspector are derived from the abstract `Inspector2` base class. Request Inspectors must also implement the `IRequestInspector2` interface, while Response Inspectors implement the `IResponseInspector2` interface. The `Inspector2` base class contains just two methods you must implement:

```
public abstract void AddToTab(TabPage o);
public abstract int GetOrder();
```

The `AddToTab` method is called when Fiddler has created a TabPage for your Inspector. In your implementation of this method, create your UI and add it to the `TabPage` provided. Most of Fiddler's default Inspectors consist of one class that implements the Inspector interfaces and one `UserControl` that contains all of the UI for the Inspector. When `AddToTab` is called, it creates an instance of the `UserControl` and adds it to the `TabPage`:

```
public override void AddToTab(TabPage oPage)
{
  // Title my tab
  o.Text = "Raw";

  // Create my UserControl and add it to my tab
  myControl = new RawView(this);
  oPage.Controls.Add(myControl);
  oPage.Controls[0].Dock = DockStyle.Fill;
}
```

The `GetOrder` method is called when Fiddler sorts the tabs for display within the UI. Inspectors with lower numbers will display to the left of the tab set while Inspectors with larger numbers will display toward the right. Fiddler itself returns integers between -1000 and 110 for its own Inspectors. You may return any value you like, although you should strive to use a unique number. In the event that two Inspectors return the same value, ordering is non-deterministic and can change between instances.

In addition to the abstract methods your Inspector *must* implement, the base class exposes a number of virtual methods which you *may* implement if you'd like. These include:

```
public virtual void ShowAboutBox()
public virtual void SetFontSize(float flSizeInPoints)
public virtual InspectorFlags GetFlags()
```

```
public virtual int ScoreForSession(Session oS)
public virtual int ScoreForContentType(string sMIMEType)

public virtual void AssignSession(Session oS)
public virtual bool CommitAnyChanges(Session oS)
public virtual bool UnsetDirtyFlag()
```

The ShowAboutBox method runs when the user right-clicks on the Inspector's tab and clicks **Inspector Properties** on the context menu. If you don't override this method, when the user clicks the menu item, a message box will show the Inspector's full type name and information about the Assembly that contains it.

The SetFontSize method runs if the user changes Fiddler's font-size at runtime; override this method to adjust your Inspector's UI font size. This method was created before the Fiddler Preference System was created, and Inspectors may instead watch the preference fiddler.ui.font.size.

The GetFlags method retrieves flags that describe the Inspector's behavior. If overridden, your Inspector may return one or more values from the InspectorFlags enumeration:

None	This Inspector has no special behaviors.
AlwaysCommitEdits	Fiddler should always commit edits, even when the Inspector should be in a readonly state. This flag is used by the Transformer, but should not be used in other Inspectors.
HideInAutoResponder	Do not show this Inspector in the window launched by the AutoResponder's **Edit Response...** command.
HideInNewWindow	Do not show this Inspector in the window opened by the Web Sessions List context menu's **Inspect in New Window...** command.

The ScoreForSession method runs when the user double-clicks or hits Enter on a Session in the Web Sessions list. When this action occurs, each Inspector is polled to determine how eager it is to display a given request or response; the higher the value, the stronger the Inspector's desire to handle the Session. This method enables an Inspector to evaluate any aspect of a Session in making its decision. It should return 0 if it has no interest in a given Session (meaning *"I can't handle that at all"*) and should return 100 if it is confident that it is the *best* handler for a given Session.

The ability to consider any aspect of a session is a powerful one, as it enables your Inspector to consider factors beyond HTTP headers when calculating its eagerness to render a Session. For instance, the WebView Inspector is able to render previews of WOFF Font files, but most servers are not configured to return the correct Content-Type for such files. Therefore, the WebView Inspector checks the first 4 bytes of any response body to detect the WOFF signature bytes.

```
static byte[] arr_WOFF_MAGIC =
        new byte[4] {(byte)'w', (byte)'O', (byte)'F', (byte)'F'};

public override int ScoreForSession(Session oS)
```

```
{
    // Check for WOFF Magic Bytes
    if (Utilities.HasMagicBytes(oS.responseBodyBytes, arr_WOFF_MAGIC)) {
      return 60;
    }

    // If not found, consult the response's Content-Type
    return ScoreForContentType(oS.oResponse.MIMEType);
}
```

Avoid performing any expensive computations in your ScoreForSession method, as it runs often and users expect that inspecting a Session will occur instantly. For example, your implementation of this method should not attempt to search a response body of arbitrary size for specific text, and should not perform network or disk operations.

If you do not override the ScoreForSession method, the base implementation calls the ScoreFor ContentType method, passing the Content-Type header.

The ScoreForContentType method predates the introduction of the ScoreForSession method, but it performs the same general function—it allows the Inspector to indicate how applicable it is for a given Session. Again, scores between 0 and 100 should be returned. Avoid returning an overly-confident value for a general type; for instance, the JSON Inspector returns only 55 when the type is application/json while the ImageView Inspector returns 80 for image types. Only return 100 if the MIME Content-Type is something that your extension will *uniquely* understand—for instance, if you have invented a custom MIME type and no other Inspector could be expected to be useful for your type.

The WebView Inspector's implementation of ScoreForContentType is as follows:

```
public override int ScoreForContentType(string sMIMEType)
{
    if (sMIMEType.StartsWith("audio/", StringComparison.OrdinalIgnoreCase)) {
      return 60;
    }

    if (sMIMEType.StartsWith("video/", StringComparison.OrdinalIgnoreCase)) {
      return 60;
    }

    // Just in case a site sent a malformed MP3 type, check the whole string
    if (sMIMEType.IndexOf("mp3", StringComparison.OrdinalIgnoreCase) > -1) {
      return 60;
    }

    return 0;
}
```

If you do not implement the ScoreForContentType method, a default score of 0 is assumed and a different Inspector will be activated by default. The user may still manually choose your Inspector whenever needed.

The IRequestInspector2 and IResponseInspector2 interfaces both inherit from the IBaseInspector2 interface, which contains the following properties and method that your Inspectors must implement:

```
bool bReadOnly { get; set; }
bool bDirty { get; }
byte[] body { get; set; }
void Clear();
```

The inherited IRequestInspector2 interface adds one property:

```
HTTPRequestHeaders headers { get; set; }
```

Similarly, the inherited IResponseInspector2 interface adds one property:

```
HTTPResponseHeaders headers { get; set; }
```

Inspectors may be readonly or read/write. Read/write Inspectors enable the user to modify the request or response under inspection when the Session is paused at a breakpoint. An Inspector's bReadOnly property is set to control whether the Inspector should permit the user to modify the request or response; readonly inspectors can simply ignore changes to the property. When bReadOnly is set to false, your Inspector should not permit the user to modify the headers or body. You can communicate the readonly status to the user by setting controls to readonly mode, and setting their background color to the color value stored in the CONFIG.colorDisabledEdit field. When bReadOnly is set to true, your Inspector may enable read/write mode for controls and allow the user to change the headers or body. If an Inspector is "display only" without modification capabilities, the bReadOnly property setter can be a no-op.

An Inspector's bDirty property is queried by Fiddler before it attempts to commit any modifications the Inspector has made to the headers or body. If your Inspector doesn't permit edits, or if the user has not made any modifications, return false when this property is queried.

The headers property allows Fiddler to provide the HTTPRequestHeaders or HTTPResponseHeaders for the Session being inspected. When a Session is assigned to your Inspector, the headers property will be set first. When Fiddler attempts to commit any changes to the inspected Session because the Inspector's bDirty property returned true, Fiddler will query the headers property for the headers. If the Inspector does not wish to make any changes to the headers, simply return null in the getter for this property.

Warning: Fiddler does not currently clone the Session's headers when assigning to the headers property. Your Inspector must be coded to either clone the headers when assigned, or must avoid making any changes to the headers object reference it receives.

The **body** property accepts a byte array that contains the request or response body for the Session being inspected. When a Session is assigned to your Inspector, the body property will be set after the headers. When Fiddler attempts to commit any changes to the Session because the Inspector's bDirty property returned true, Fiddler will query the body property for the new byte array to use. If the Inspector does not wish to make any changes to the body, simply return null in the getter for this property. To store an empty body, return new byte[0].

Warning: Fiddler does not currently clone the Session's body when assigning to the body property. Your Inspector must be coded to either clone the body array when assigned, or must avoid making any changes to the bytes in the body array reference it receives.

The Clear method is called by Fiddler when the user has unselected the current Session and your Inspector should be reset. In response to this method call, clear all data from the Inspector's UI, and indicate to the user that no Session is selected.

Inspect Session Objects

In the original Inspectors API, the Inspectors were never provided a reference to the Session object under Inspection-- only the headers and body would be provided. This provided for a simple, easily understood API contract, but this simplicity presented a number of shortcomings. For instance, it was impossible for an Inspector to get or set flags on the Session object, and even examining properties of the Session was impossible. For instance, the Caching Response Inspector was unable to determine whether the inspected traffic used HTTPS because the URL (and thus the protocol scheme) only appears in the *request* headers, which were never available to a Response Inspector.

To resolve these shortcomings, the Inspector2 base class was augmented with three additional virtual methods:

```
public virtual void AssignSession(Session oS)
public virtual bool CommitAnyChanges(Session oS)
public virtual bool UnsetDirtyFlag()
```

These methods allow an Inspector to be passed a Session object rather than having individual header and body properties set using the IRequestInspector2 and IResponseInspector2 interfaces. If your Inspector *does not* override these virtual methods, Fiddler will simply access the headers and body properties on the interface, and you need not implement any of the four virtual methods. If your Inspector *does* override the AssignSession method, it must still implement all of the legacy properties because not all codepaths in Fiddler call the newer virtual methods. Specifically, when editing a response using the AutoResponder tab, no Session object is available, so the legacy properties will be used.

The AssignSession method is called when the user selects a Session in the Web Sessions list when your Inspector's tab is visible. In your overridden method, your Inspector should update its UI based on the headers and/or body of the Session. Note that your Inspector must *itself* examine the Session's state to determine whether the Inspector should be readonly, as shown in the following Response Inspector's code:

```
public override void AssignSession(Session oSession) {
  if ((null == oSession) || !oSession.bHasResponse) {
    Clear(); return;
  }

  UpdateUIFromHeaders(oSession.oResponse.headers);
  UpdateUIFromBody(oSession.responseBodyBytes);

  bool bIsReadOnly = ((oSession.state != SessionStates.HandTamperResponse)
                  && !oSession.oFlags.ContainsKey("x-Unlocked"));

  UpdateReadOnlyState(bIsReadOnly);
}
```

If you do not override the AssignSession method, the base Inspector2 class' implementation will automatically assign to the headers, body, and bReadOnly properties instead:

```
public virtual void AssignSession(Session oS) {
  if (this is IRequestInspector2) {
    IRequestInspector2 oRI = (this as IRequestInspector2);
    oRI.headers = oS.oRequest.headers;
    oRI.body = oS.requestBodyBytes;
    oRI.bReadOnly = ((oS.state != SessionStates.HandTamperRequest)
                  && !oS.oFlags.ContainsKey("x-Unlocked"));
    return;
  }

  if (this is IResponseInspector2)
  //...
```

The CommitAnyChanges method is called when the Inspector should commit any changes to the request or response. If the Inspector has any uncommitted edits, they should be stored to the Session when this method is called and it should return true. If no changes were committed, return false. If you do not override this method, after Fiddler consults the bDirty property of the Inspector, and if it is true, and if the Session is in a state that permits editing, the default implementation will update the Session's headers and body using those properties of the Inspector.

The UnsetDirtyFlag method is called when Fiddler wishes to mark your Inspector as non-dirty (e.g. because it updated the Session's headers and body from those properties of the Inspector). If your Inspector overrides this method and can successfully clear its dirty state, do so and return true. This method exists because some Inspectors may not be able to easily reset their dirty state, and thus the bDirty property is readonly-- only the Inspector may change it. The benefit of implementing this method is that it prevents unneeded *"Do you want to save changes?"* prompts when the user edits an AutoResponder response using a popup Inspectors window.

Deal with HTTP Compression and Chunking

Some Inspectors do not contain code to parse a chunked or compressed response body into a higher-level format like an audio file. In those Inspectors, the user is simply encouraged to decode the response manually before inspecting:

```
if (oHeaders.Exists("Transfer-Encoding") || oHeaders.Exists("Content-Encoding"))
{
  lblDisplayMyEncodingWarning.Visible = true;
  return;
}
```

Fiddler allows the user to easily remove the compression and chunking by clicking the yellow notification bar or by using the **Transformer** Inspector.

However, it is possible to make a copy of the body and decode it for your Inspector's private use. Be wary of the cost of decoding large bodies; you'd be better off having the user do it manually just once instead of every time the body is loaded in your Inspector.

There are three ways to get the uncompressed and unchunked body.

Decode a Copy of the Body

All Inspectors are provided a copy of the headers and body. Using this information, the body may be cloned and decoded using the Utilities.utilDecodeHTTPBody static method. If the body needs to be interpreted as a string, the getEntityBodyEncoding and GetStringFromArrayRemovingBOM methods can be used to convert the body bytes to a string.

Here's what the JSON Inspector does in its body property setter. In this example, the oHeaders object is a reference to the headers stored by the headers property setter, and the incoming value object refers to the new body byte array that is being assigned to the Inspector:

```
if (null != oHeaders)
{
  // Check for no body
  if (Utilities.IsNullOrEmpty(value)) return;

  if (!oHeaders.ExistsAndContains("Content-Type", "application/json")
      && !oHeaders.ExistsAndContains("Content-Type", "javascript"))
  {
    // Not JSON
    return;
  }

  if (oHeaders.Exists("Transfer-Encoding") || oHeaders.Exists("Content-Encoding"))
  {
```

```
    // Create a copy of the body to avoid corrupting the original
    byte[] arrCopy = (byte[])value.Clone();
    try
    {
      // Decode. Warning: Will throw if value cannot be decoded
      Utilities.utilDecodeHTTPBody(oHeaders, ref arrCopy);
      value = arrCopy;
    }
    catch
    {
      // Leave value alone.
    }
  }
}

// Okay, now the body stored in "value" is unchunked
// and uncompressed. We need to convert it to a string,
// keeping in mind that the HTTP response might have
// been in a non-Unicode codepage.

oEncoding = Utilities.getEntityBodyEncoding(oHeaders, value);
sJSON = Utilities.GetStringFromArrayRemovingBOM(value, oEncoding);
myControl.SetJSON(sJSON);

//...
```

The headers are not updated by this code, which means that they may refer to encodings that have been removed from the Inspector's copy of the body.

Use the GetRe*BodyAsString Methods

If your Inspector overrides the `AssignSession` method, then you can get the body as a string using one of the following two methods:

```
string sRequestBody = oSession.GetRequestBodyAsString();
string sResponseBody = oSession.GetResponseBodyAsString();
```

These methods consult the headers to determine what encodings are in use, then copy the body bytes to a temporary array and decode them. Next, the `Content-Type` header and the body are inspected for clues as to which character set the content uses, and the body bytes are converted to a .NET string (Unicode) and returned as the result of the function.

.NET strings are immutable. You don't need to worry about corrupting the original HTTP body by manipulating the returned string, since any modifications will yield a new string.

Use the utilDecode* Methods

If your Inspector overrides the `AssignSession` method, then your code may call the Session object's `utilDecodeRequest` and `utilDecodeResponse` methods to decode the request or response bodies respectively. These methods will decompress and unchunk the body and update the Session's headers to remove the reference to the now-removed encodings.

Your Inspector **should not** automatically call these methods when a Session is assigned to your Inspector. If it did, your Inspector would permanently change the Session even when the Inspector is meant to be in a readonly state. Instead, call these methods only if the user takes an explicit action, like clicking on a button or link that indicates that a permanent change will be made.

Inspector Assemblies

When looking for Inspectors, Fiddler loads all assembly .DLLs from the %PROGRAMFILES%\Fiddler2\ Inspectors and %USERPROFILE%\Documents\Fiddler2\Inspectors folders and enumerates all public classes within them to find Request and Response Inspectors.

Install to the %PROGRAMFILES% subfolder to make your Inspectors available to all users on the machine, or the %USERPROFILE% subfolder to make them available only to the current user.

In addition to placing your Inspector assemblies in the appropriate folder, you must also mark your assembly to indicate the minimum version of Fiddler required by your Inspectors. Set the RequiredVersion attribute as follows:

```
// These Inspectors require methods introduced in v2.5.0.0...
[assembly: Fiddler.RequiredVersion("2.5.0.0")]
```

If Fiddler loads an assembly for which the RequiredVersion attribute indicates a later version of Fiddler is needed, the user will be notified that an update is required and no Inspectors will be loaded from the assembly. Assemblies in the \Inspectors\ folder which lack a RequiredVersion attribute are silently ignored.

Fiddler skips enumeration of DLLs named with a leading underscore character (_) when loading Inspectors. Many Inspectors rely upon 3rd party assemblies that do not themselves contain any Fiddler-related code. To avoid the performance cost of Fiddler enumerating such assemblies to look for Inspectors, name those assemblies using a leading underscore.

BUILD EXTENSIONS

When you need to add functionality to Fiddler and an Inspector isn't the appropriate way to expose that functionality, build an extension instead. Extensions can enhance Fiddler with anything from simple features (like a new menu item) to extremely complicated business logic and reporting infrastructures.

Getting started is easy. The simplest Fiddler extension must implement only one interface whose methods are called to load and unload the extension:

```
public interface IFiddlerExtension
{
    void OnLoad();
    void OnBeforeUnload();
}
```

The OnLoad function is called when Fiddler has finished loading and its UI is fully available. At this point, you can safely add menu items, tabbed pages, or other elements to the Fiddler UI. The OnBeforeUnload function will be called when Fiddler is shutting down and unloading all extensions.

The IAutoTamper interface inherits from the IFiddlerExtension interface, and permits your extension to receive callbacks as each Session is processed, enabling modifications, logging, or other operations.

```
public interface IAutoTamper : IFiddlerExtension
{
    void AutoTamperRequestBefore(Session oSession);
    void AutoTamperRequestAfter(Session oSession);
    void AutoTamperResponseBefore(Session oSession);
    void AutoTamperResponseAfter(Session oSession);
    void OnBeforeReturningError(Session oSession);
}
```

The difference between the *Before and *After methods is that the former execute before the user has a chance to manually tamper with a breakpointed Session using the Inspectors, while the latter methods execute after any such modifications are completed. If you to permit the user to manually undo any modifications your method makes, use the *Before methods, otherwise, use the *After methods.

The IAutoTamper2 interface inherits from IAutoTamper and adds one additional method that is called when Fiddler has read the server's response headers, (usually) before the response body is available:

```
public interface IAutoTamper2 : IAutoTamper
{
    void OnPeekAtResponseHeaders(Session oSession);
}
```

A common use of the `OnPeekAtResponseHeaders` method is to examine the response's headers to decide whether the response should be buffered or streamed. For instance, to stream all image files, you could write the following code:

```
void OnPeekAtResponseHeaders(Session oSession)
{
  if (oSession.oResponse.MIMEType.StartsWith("image/"))
  {
    bBufferResponse = false;
  }
}
```

Be careful not to attempt to read the `responseBodyBytes` array in this method, because a Null Reference Exception is likely to ensue. Additionally, you should avoid manipulating headers related to the response's length (e.g. `Content-Length`, `Transfer-Encoding`, `Connection`) because doing so is likely to impair the subsequent attempt to read to the response body from the server.

The `IAutoTamper3` interface inherits from `IAutoTamper2` and adds one additional method that is called when Fiddler has read the client's request headers, (usually) before the request body is available:

```
public interface IAutoTamper3 : IAutoTamper2
{
    void OnPeekAtRequestHeaders(Session oSession);
}
```

This method is only useful in certain niche scenarios; in most cases, the availability of the request's headers alone is not sufficient to do anything useful.

Understand Threading

The `IAutoTamper` interfaces' methods are called on background, non-UI threads. If you wish to update UI, you *must* use `Invoke` or `BeginInvoke` to update the UI. Also, note that the `IAutoTamper` interfaces' methods can be called *before* the `OnLoad` event fires-- Fiddler allows traffic to flow before the UI is fully available. Therefore, most extensions will initialize objects and UI inside their constructor and wait until `OnLoad` only to insert their UI into the main Fiddler UI.

Integrate with QuickExec

Extensions that implement the `IHandleExecAction` interface are called when the user has entered a command into the QuickExec box or invoked a command using the `ExecAction.exe` command-line tool.

```
public interface IHandleExecAction
{
    bool OnExecAction(string sCommand);
}
```

If your extension would like to handle the command (and prevent further processing by other extensions and Fiddler itself) return `true` from your implementation of this method. The `Utilities` class includes a helper function for interpreting the `sCommand` parameter:

```
public static string[] Parameterize(string sCommand)
```

The `Parameterize` method tokenizes a string into tokens. The string is split by whitespace characters, unless the spaces are contained within quotation marks, in which case the entire quoted string is stored as a token. Use a backslash character (\) to escape quotation marks so that they may appear literally within a string.

Example Extension

The following is a simple extension which examines all responses as they are received. It determines whether the responses attempt to set cookies, and if so, whether a valid P3P Compact Policy statement has been provided. This example adds an item to the top-level menu, adds a column to the Web Sessions list, and modifies Sessions as they are processed.

```csharp
using Fiddler;
using System;
using System.Text;
using System.IO;
using System.Globalization;
using System.Windows.Forms;
using System.Text.RegularExpressions;

[assembly: Fiddler.RequiredVersion("2.5.0.0")]
[assembly: AssemblyVersion("1.0.1.0")]
[assembly: AssemblyDescription("Scans for Cookies and P3P")]

public class TagCookies : IAutoTamper2
{
    private bool bEnabled = false;
    private bool bEnforceP3PValidity = false;
    private bool bCreatedColumn = false;
    private MenuItem miEnabled;
    private MenuItem miEnforceP3PValidity;
    private MenuItem mnuCookieTag;

    private enum P3PState
    {
        NoCookies,
        NoP3PAndSetsCookies,
        P3POk,
        P3PUnsatisfactory,
        P3PMalformed
    }

    public void OnLoad()
```

```
{
    /* NB: OnLoad might not get called until ~after~ one of
       the AutoTamper methods was called, because sessions are
       processed while Fiddler is loading.
       This is okay for us, because we created our mnuCookieTag
       in the constructor and its simply not visible anywhere
       until this method is called and we merge it onto the
       Fiddler Main menu. */

    FiddlerApplication.UI.mnuMain.MenuItems.Add(mnuCookieTag);
}

// We don't need to do anything on unload, since Fiddler only presently
// unloads extensions at shutdown, and the GC will dispose of our UI.
public void OnBeforeUnload() { /*noop*/ }

private void InitializeMenu()
{
    this.miEnabled = new MenuItem("&Enabled");
    this.miEnforceP3PValidity = new MenuItem("&Rename P3P header if invalid");

    this.miEnabled.Index = 0;
    this.miEnforceP3PValidity.Index = 1;

    this.mnuCookieTag = new MenuItem("Privacy");
    this.mnuCookieTag.MenuItems.AddRange(new MenuItem[] {
      this.miEnabled, this.miEnforceP3PValidity });

    this.miEnabled.Click += new System.EventHandler(this.miEnabled_Click);
    this.miEnabled.Checked = bEnabled;

    this.miEnforceP3PValidity.Click +=
      new System.EventHandler(this.miEnforceP3PValidity_Click);

    this.miEnforceP3PValidity.Checked = bEnforceP3PValidity;
}

public void miEnabled_Click(object sender, EventArgs e)
{
    miEnabled.Checked = !miEnabled.Checked;
    bEnabled = miEnabled.Checked;
    this.miEnforceP3PValidity.Enabled = bEnabled;
    if (bEnabled) { EnsureColumn(); }
    FiddlerApplication.Prefs.SetBoolPref("extensions.tagcookies.enabled",
                                    bEnabled);
}

public void miEnforceP3PValidity_Click(object sender, EventArgs e)
{
    miEnforceP3PValidity.Checked = !miEnforceP3PValidity.Checked;
    bEnforceP3PValidity = miEnforceP3PValidity.Checked;
    FiddlerApplication.Prefs.SetBoolPref(
```

```
                    "extensions.tagcookies.EnforceP3PValidity", bEnforceP3PValidity);
    }

    private void EnsureColumn()
    {
        // If we already created the column, bail out.
        if (bCreatedColumn) return;

        // Add a new Column to the Web Sessions list, titled "Privacy Info",
        // that will automatically fill with each Session's X-Privacy flag string
        FiddlerApplication.UI.lvSessions.AddBoundColumn(
                                            "Privacy Info", 1, 120, "X-Privacy");
        bCreatedColumn = true;
    }

    public TagCookies()
    {
        this.bEnabled = FiddlerApplication.Prefs.GetBoolPref(
          "extensions.tagcookies.enabled", false);

        this.bEnforceP3PValidity = FiddlerApplication.Prefs.GetBoolPref(
           "extensions.tagcookies.EnforceP3PValidity", true);

        InitializeMenu();

        if (bEnabled)
        { EnsureColumn(); }
        else
        { this.miEnforceP3PValidity.Enabled = false; }
    }

    private void SetP3PStateFromHeader(string sValue, ref P3PState oP3PState)
    {
        // If there was no P3P header, bail out
        if (string.IsNullOrEmpty(sValue)) { return; }

        string sUnsatCat = String.Empty;
        string sUnsatPurpose = String.Empty;
        sValue = sValue.Replace('\'', '"');

        string sCP = null;

        // Use a Regular Expression to search the header for a CP attribute
        Regex r = new Regex("CP\\s?=\\s?[\"]?(?<TokenValue>[^\";]*)");
        Match m = r.Match(sValue);
        if (m.Success && (null != m.Groups["TokenValue"]))
        {
            sCP = m.Groups["TokenValue"].Value;
        }

        // If we didn't find a Compact Policy statement, bail out.
        if (String.IsNullOrEmpty(sCP)) { return; }
```

```csharp
        // Okay, we've got a compact policy string. Evaluate each token.
        oP3PState = P3PState.P3POk;
        string[] sTokens = sCP.Split(new char[] { ' ' },
            StringSplitOptions.RemoveEmptyEntries);

        foreach (string sToken in sTokens)
        {
            // Reject clearly invalid tokens...
            if ((sToken.Length < 3) || (sToken.Length > 4))
            {
                oP3PState = P3PState.P3PMalformed;
                return;
            }

            // Track any tokens with "Unacceptable" privacy category
            if (",PHY,ONL,GOV,FIN,".IndexOf("," + sToken + ",",
                StringComparison.OrdinalIgnoreCase) > -1)
            {
                sUnsatCat += (sToken + " ");
                continue;
            }

            // Track any tokens with "Unacceptable" privacy purposes
            if (",SAM,OTR,UNR,PUB,IVA,IVD,CON,TEL,OTP,".IndexOf("," + sToken + ",",
                StringComparison.OrdinalIgnoreCase) > -1)
            {
                sUnsatPurpose += (sToken + " ");
                continue;
            }

            // TODO: Check each token against the list of 70-some valid tokens and
            // reject if it's not found.
        }

        // If a cookie contains an unsatisfactory purpose and an unsatisfactory
        // category, tag it. Learn more about "Unsatisfactory cookies" at
        // http://msdn.microsoft.com/en-us/library/ie/ms537343(v=vs.85).aspx
        if ((sUnsatCat.Length > 0) && (sUnsatPurpose.Length > 0))
        {
            if (oP3PState == P3PState.P3POk)
            {
                oP3PState = P3PState.P3PUnsatisfactory;
            }
        }
    }
}

// On each HTTP response, examine the response headers for attempts to set
// cookies, and check for a P3P header too. We do this
// in OnPeekAtResponseHeaders rather than OnBeforeResponse because we only
// need the headers and do not need to wait for the responseBodyBytes to
// be available.
```

```
public void OnPeekAtResponseHeaders(Session oS)
{
    // If our extension isn't enabled, bail fast
    if (!bEnabled) return;

    P3PState oP3PState = P3PState.NoCookies;
    if (!oS.oResponse.headers.Exists("Set-Cookie")) { return; }

    oP3PState = P3PState.NoP3PAndSetsCookies;

    if (oS.oResponse.headers.Exists("P3P"))
    {
        SetP3PStateFromHeader(oS.oResponse.headers["P3P"], ref oP3PState);
    }

    // Based on the cookie/P3P state, set the background color of item in the
    // Web Sessions list. Also set the X-Privacy flag which is shown in the
    // column that we created.
    switch (oP3PState)
    {
        case P3PState.P3POk:
            oS["ui-backcolor"] = "#ACDC85";
            oS["X-Privacy"] = "Sets cookies & P3P";
            break;

        case P3PState.NoP3PAndSetsCookies:
            oS["ui-backcolor"] = "#FAFDA4";
            oS["X-Privacy"] = "Sets cookies without P3P";
            break;

        case P3PState.P3PUnsatisfactory:
            oS["ui-backcolor"] = "#EC921A";
            oS["X-Privacy"] = "Sets cookies; P3P unsat. for 3rd-party use";
            break;

        case P3PState.P3PMalformed:
            oS["ui-backcolor"] = "#E90A05";
            if (bEnforceP3PValidity)
            {
                oS.oResponse.headers["MALFORMED-P3P"] =
                    oS.oResponse.headers["P3P"];
                oS["X-Privacy"] = "MALFORMED P3P: " +
                    oS.oResponse.headers["P3P"];

                // Delete invalid header to prevent the client from seeing it.
                oS.oResponse.headers.Remove("P3P");
            }
            break;
    }
}

// Our extension doesn't need any of the other AutoTamper* methods.
```

```
        public void AutoTamperRequestBefore(Session oS) {/*noop*/}
        public void AutoTamperRequestAfter(Session oS) {/*noop*/}
        public void AutoTamperResponseAfter(Session oS) {/*noop*/}
        public void AutoTamperResponseBefore(Session oS) {/*noop*/}
        public void OnBeforeReturningError(Session oS) {/*noop*/}
    }
```

If your extension needs to extend to the Web Sessions list's context menu, add your new menu items to `FiddlerApplication.UI.mnuSessionContext`. If your extension needs to create a new top-level tab, it can add one to the `tabsViews` control. Here's how the Timeline tab adds its tab with a title and icon:

```
    public void OnLoad() {
        oPage = new TabPage("Timeline");
        oPage.ImageIndex = (int)Fiddler.SessionIcons.Timeline;
        FiddlerApplication.UI.tabsViews.TabPages.Add(oPage);
    }
```

If your tab contains any non-trivial UI, you should use the pattern described in the "Best Practice: Use Delay Load" section to ensure that the heavyweight initialization only occurs if and when the user switches to your new tab.

Extension Assemblies

When looking for extensions, Fiddler loads all assembly .DLLs from the %PROGRAMFILES%\Fiddler2 \Scripts and %USERPROFILE%\Documents\Fiddler2\Scripts folders and enumerates all public classes within them to find extensions.

Install to the %PROGRAMFILES% subfolder to make your extension available to all users on the machine, or the %USERPROFILE% subfolder to install it for the current user only.

In addition to placing your extension assemblies in the appropriate folder, you must also mark your assembly to indicate the minimum version of Fiddler required by your extension. Set the RequiredVersion attribute as follows:

```
    // We require methods introduced in v2.5.0.0...
    [assembly: Fiddler.RequiredVersion("2.5.0.0")]
```

If Fiddler loads an assembly for which the RequiredVersion attribute indicates a later version of Fiddler is needed, the user will be notified that an update is required and no extensions will be loaded from the assembly. Assemblies in the \Scripts\ folder which lack a RequiredVersion attribute are silently ignored.

Fiddler skips enumeration of DLLs named with a leading underscore character (_) when loading extensions. Many extensions rely upon 3rd party assemblies that do not themselves contain any Fiddler-related code. To avoid the performance cost of Fiddler enumerating such assemblies to look for extensions, name those assemblies using a leading underscore.

BUILD IMPORT AND EXPORT TRANSCODERS

One of the most common goals when building an extension is to export captured data out of Fiddler, or import data captured using other tools. While there's no reason you *can't* build such an extension using the general IFiddlerExtension interface, there are shortcomings in doing so:

- Such extensions have a performance cost, even when unused
- Such extensions require a lot of boilerplate code
- Inconsistent import/export UI leads to user confusion

To combat these shortcomings, Fiddler offers a specific extension type called a **Transcoder**. Fiddler ships with a number of these Transcoders by default, and developers can build new Transcoders easily. A Transcoder is simply an object that implements either or both of the ISessionImporter and ISession Exporter interfaces. Transcoder Assemblies are only loaded when invoked by the user via the **Import Sessions** and **Export Sessions** entry points on the File menu. Delay-loading means that Transcoders do not have a performance impact on Fiddler boot time or memory usage.

Direct Fiddler to load your Transcoder assemblies
Fiddler loads Transcoder assembly DLLs from the %PROGRAMFILES%\Fiddler2\ImportExport\ and %USERPROFILE%\Documents\Fiddler2\ImportExport\ folders. Install to the %PROGRAMFILES% location to make your Transcoder available to all users on the machine, or the %USERPROFILE% folder to install it for the current user only.

Be sure to set the RequiredVersion attribute as follows:

```
// These Transcoders require methods introduced in v2.5.0.0...
[assembly: Fiddler.RequiredVersion("2.5.0.0")]
```

...and ensure that your Transcoder classes are marked public.

The ProfferFormat Attribute
Each Transcoder class must be decorated with one or more ProfferFormat attributes that specify Format Name and FormatDescription strings that describe the Transcoder. These strings are shown to the user in the Select Format window. For instance, the HTTPArchive format exporter is decorated with two ProfferFormat attributes:

```
[ProfferFormat("HTTPArchive v1.1", "A lossy JSON-based HTTP traffic
archive format. Standard is documented @ http://groups.google.com/group/http-
archive-specification/web/har-1-1-spec")]
```

```
[ProfferFormat("HTTPArchive v1.2", "A lossy JSON-based HTTP traffic
archive format. Standard is documented @ http://groups.google.com/group/http-
archive-specification/web/har-1-2-spec")]
```

```
public class HTTPArchiveFormatExport: ISessionExporter
{
    //...
```

Each of these two attributes identifies a format supported by the Transcoder, and each is displayed in the Select Format window's dropdown:

When the user invokes the Transcoder, the FormatName is provided to the ImportSessions or Export Sessions method so that a Transcoder that supports multiple formats may know which format the user has requested.

An additional overload of the ProfferFormat attribute allows you to specify the file extensions commonly used by a given import format. For instance, the Packet Capture importer uses the following declaration:

```
[ProfferFormat("Packet Capture", "The PCAP and CAP formats are...",
               ".cap;.pcap;.pcapng")]
```

The third parameter lists file extensions which are imported by only this extension. Fiddler uses the extension information if the user runs fiddler.exe FileToLoad.pcap or holds the Control key while dropping a file with the specified extension to the Web Sessions list. When using this parameter, do not attempt to register for generic extensions like .xml.

The ISessionImporter Interface
Transcoders that implement the ISessionImporter interface are invoked when the user invokes the **File > Import Sessions...** menu command. The interface defines one method:

```
public interface ISessionImporter : IDisposable
{
    Session[] ImportSessions(string sFormatName,
        Dictionary<string, object> dictOptions,
        EventHandler<ProgressCallbackEventArgs> evtProgressNotifications);
}
```

... and it also inherits the Dispose method from IDisposable.

The `ImportSessions` method should return an array of `Session` objects created from the import of the data, or `null` if there was an error in loading the data.

When the user chooses **File** > **Import Sessions…**, Fiddler will call the Transcoder and then add the Sessions returned by the Transcoder to the Web Sessions list.

The ISessionExporter Interface

Transcoders that implement the `ISessionExporter` interface are called when the user invokes the **File** > **Export Sessions** menu commands. The interface defines one method:

```
public interface ISessionExporter : IDisposable
{
    bool ExportSessions(string sFormatName,
      Session[] oSessions,
      Dictionary<string, object> dictOptions,
      EventHandler<ProgressCallbackEventArgs> evtProgressNotifications);
}
```

… and it also inherits the `Dispose` method from `IDisposable`.

The `ExportSessions` method should return `true` if the export of the Sessions passed in the `oSessions` parameter is successful. If the data could not be exported for some reason, the Transcoder should log an explanation to Fiddler's Log and return `false`.

Handle Options

The `ImportSessions` and `ExportSessions` methods' second parameter is a `string-to-object Dictionary` that permits callers (FiddlerScript, Extensions, or a FiddlerCore-based application) to pass options into the Transcoder.

The provided `dictOptions` dictionary may be `null`, or may contain a set of string-keyed objects. Most Importers support specification of a filename like this:

```
dictOptions["Filename"] = "C:\\test.file";
```

When a filename is provided through this mechanism, the Transcoder can suppress its normal UI and respect the provided option. Similarly, many Transcoders support a `Silent` key, which, if present, ensures that no warning or error UI is shown to the user.

Other Transcoders have other options, depending on their individual needs. For instance, FiddlerScript can invoke the HTTPArchive Transcoder, passing in the filename string and maximum response size integers thusly:

```
var oSessions = FiddlerApplication.UI.GetAllSessions();
var oExportOptions = FiddlerObject.createDictionary();
oExportOptions.Add("Filename", "C:\\users\\ericlaw\\desktop\\out1.har");
```

```
oExportOptions.Add("MaxTextBodyLength", 1024);
oExportOptions.Add("MaxBinaryBodyLength", 16384);

FiddlerApplication.DoExport("HTTPArchive v1.2", oSessions, oExportOptions, null);
```

As you can see in this example, the DoExport method on the FiddlerApplication object enables script or an extension to invoke a Transcoder by passing the FormatName. Similarly, the DoImport method permits invocation of a Transcoder to import Sessions.

The HTTPArchive Transcoder's code checks whether its caller has set any options like so:

```
public bool ExportSessions(string sFormat, Session[] oSessions,
  Dictionary<string, object> dictOptions,
  EventHandler<ProgressCallbackEventArgs> evtProgressNotifications)
{

  //...
  string sFilename = null;
  int iMaxTextBodyLength = DEFAULT_MAX_TEXT_BYTECOUNT;
  int iMaxBinaryBodyLength = DEFAULT_MAX_BINARY_BYTECOUNT;

  if (null != dictOptions)
  {
    if (dictOptions.ContainsKey("Filename"))
    {
      sFilename = dictOptions["Filename"] as string;
    }

    if (dictOptions.ContainsKey("MaxTextBodyLength"))
    {
      iMaxTextBodyLength = (int)dictOptions["MaxTextBodyLength"];
    }

    if (dictOptions.ContainsKey("MaxBinaryBodyLength"))
    {
      iMaxBinaryBodyLength = (int)dictOptions["MaxBinaryBodyLength"];
    }
  }

//...
```

Provide Progress Notifications

A caller may subscribe to progress notifications from your Transcoder by passing in an EventHandler delegate via evtProgressNotifications. As the import or export proceeds, your Transcoder should periodically supply ProgressCallbackEventArgs objects to report on the progress the operation.

```
public class ProgressCallbackEventArgs: EventArgs
{
  public ProgressCallbackEventArgs(float flCompletionRatio, string sProgressText)
  public string ProgressText { get; }
```

```
    public string PercentComplete { get; }
    public bool Cancel { get; set; }
  }
```

When creating the `EventArgs` object, set `flCompletionRatio` to the fraction of the operation that is complete (ranging from 0 to 1.0). If the completion ratio cannot be determined, simply set `flCompletionRatio` to 0 or a "guess" between 0 and 1.0. Set `sProgressText` to provide status text (for instance "Adding Session #1234" or "Compressing output."

After constructing the `EventArgs`, invoke the provided event handler if it is non-`null`.

If the handler sets the `Cancel` property to `true`, your Transcoder should gracefully abort the current operation as soon as possible, returning `null` or `false` to the caller.

Notes on Threading and Transcoders in FiddlerCore

Currently, methods of the `ISessionImporter` and `ISessionExporter` interfaces are called on the application's UI thread. This is almost certain to change in the future, so you should ensure that your classes are thread-safe and that they do not attempt to directly manipulate any UI.

Transcoders may be cross-compiled to work with FiddlerCore which has no UI and thus any attempt to manipulate the Fiddler UI will throw an exception. To cross-compile with FiddlerCore, create two variants of your project, one referencing `Fiddler.exe` and one referencing `FiddlerCore.dll`. For both hosts, it is also advisable to support the `Filename` key (with string value of a fully-qualified path) in the `dictOptions` parameter, and consider supporting a key named `Silent` (with a boolean value).

Beyond Files

While most Transcoder objects are designed to import or export *files* of various formats, there's no requirement that files are the source or destination of Transcoding. For instance, you can build a Transcoder whose `ISessionExporter` implementation stores the captured traffic to a remote database by calling a web service. Similarly, you could develop an `ISessionImporter` that reloads previously-stored traffic out of that database and adds it back to the Web Sessions list.

Example Transcoder

To build a simple Transcoder, follow these steps:

1. Start Visual Studio (version 2005 or later).

2. Create a new **Project** of type **Visual C# Class Library**.

3. Right-click the project's **References** folder in the **Solution Explorer**.

4. Choose the **Browse** tab and find `Fiddler.exe` in the %PROGRAMFILES%\Fiddler2\ folder. If you want to build a version of your Transcoder that works with FiddlerCore instead, reference `FiddlerCore.dll`.

5. Click **Ok** to add the reference.

6. In the Solution Explorer, right click the project. Choose **Properties**.

7. On the **Application** tab, ensure that the project's **Target Framework** is **.NET Framework 2.0**. Note that if you need to change this value, Visual Studio may prompt you to reload the project.

8. On the **Build** tab, ensure that the **Platform Target** is **Any CPU**.

9. On the **Build Events** tab, add the following as the **Post-build event** command line:

```
copy "$(TargetPath)"
    "%USERPROFILE%\Documents\Fiddler2\ImportExport\$(TargetFilename)"
```

This will ensure that every time you successfully build your project, your new assembly is copied to the proper location for Fiddler to load. You will, of course, need to close Fiddler between each build or the command to copy the assembly to the target folder will fail with a "File in use" error.

10. On the **Debug** tab, click **Start external program** and enter %PROGRAMFILES%\Fiddler2 \Fiddler.exe as the target program. When you hit F5 to test your Transcoder, Fiddler will launch.

11. Save the project.

Modify the default class1.cs (or create a new class) in your project as follows:

```
using System;
using System.IO;
using System.Text;
using System.Collections.Generic;
using System.Windows.Forms;
using Fiddler;

[assembly: AssemblyVersion("1.0.0.0")]
[assembly: Fiddler.RequiredVersion("2.5.0.0")]

// Note that this Transcoder only works when loaded by Fiddler itself; it will
// not work from a FiddlerCore-based application. The reason is that the output
// uses the columns shown in Fiddler's Web Sessions list, and FiddlerCore has
// no such list.

// Ensure your class is public, or Fiddler won't see it!
[ProfferFormat("Tab-Separated Values", "Session List in Tab-Delimited Format")]
[ProfferFormat("Comma-Separated Values",
    "Session List in Comma-Delimited Format; import into Excel or other tools")]
public class CSVTranscoder : ISessionExporter
{
  public bool ExportSessions(string sFormat, Session[] oSessions,
      Dictionary<string, object> dictOptions,
      EventHandler<ProgressCallbackEventArgs> evtProgressNotifications)
```

```
{
    bool bResult = false;
    string chSplit;

    // Determine if we already have a filename
    // from the dictOptions collection
    string sFilename = null;
    if (null != dictOptions && dictOptions.ContainsKey("Filename"))
    {
        sFilename = dictOptions["Filename"] as string;
    }

    // If we don't yet have a filename, prompt the user
    // with a File Save dialog, using the correct file extension
    // for the export format they selected
    if (sFormat == "Comma-Separated Values")
    {
        chSplit = ",";
        if (string.IsNullOrEmpty(sFilename))
            sFilename = Fiddler.Utilities.ObtainSaveFilename(
                "Export As " + sFormat, "CSV Files (*.csv)|*.csv");
    }
    else
    {
        // Ensure caller asked for Tab-delimiting.
        if (sFormat != "Tab-Separated Values") return false;
        chSplit = "\t";
        if (string.IsNullOrEmpty(sFilename))
            sFilename = Fiddler.Utilities.ObtainSaveFilename(
                "Export As " + sFormat, "TSV Files (*.tsv)|*.tsv");
    }

    // If we didn't get a filename, user cancelled. If so, bail out.
    if (String.IsNullOrEmpty(sFilename)) return false;

    try
    {
        StreamWriter swOutput = new StreamWriter(sFilename, false,
                                                 Encoding.UTF8);
        int iCount = 0;
        int iMax = oSessions.Length;

        // Write column headers
        bool bFirstCol = true;
        foreach (ColumnHeader oLVCol in FiddlerApplication.UI.lvSessions.Columns)
        {
            if (!bFirstCol)
            {
                swOutput.Write(chSplit);
            }
            else
            {
```

```csharp
            bFirstCol = false;
        }

        // Remove any delimiter characters from the value
        swOutput.Write(oLVCol.Text.Replace(chSplit, ""));
}

swOutput.WriteLine();

#region WriteEachSession
foreach (Session oS in oSessions)
{
    iCount++;

    // The ViewItem object is the ListViewItem in the Web Sessions list
    // Obviously, this doesn't exist in FiddlerCore-based applications
    if (null != oS.ViewItem)
    {
        bFirstCol = true;
        ListViewItem oLVI = (oS.ViewItem as ListViewItem);
        if (null == oLVI) continue;
        foreach (ListViewItem.ListViewSubItem oLVC in oLVI.SubItems)
        {
            if (!bFirstCol)
            {
                swOutput.Write(chSplit);
            }
            else
            {
                bFirstCol = false;
            }

            // Remove any delimiter characters from the value
            swOutput.Write(oLVC.Text.Replace(chSplit, ""));
        }

        swOutput.WriteLine();
    }

    // Notify the caller of our progress
    if (null != evtProgressNotifications)
    {
        ProgressCallbackEventArgs PCEA =
          new ProgressCallbackEventArgs((iCount / (float)iMax),
            "wrote " + iCount.ToString() + " records.");
        evtProgressNotifications(null, PCEA);

        // If the caller tells us to cancel, abort quickly
        if (PCEA.Cancel) { swOutput.Close(); return false; }
    }
}
#endregion WriteEachSession
```

```
            swOutput.Close();
            bResult = true;
        }
        catch (Exception eX)
        {
            // TODO: Replace alert with FiddlerApplication.Log.LogFormat(...
            MessageBox.Show(eX.Message, "Failed to export");
            bResult = false;
        }
        return bResult;
    }

    public void Dispose() { /*no-op*/ }
}
```

This simple example defines an ISessionExporter that offers two text formats: "Comma-separated values" and "Tab-separated values." When ExportSessions is called, the method examines the dictOptions provided and prompts the user for any missing information (like the target filename) required to complete the export. It then processes each Session in the oSessions array, reporting progress of the export back to Fiddler using the callback event handler provided.

FiddlerCore

OVERVIEW

As you've seen in prior chapters, you can extend Fiddler's functionality with both script and .NET code, and this is the best approach for building new functionality for most users. However, in some scenarios, like test automation, it would be more natural to add proxy functionality into an existing tool or test harness instead of using the entirety of Fiddler for the job.

Enter **FiddlerCore**. FiddlerCore is a class library that you can reference in your .NET applications to add Fiddler-like proxy functionality to .NET programs with none of the Fiddler user-interface. This diagram shows the difference between extending Fiddler with your code and extending your code with FiddlerCore:

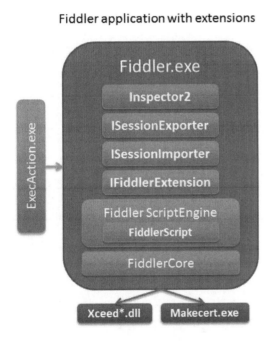

If you've previously built a Fiddler extension, you'll find that programming against FiddlerCore is an easy adjustment. Many FiddlerCore-based applications are first prototyped as a Fiddler extension before being moved into a standalone program. Building your code on Fiddler first allows you to easily see what is happening to web traffic using Fiddler's Inspectors. Once you're using FiddlerCore, you can only see the web traffic by adding logging functionality to your application (unless you chain your FiddlerCore application to an upstream or downstream Fiddler instance!).

Legalities and Licenses

Before adopting any library, you should always understand its license terms. FiddlerCore's license terms are included in its installer; Telerik offers both commercial and non-commercial licenses for the core proxy engine.

FiddlerCore's certificate generation code (used to intercept HTTPS traffic) requires Microsoft's `makecert.exe` on platforms prior to Windows 7. That utility is a licensed Visual Studio 2008 redistributable[3], so if you have a license to that tool you may redistribute `makecert` with your FiddlerCore-based applications. If you do not have the appropriate license, you should either speak to your lawyer or supply a different certificate generation library. If you do not need to decrypt HTTPS traffic, your program does not need to take a dependency on `makecert`.

One alternative to `makecert` is the "Bouncy Castle" library included with the default FiddlerCore installation package. You should consult that library's license terms if you wish to use it instead of Microsoft's `makecert` utility.

FiddlerCore may also use the ZIP library of your choice for saving and loading SAZ archive files. You can use the .NET Framework's built-in classes, the DotNetZip open-source library (recommended), or a commercial library like Xceed Compression. Again, you should consult the license terms of any library you choose to use in your application.

Get Started with FiddlerCore

You can download FiddlerCore from `http://www.telerik.com/fiddler/fiddlercore/`. The download package contains three copies of the library, one compiled for the v4 .NET Common Language Runtime, and two compiled for the v2 .NET CLR with either the v2 or v3.5 Framework. The package also contains source code for a demonstration program which exercises FiddlerCore's functionality, the `makecert.exe` utility, and a certificate-generating assembly based on the Bouncy Castle library. If you instead choose to install FiddlerCore using the NuGet package manager, only the core libraries are included.

You should also take the opportunity to download the separate documentation package, which will install the `FiddlerCore.chm` file. This file is an HTML Help file[4] that shows all of the classes, properties, methods, and fields available in FiddlerCore for your application to call.

After installing these packages, you'll have a new folder named `FiddlerCoreAPI` on your desktop.

Compile the Sample Application

Explore the `SampleApp` subfolder of the `FiddlerCoreAPI` folder, and open the `Demo.csproj` file to launch Visual Studio. The Demo project contains a Console Application which demonstrates FiddlerCore's basic

---

[3] See redist.txt in the Microsoft Visual Studio program files folder.
[4] Built using the very cool Sandcastle Help File Builder tool. `https://github.com/EWSoftware/SHFB`

functionality. Scroll to the `static void Main` function in `Program.cs` to see how FiddlerCore is configured and used.

The very first thing you'll need to do is attach the event listeners that handle events raised by FiddlerCore. A key concept to understand is that FiddlerCore calls most event handlers on the background threads in which Sessions are processed, so if you make any calls that modify shared objects (e.g. a list of Sessions) or update the application's UI, you must do so using thread-safe mechanisms. To update shared data-structures, use a `Mutex` or `lock`; to update WinForms-based UI, use the `BeginInvoke` method on the control being updated.

Supplying event handlers for FiddlerCore's `OnNotification` and `LogString` events allows you to see error messages and other information useful for troubleshooting problems in your application:

```
FiddlerApplication.OnNotification += delegate(object s,
  NotificationEventArgs oNEA)
{
  Console.WriteLine("** NotifyUser: " + oNEA.NotifyString);
};

FiddlerApplication.Log.OnLogString += delegate(object s, LogEventArgs oLEA)
{
  Console.WriteLine("** LogString: " + oLEA.LogString);
};
```

The next step is to attach handlers that fire as each Session is processed. It's common to attach handlers for the `BeforeRequest` and `BeforeResponse` events.

One of the most common behaviors of the `BeforeRequest` handler is to set the `bBufferResponse` property to `false` if you want responses to stream to the client, or to `true` if you want the `BeforeResponse` handler to be able to modify the response before the client gets it. If your application will keep a list of Sessions, you should add the new `Session` to your list in the `BeforeRequest` handler.

```
FiddlerApplication.BeforeRequest += delegate(Session oS)
{
  // Buffer response to allow response tampering
  oS.bBufferResponse = true;

  // Use a thread-safe mechanism to update my List<Session>
  Monitor.Enter(oAllSessions);
  oAllSessions.Add(oS);
  Monitor.Exit(oAllSessions);
};
```

A `BeforeResponse` handler enables you to modify a Session's response:

```
FiddlerApplication.BeforeResponse += delegate(Fiddler.Session oS)
{
```

```
      oS.utilDecodeResponse();
      // Note: This change only takes effect properly if
      // oS.bBufferResponse was set to true earlier!
      oS.utilReplaceInResponse("<title>", "<title>INJECTED!!");
   };
```

After your handlers are ready, your next step is to start the FiddlerCore proxy instance. First calculate the desired behavior flags:

```
   // The default flags are your best bet
   FiddlerCoreStartupFlags oFCSF = FiddlerCoreStartupFlags.Default;

   // ...but if, say, we don't want FiddlerCore to Decrypt
   // HTTPS traffic, we can unset that flag at this point
   oFCSF = (oFCSF & ~FiddlerCoreStartupFlags.DecryptSSL);
```

Then call the `Startup` method, passing in the desired port and your flags:

```
   // Start listening on port 8877
   FiddlerApplication.Startup(8877, oFCSF);
```

If you don't care which port FiddlerCore listens on, avoiding errors if that port is already in use, pass 0 for the port and FiddlerCore will automatically select an available port. The port chosen can be retrieved using the property `FiddlerApplication.oProxy.ListenPort`.

When using the default flags, the `Startup` method will immediately register the new proxy as the system's default proxy. Any `BeforeRequest` and `BeforeResponse` event handlers will begin to fire as traffic is captured.

After you're done with FiddlerCore, you should call the `Shutdown` method to unregister as the system proxy and close the listening proxy port:

```
   FiddlerApplication.Shutdown();
```

Note that the `Shutdown` method cannot gracefully terminate any in-progress Web Sessions. Those Sessions' background threads will continue to run (potentially calling into your handlers) but will likely eventually be aborted by either an `ObjectDisposedException` or `NullReferenceException` when they attempt to access the now-null `FiddlerApplication.oProxy` object. If you'd prefer, you might instead call:

```
   FiddlerApplication.oProxy.Detach();
```

…to unregister as the system proxy. Wait a few seconds to permit in-progress Sessions to complete before calling the `Shutdown` method.

FiddlerCoreStartupFlags

The `FiddlerCoreStartupFlags` enumeration allows you to specify the behavior of the FiddlerCore proxy endpoint. The enumeration exposes the following flags:

`None`	No options are set.
`RegisterAsSystemProxy`	Register as the system proxy when `Startup()` is called.
`DecryptSSL`	Decrypt HTTPS traffic that flows through the proxy.
`AllowRemoteClients`	Permit connections from remote PCs or devices. You may need to enable a firewall exception for your application to receive remote traffic.
`ChainToUpstreamGateway`	Automatically adopt the system's existing proxy settings as an upstream gateway proxy.
`MonitorAllConnections`	Register as the default proxy for all WinINET connections, including dialup and VPN connections. When not set, only the LAN connection is set to point at the FiddlerCore proxy instance.
`HookUsingPACFile`	When registering as the default proxy, use `http://FiddlerCoreIP:port/proxy.pac` as the proxy configuration script URL.
`CaptureLocalhostTraffic`	Add `<-loopback>` to the system's proxy exceptions list, enabling IE9+ to send loopback traffic to FiddlerCore.
`CaptureFTP`	Register as the system proxy for FTP traffic.
`OptimizeThreadPool`	Improve FiddlerCore's throughput by internally calling the `ThreadPool.SetMinThreads` method.
`Default`	This flag encompasses the following flags: `RegisterAsSystemProxy` | `DecryptSSL` | `AllowRemoteClients` | `ChainToUpstreamGateway` | `MonitorAllConnections` | `CaptureLocalhostTraffic` | `OptimizeThreadPool`

Using `FiddlerCoreStartupFlags.Default` is the recommended approach as it sets the options desired by most applications. Even if you don't want all of the flags in the default set, your best bet is to start with `Default` and use bit-manipulation to mask off unwanted options:

```
FiddlerCoreStartupFlags oFlags =
    (FiddlerCoreStartupFlags.Default & ~FiddlerCoreStartupFlags.DecryptSSL);
```

This approach has the benefit that your application will automatically be opted-in (upon recompile) to new default options as they are added to improved versions of FiddlerCore.

THE FIDDLERAPPLICATION CLASS

The static `FiddlerApplication` class provides many useful event handlers, static methods, and properties that control FiddlerCore's behavior. Most of these APIs are also available for use by extensions running inside Fiddler itself.

FiddlerApplication Events

`FiddlerApplication` raises events from the FiddlerCore engine and each Session as it is processed. Most of these events fire on background threads so you must take care to ensure that your handlers are thread-safe. Use `BeginInvoke` or `Invoke` to update any user-interface elements on the UI thread.

OnReadRequestBuffer Event

This event fires on every read of the client's request stream. It is generally not handled because the event provides only a raw buffer of bytes which hasn't yet been parsed into headers and body.

The event can be useful when low-level logging (of say, packet-level timing information) is desired.

```
FiddlerApplication.OnReadRequestBuffer += new
  EventHandler<RawReadEventArgs>(OnRequestRead);

static void OnRequestRead(object sender, RawReadEventArgs e)
{
  Console.WriteLine(String.Format("Read {0} request bytes for Session {1}",
    e.iCountOfBytes, e.sessionOwner.id));
}
```

RequestHeadersAvailable Event

This event fires after FiddlerCore has read the complete set of request headers from the client; only the headers are available and attempts to examine the `requestBodyBytes` will result in a Null Reference Exception. Your event handler might decide (based on the request URL) that the Session is not of interest and call the `Ignore()` method on the Session to suppress further updates on its processing.

BeforeRequest Event

This event fires after the request has been completely read from the client, before the server is contacted. This provides the opportunity to modify the client's request or generate a local response without contacting the server.

OnValidateServerCertificate Event

This event fires as FiddlerCore evaluates a HTTPS server's certificate. Your event handler may accept or reject the server's certificate based on the criteria of your choosing. For instance, you could require that the certificate chain be deemed valid by .NET and further require that the chain be validated by a Certificate Notary Service:

```
FiddlerApplication.OnValidateServerCertificate += new
  System.EventHandler<ValidateServerCertificateEventArgs>(CheckCert);

void CheckCert(object sender, ValidateServerCertificateEventArgs e)
{
  // If there's an obvious issue with the presented certificate,
  // it will be rejected unless overridden here.
  if (SslPolicyErrors.None != e.CertificatePolicyErrors)
  {
    return;     // Certificate will be rejected
  }

  // Check if the Convergence Certificate Notary services have
  // an opinion about this certificate chain.
  bool bNotariesAffirm = GetNotaryConsensus(e.Session,
    e.ServerCertificate, e.ServerCertificateChain);

  FiddlerApplication.Log.LogFormat("Notaries have indicated that the "
    + "certificate presented for {0} is {1}", e.ExpectedCN,
    bNotariesAffirm ? "VALID" : "INVALID");

  if (!bNotariesAffirm)
  {
    e.ValidityState = CertificateValidity.ForceInvalid;
    return;
  }

  e.ValidityState = CertificateValidity.ForceValid;
}
```

OnReadResponseBuffer Event

This event fires on every read of the server's response stream. It is generally not handled because the event provides only a raw buffer of bytes which hasn't yet been parsed into headers and body.

The event can be useful when low-level logging (of say, timing information) is desired.

```
FiddlerApplication.OnReadResponseBuffer += new
  EventHandler<RawReadEventArgs>(OnRead);

static void OnRead(object sender, RawReadEventArgs e) {
  Console.WriteLine(String.Format("Read {0} response bytes for Session {1}",
    e.iCountOfBytes, e.sessionOwner.id));

  // NOTE: arrDataBuffer is a fixed-size array. Only bytes 0 to
  // iCountOfBytes should be read/manipulated.

  // Just for kicks, lowercase every ASCII char. Note that this will
  // obviously mangle any binary MIME files and break many types of markup
  for (int i = 0; i < e.iCountOfBytes; i++) {
    if ((e.arrDataBuffer[i] > 0x40) && (e.arrDataBuffer[i] < 0x5b))
    {
```

```
        e.arrDataBuffer[i] = (byte)(e.arrDataBuffer[i] + (byte)0x20);
      }
    }
  }
```

ResponseHeadersAvailable Event

This event fires when FiddlerCore has read the complete set of response headers from the server. It provides the opportunity to set the Session's bBufferResponse property based on the contents of the headers:

```
FiddlerApplication.ResponseHeadersAvailable += delegate(Session oS)
{
  // Disable streaming for HTML responses on a target server so that
  // we can modify those responses in the BeforeResponse handler
  if (oS.HostnameIs("example.com") && oS.oResponse.MIMEType.Contains("text/html"))
  {
    oS.bBufferResponse = true;
  }

  // Or, enable streaming for responses that need to stream
  string sContentType = oS.oResponse.headers["Content-Type"];
  if (sContentType.OICStartsWithAny("text/event-stream",
          "multipart/x-mixed-replace", "video/", "audio/",
          "application/x-mms-framed"))
  {
      oS.bBufferResponse = false;
  }
};
```

When this event fires, the response body is not yet available from the server. Attempting to modify the responseBodyBytes or modify headers that influence the download of the body (Content-Length, Transfer-Encoding, and Connection) inside this event will almost certainly cause an error.

BeforeResponse Event

This event fires after the response has been completely read from the server. If you plan to modify the server's response in your handler for this event, you must first disable streaming of the response by setting oSession.bBufferResponse to true in the ResponseHeadersAvailable or BeforeRequest events.

If the Session's bBufferResponse property is false, as it is by default in FiddlerCore, the response will stream to the client as it is read from the server, *before* your BeforeResponse event handler has the chance to modify it. On streaming responses, the BeforeResponse event handler (non-intuitively but necessarily) fires *after* the response is sent to the client.

BeforeReturningError Event

This event fires when FiddlerCore generates an error (e.g. a DNS lookup failure notice) to return to the client. The event provides the opportunity to customize the error message that will be returned to the client.

```
FiddlerApplication.BeforeReturningError += delegate(Session oS)
```

```
{
    string sErrMsg = oS.GetResponseBodyAsString();

    oS.utilSetResponseBody("<!doctype html><title>AcmeCorp Error Page</title>"
        + "<body>Sorry, this page or service is presently unavailable. Please try"
        + " again later. <br /><pre>" + sErrMsg + "</pre></html>");
};
```

Your event handler might also take other actions, like logging the error to a database.

AfterSessionComplete Event

This event fires when the processing of a Session is complete. It provides the opportunity to perform any necessary logging of the final state of the Session.

OnWebSocketMessage

This event fires when a request or response message is received on a WebSocket connection. It provides the opportunity to modify the contents of the message or prevent it from being transmitted.

FiddlerAttach Event

This event fires when FiddlerCore has registered as the system's default proxy.

FiddlerDetach Event

This event fires when FiddlerCore has unregistered as the system's default proxy.

OnClearCache Event

This event fires when the `Fiddler.WinINETCache.ClearCacheItems` method is called; properties of the EventArgs object indicate what elements of the cache should be cleared. The event allows your application to provide its own handling (e.g. clearing an auxiliary cache) instead of or in addition to the default handling, in which FiddlerCore deletes the requested items from the WinINET cache.

OnNotification Event

This event fires when FiddlerCore logs a notification event. Since FiddlerCore runs in silent mode by default, most notifications of errors or configuration problems are raised using this event.

Developers often contact me to complain that *"FiddlerCore isn't working properly."* After attaching a handler for this event, the source of the problem is often obvious.

FiddlerApplication Methods

Startup()

This method is used to configure the default FiddlerCore proxy listener and instruct it to begin capturing requests. Various overloaded versions of this method are available—I strongly recommend that you use the overload that accepts `FiddlerCoreStartupFlags` and recommend that you specify `FiddlerCoreStartupFlags.Default`.

Shutdown()

This method detaches the default FiddlerCore listener (if attached) and disposes it.

IsStarted()

This method returns true if the default FiddlerCore listening endpoint has been created, otherwise it returns false.

IsSystemProxy()

This method returns true if FiddlerCore is running and attached as the system proxy, otherwise it returns false.

CreateProxyEndpoint()

This method allows you to create additional FiddlerCore proxy endpoints that can accept requests from clients. When calling this method, supply a port number and a boolean indicating whether remote connections should be permitted.

You may also supply either a string containing a hostname or an X509Certificate2. If either is supplied, the endpoint will automatically perform a HTTPS handshake with the client on each connection, presenting either the provided certificate or an automatically generated certificate containing the specified hostname. Use this overload when running FiddlerCore as a reverse proxy for a HTTPS site.

```
Proxy oSecureEP = FiddlerApplication.CreateProxyEndpoint(8777, true, "localhost");
if (null != oSecureEP)
{
  FiddlerApplication.Log.LogString("Created secure endpoint listening "
    + "on port 8777, which will send a HTTPS certificate for 'localhost'");
}
```

If you do not supply a hostname or certificate, the endpoint will act as a normal proxy endpoint and will not masquerade as a HTTPS server.

Sessions accepted by the endpoints created using this method will be processed using the normal Session-processing pipeline. Your Session-processing event handlers can determine which endpoint a given request was received upon by examining its LocalPort property:

```
FiddlerApplication.Log.LogFormat("Session {0} received by EndPoint on Port #{1}",
  oSession.id,
  (null != oSession.oRequest.pipeClient) ?
     "n/a" : oSession.oRequest.pipeClient.LocalPort
);
```

DoImport()

This method enables import of Sessions using the Importer architecture. When calling this method, supply an Import Format name, a StringDictionary containing options, and a progress event callback to receive updates on the progress of the import.

DoExport()

This method enables export of Sessions using the Exporter architecture. When calling this method, supply an Export Format name, the array of Sessions, a `StringDictionary` containing options, and a progress event callback to receive updates on the progress of the export.

GetVersionString()

This method returns a string describing the FiddlerCore version. For instance:

```
FiddlerCore/4.5.0.0 (+SAZ)
```

GetDetailedInfo()

This method returns a string describing the FiddlerCore version and the configuration of the default listening endpoint. This method is used by logging or for display in an application's About box.

ResetSessionCounter()

This method resets the Session ID counter to 0. Use this method sparingly, because duplicate Session IDs can be very confusing.

FiddlerApplication Properties and Fields

isClosing

This boolean is set to `true` when the application is shutting down. When set to `true`, FiddlerCore will attempt to avoid unnecessary processing of Sessions and will suppress errors as gracefully as possible.

Log

This object provides access to Fiddler's logging system. The `LogString` and `LogFormat` methods allow your code to record new messages. The `OnLogString` event permits your application to detect when messages are logged. See the **Logging** section on page 251 for more information.

oDefaultClientCertificate

When set, FiddlerCore will use the supplied `X509Certificate` when performing client authentication to a HTTPS server.

oProxy

This object represents Fiddler's default listening proxy endpoint. Its `SendRequest` methods allow your application to generate and inject new requests into the processing pipeline.

oTranscoders

This object represents Fiddler's Import/Export subsystem. Your application may register Transcoder assemblies using the `ImportTranscoders` method on this object. Invoke Import or Export operations using the `DoImport` and `DoExport` methods of the `FiddlerApplication` object.

Prefs

This object provides access to Fiddler's Preferences system. See **Programming with Preferences** on page 253 for more information.

The Rest of the Fiddler API

With the exception of a few FiddlerCore-specific APIs, Fiddler and FiddlerCore share a common object model. Code developed as a Fiddler extension can often be ported to run in a FiddlerCore-based application simply by eliminating any dependencies upon Fiddler user-interface objects.

COMMON TASKS WITH FIDDLERCORE

Keep Track of Sessions

Unlike Fiddler, FiddlerCore does not keep a Session list automatically. If you want a Session list, simply create a `List<Fiddler.Session>` and add new Sessions to it as they are captured. The multi-threaded nature of FiddlerCore means that you must `Invoke` to a single thread, use thread-safe data structures, or use a `Monitor` or other synchronization mechanism (as shown below) to update or enumerate a list of Sessions safely.

```
// Inside your main object, create a list to hold the Sessions
// The generic list type requires you are #using System.Collections.Generic
List<Fiddler.Session> oAllSessions = new List<Fiddler.Session>();

// Add Sessions to the list as they are captured
Fiddler.FiddlerApplication.BeforeRequest += delegate(Fiddler.Session oS)
{
  Monitor.Enter(oAllSessions);
  oAllSessions.Add(oS);
  Monitor.Exit(oAllSessions);
};
```

Keep in mind that `oAllSessions` can quickly balloon out the memory use within your application because Sessions cannot be garbage-collected while they are referenced in the list. You should periodically trim the list to keep it of a reasonable size. Alternatively, if you only care about request URLs or headers, you could keep a `List<>` of those types rather than storing references to `Session` objects.

Get Traffic to FiddlerCore

Like Fiddler itself, FiddlerCore runs as a local proxy instance, and it only sees traffic that is sent to it. If the `RegisterAsSystemProxy` flag is set when you call the `FiddlerApplication.Startup` method, FiddlerCore will automatically register as the system proxy, just like Fiddler does. If you do not configure FiddlerCore as the system proxy, you can manually configure most applications to point at your FiddlerCore instance. FiddlerCore offers the unique ability to register as the WinINET proxy for just the process in which it is running. This is a useful capability for scenarios where you have a Web Browser control in your .NET application and want to use FiddlerCore to only capture or modify the traffic from that Web Browser control (and any other WinINET APIs).

To make use of this capability, call the `SetProxyInProcess` method with your listening endpoint's address and port, and a proxy-bypass list:

```
Fiddler.URLMonInterop.SetProxyInProcess("127.0.0.1:7777", "<-loopback>");
```

When capture is complete, you may reset the current process back to the default system proxy:

```
Fiddler.URLMonInterop.ResetProxyInProcessToDefault();
```

Trust the FiddlerCore Certificate

If your FiddlerCore application needs to decrypt HTTPS traffic, you can have your application automatically generate a root certificate and prompt the user to trust it:

```
private bool CreateAndTrustRoot() {
  // Ensure root exists
  if (!Fiddler.CertMaker.rootCertExists())
  {
    bCreatedRootCertificate = Fiddler.CertMaker.createRootCert();
    if (!bCreatedRootCertificate) return false;
  }

  // Ensure root is trusted
  if (!Fiddler.CertMaker.rootCertIsTrusted()) {
    bTrustedRootCert = Fiddler.CertMaker.trustRootCert();
    if (!bTrustedRootCert) return false;
  }

  return true;
}
```

Note that trustRootCert only affects the Windows Certificate Store and has no impact on Firefox's certificate store or those used when Fiddler is running on the Mono Framework on Mac or Linux.

If you prefer to trust the FiddlerCore root certificate on a machine-wide basis instead, call createRootCert and then call GetRootCertificate to retrieve the new root certificate. Then call the following method:

```
private static bool setMachineTrust(X509Certificate2 oRootCert) {
  try
  {
    X509Store certStore = new X509Store(StoreName.Root,
                                        StoreLocation.LocalMachine);
    certStore.Open(OpenFlags.ReadWrite);
    try
    {
      certStore.Add(oRootCert);
    }
    finally
    {
      certStore.Close();
    }
    return true;
  }
  catch (Exception eX) {
    return false;
  }
}
```

Note that your application must be running with Admin-level privileges to add certificates to the machine-wide root certificate store.

Generate Responses

Fiddler's AutoResponder tab allows users to replay a previously captured Session. Hosters of FiddlerCore can reproduce the behavior of this feature in their applications. The following snippet identifies requests for replaceme.txt and returns a previously captured response stored in a Session object named SessionIWantToReturn.

```
Fiddler.FiddlerApplication.BeforeRequest += delegate(Fiddler.Session oS)
{
  if (oS.uriContains("replaceme.txt"))
  {
    oS.utilCreateResponseAndBypassServer();
    oS.responseBodyBytes = Utilities.Dupe(SessionIWantToReturn.responseBodyBytes);
    oS.oResponse.headers =
      (HTTPResponseHeaders) SessionIWantToReturn.oResponse.headers.Clone();
  }
};
```

Other Resources

See http://fiddler.wikidot.com/fiddlercore for more information on building FiddlerCore-based applications.

Appendices

APPENDIX A: TROUBLESHOOTING

Throughout its existence, Fiddler has been painstakingly refined to address most of the common problems users have encountered. However, there are some circumstances in which manual troubleshooting steps may be required.

Missing Traffic

The single most common complaint I hear from users is: *"Fiddler used to work but now it doesn't show anything. Please help!"*

In virtually all cases, the problem is that a filter is set that is causing the traffic to be hidden. Sometimes, the filter was set inadvertently, and sometimes the user merely set it a while ago and forgot about it.

Fortunately, it's easy to troubleshoot filters—just click the **Troubleshoot...** option on the **Help** menu. When Filter Troubleshooting is enabled, the Web Sessions list will include all Sessions that would ordinarily be hidden, rendering each filtered Session using the strikethrough font. The Comments column for each filtered Session shows which filter was responsible for hiding the traffic, allowing you to adjust your filters as needed. For instance, the following Sessions were hidden because they were sent by a web browser process, and the status bar's Process Filter is set to show only **Non-Browser** traffic:

If you don't see the missing Sessions even after enabling Filter Troubleshooting, your next step is to try to visit http://ipv4.fiddler:8888/ in the client application. If your client's traffic is being proxied by Fiddler, you will see an entry in the Web Sessions list and the browser will show an "echo" page:

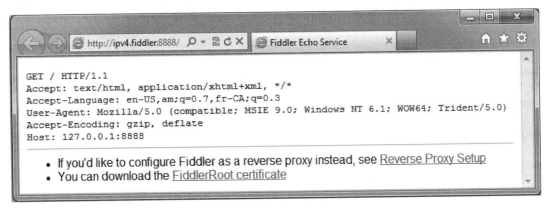

If you don't see this page, that suggests that the client application isn't correctly configured to have its traffic proxied. Ensure that you are not connected to the target network using Microsoft DirectAccess—that technology will bypass the local Fiddler proxy server.

Your next step should be to try the URL http://localhost:8888/, assuming the client and Fiddler are running on the same computer. If that URL cannot be reached, it means that your client application is unable to contact Fiddler, either because Fiddler is not properly running, or there is a firewall or other problem preventing Fiddler from receiving the traffic. You should check your firewall configuration, and see if you get different results from other clients or when running on a different computer.

Interference from Security Software

In rare instances, security software like firewalls, anti-malware, and antivirus programs can interfere with the proper download, installation, and running of Fiddler.

Problems Downloading Fiddler

Some enterprise firewalls or security gateways will block your ability to download software from the Fiddler websites (e.g. `getfiddler.com` and `fiddler2.com`); instead of a successful download, you'll instead see a blocking error page. Overzealous security suites may consider network debugging software like Fiddler a "hacking tool" and thus not something needed by common users. In most cases, there's little an end-user can do to get around the block, short of protesting to their IT administrator or downloading Fiddler to a USB memory stick using an unmanaged network connection.

Problems Installing Fiddler

Some security programs running locally attempt to protect the system from setup programs; these products often change the access control lists on registry keys and filesystem locations which prevent successful install of Fiddler. In such cases, you will usually see a message from the Fiddler installer complaining "A system administrator must install this tool" despite the fact that you are, in fact, an administrator. To address this problem, you can either temporarily disable the security software, or perform an XCOPY install of Fiddler, described on page 12.

Problems Running Fiddler

After Fiddler has been successfully installed, security software may still interfere with it.

Some security packages attempt to filter web-traffic using their own locally-running proxy server; for instance, some products from AVG and McAfee do this. The problem with such proxies is that they can overwrite the proxy settings that allow Fiddler to capture your traffic. Even if they properly chain to Fiddler, all traffic will be coming from that proxy process (e.g. `avp.exe` or `tmproxy.exe`) rather than the original client process, breaking Fiddler's Process Filters (e.g. nothing will show if Fiddler is configured to show only **Web Browser** traffic). You may be able to live with this limitation, or you may choose to disable the web filtering component of your security software.

Other packages impose firewall restrictions that prevent traffic from being sent to Fiddler or that prevent traffic from Fiddler from being sent to the Internet. By default, Fiddler's installer attempts to register an exception with the Windows Firewall, but this exception will not be respected by other firewalls. If you encounter this problem, you will either not see any requests in Fiddler (because the traffic didn't make it to Fiddler) or you will see all requests fail with HTTP/502 errors, the body of which will read:

```
[Fiddler] The socket connection to example.com failed. <br /> An attempt was
made to access a socket in a way forbidden by its access permissions.
```

You can typically use your firewall's configuration interface to add an exception for Fiddler.exe or its port 8888.

Lastly, you may find that security software prevents Fiddler from successfully registering as the system proxy server. When you click **Tools** > **WinINET Options** > **LAN Settings** while Fiddler is running, you should see the proxy settings set to 127.0.0.1:8888. If you don't see Fiddler properly listed, it's possible that your security software is blocking access to the proxy-configuration registry keys. To resolve this, you may be able to turn off a "registry protection" option in your software, or might possibly resolve the issue by running Fiddler as an Administrator.

Corrupted Proxy Settings

If Fiddler crashes or is terminated without shutting down properly, your system's proxy settings will likely remain pointed at Fiddler. If you subsequently start your browser or use other applications that respect the proxy settings, you will likely see connection errors.

To resolve this problem, simply restart Fiddler. On startup, Fiddler will detect that the system proxy settings were already pointed at Fiddler and note that fact. Later, when Fiddler is gracefully shut down, the proxy settings will be restored to the Windows default ("Automatically detect proxy") settings.

Alternatively, rather than restarting Fiddler, you can manually adjust your proxy settings by opening the Internet Options Control Panel from your system Control Panel or by clicking **Tools** > **Internet Options** in Internet Explorer. Click the **Connections** tab, then click the **LAN Settings** button at the bottom. Ensure that when Fiddler is not running, the proxy settings are not configured to point to 127.0.0.1:8888. If they are, adjust the proxy settings to point to your network's proxy, or clear all of the checkboxes if your network does not require a proxy.

If you have connection problems in Firefox when Fiddler isn't running, check Firefox's **Tools** > **Options** > **Advanced** > **Network** > **Connection Settings** screen to ensure that the settings are correct for your network.

Resetting Fiddler

In order to prevent data loss, reinstalling or uninstalling Fiddler will not remove its settings from the registry and filesystem. This means that you cannot resolve simple problems (for instance, a "missing column" or similar issue) by reinstalling Fiddler.

If you wish to reset Fiddler's UI configuration, hold the SHIFT key while starting Fiddler, and click Yes in the following prompt:

When started with the default settings, Fiddler will restore all UI elements to their default states and sizes, unhide any hidden tabs or columns, and reset other state as appropriate. It will not, however, uninstall any plugins or reset your FiddlerScript.

To reset your FiddlerScript, simply delete or rename the file %USERPROFILE%\Documents\Fiddler2 \CustomRules.js, if it is present. The next time Fiddler is started, the default SampleRules.js file will be loaded.

Troubleshoot Certificate Problems

In rare cases, you may find that Fiddler is unable to generate HTTPS interception certificates using the MakeCert.exe utility. This problem is accompanied by an error message similar to the following:

```
-------------------------------------------
Creation of the interception certificate failed.
makecert.exe returned -1.
Error: Can't create the key of the subject ('JoeSoft')
Failed
-------------------------------------------
```

This problem might be resolved by resetting Fiddler's certificates. Click **Tools** > **Fiddler Options** > HTTPS. Untick the **Decrypt HTTPS Traffic** checkbox, then click the **Remove Interception Certificates** button to clear any Fiddler interception certificates from the Windows certificate store. Then, tick the **Decrypt HTTPS Traffic** checkbox again.

Warning: As the following instructions involve editing sensitive areas of your system, they should only be undertaken by experts.

If resetting certificates isn't successful, you may be able to fix broken MakeCert.exe functionality by using the SysInternals Process Monitor utility to find MakeCert.exe file accesses within the folder path %USERPROFILE%\Application Data\Microsoft\Crypto\RSA\<keyname>\<filename> when Fiddler fails to generate a certificate. Moving the accessed files may restore the certificate store's functionality.

If problems persist, you may be able to avoid the problem by switching to the **Certificate Maker** plugin described on page 126. This plugin does not utilize the Windows Certificate APIs for certificate generation, and thus may resolve the problem.

Wipe all traces of Fiddler

Warning: As these instructions involve editing sensitive areas of your system, they should only be undertaken by experts.

To fully clear all remnants of Fiddler from your system:

1. Uninstall Fiddler using the **Add/Remove Programs** applet in the system control panel.
   a. When prompted to delete Fiddler-related settings, choose **Yes**.
2. Uninstall any Fiddler plugins listed in the **Add/Remove Programs** list.
3. Delete the folders:
   - `%PROGRAMFILES%\Fiddler2`
   - `%USERPROFILE%\Documents\Fiddler2`
4. Use `RegEdit.exe` to remove the registry keys:
   - `HKLM\Software\Microsoft\Fiddler2`
   - `HKCU\Software\Microsoft\Fiddler2`
5. Use the Windows Certificate Manager (`CertMgr.msc`) to remove all of Fiddler's certificates from your Personal and Trusted Root Certification Authorities storage areas.
6. If you configured Firefox or Opera to trust Fiddler certificates, use the control panels in those products to remove the Fiddler certificates.
7. Inside IE's **Tools** > **Internet Options** > **Connections** > **LAN Settings**, ensure that none of the settings point to Fiddler.

Fiddler complains about the "Configuration System"

The following error message indicates that one of the .NET Framework's configuration files is corrupt:

```
--------------------------
Awww, Fiddlesticks!
--------------------------
Your Microsoft .NET Configuration file is corrupt and contains invalid data.
You can often correct this error by installing updates from WindowsUpdate and/or
reinstalling the .NET Framework.

Configuration system failed to initialize
Source: System.Configuration
at System.Configuration.ConfigurationManager.PrepareConfigSystem()
at System.Configuration.ConfigurationManager.GetSection(String sectionName)

System.Configuration.ConfigurationErrorsException: Unrecognized configuration
section system.serviceModel.
c:\WINDOWS\Microsoft.NET\Framework\v2.0.50727\Config\machine.config
```

The most common fix for this is to visit WindowsUpdate and install all available .NET Framework updates. If that doesn't work, try re-installing the .NET Framework. If that doesn't work, try editing the XML file (e.g. `machine.config`) specified by the error message to correct whatever the message is complaining about.

Fiddler randomly stops capturing traffic

The Microsoft Firewall client for ISA / Forefront TMG has an option to automatically reconfigure Internet Explorer settings. Unfortunately, this setting will cause Internet Explorer to detach from Fiddler at random times. When this occurs, a notification bar will appear to notify you that the system proxy was changed:

To prevent this problem, disable **browser automatic configuration** in the Microsoft Firewall client applet.

If there's a Firewall Client icon in your system tray, right click it and choose **Configure...** from the popup menu. If you don't see the icon, type `forefront` in the Start Menu search box to find the applet. On the Web Browser tab, uncheck the **Enable Web browser automatic configuration** checkbox.

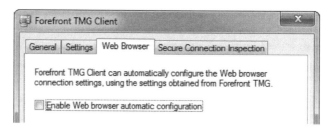

Other VPN and firewall software may have similar behavior. For instance, the Cisco AnyConnect client adjusts the system's proxy settings when connecting and disconnecting from the VPN.

Fiddler may stall when streaming RPC-over-HTTPS traffic

The HTTP and HTTPS protocols are extremely popular data transports; even scenarios that would otherwise use a simple TCP/IP connection often use HTTP or HTTPS because these protocols are usually allowed to traverse firewalls. Fiddler *may* encounter problems if other traffic is masquerading as HTTP.

For instance, one scenario where you could encounter problems is when using Microsoft Outlook with an Exchange Server configured to deliver mail using the RPC-over-HTTPS feature. You will see a request in Fiddler like so:

```
RPC_OUT_DATA /rpc/rpcproxy.dll?ex.example.com HTTP/1.1
Host: ex.example.com
```

```
Content-Type: application/rpc
Content-Length: 1073741824
```

Outlook is attempting to use the HTTPS protocol to establish a bytestream over which a bidirectional TCP/IP stream will be layered. The problem is that the client isn't *really* planning to send a one gigabyte request body—it's instead just sending a huge value to indicate that it *might* send a lot of data. Fiddler dutifully waits for the client to send the promised gigabyte of data before proceeding with the network request. Since the data is not forthcoming from the client, no connection is made, and Outlook will indicate that it's "*Trying to connect…*" forever.

Enabling the **Stream** option in Fiddler's toolbar enables *responses* to stream to the client, but in most cases Fiddler will not automatically stream *requests* to the server. Fiddler includes code to detect RPC-over-HTTPS traffic and treat it specially; this code should permit the Outlook to Exchange scenario to succeed, but it only recognizes the RPC methods and may not recognize the schemes used by other products.

To enable features that masquerade as HTTP traffic to work correctly while Fiddler is running, you can:

1. Configure the target hostname to bypass Fiddler entirely: Add `exchange.example.com` to the **Bypass Fiddler** box on the **Tools** > **Fiddler Options** > **Connections** tab, or

2. Configure Fiddler to skip decrypting connections to the target host: Add `exchange.example.com` to the **Skip Decryption** box on the **Tools** > **Fiddler Options** > **HTTPS** tab, or

3. Configure Fiddler to skip decrypting of traffic from the client application: Use the dropdown box on the **Tools** > **Fiddler Options** > **HTTPS** tab to enable decryption **for browsers only**.

APPENDIX B: COMMAND LINE SYNTAX

`Fiddler.exe` accepts zero or more command-line arguments, consisting of zero or more option flags and a single filename of a file to load on startup.

```
fiddler.exe [options] [FileToLoad]
```

The `FileToLoad` argument may either be a SAZ file or a file of an importable type (e.g. `.pcap` or `.har`).

Fiddler registers itself in Windows' `AppPaths` key so that you can launch it by typing `fiddler` in the shell's Start > Run prompt (hit `Windows+R`) instead of specifying a fully-qualified path to `fiddler.exe`.

Option Flags

Option flags may be preceded by either a / or - character.

Flag	Description
`-?`	Show the list of available command line arguments.
`-viewer`	Open a Fiddler's Viewer Mode instance.
`-quiet`	Launch in "quiet" mode, where prompts and alerts are suppressed, and the main window is minimized to the system tray. This mode is most often used when Fiddler is running as a part of an automated script.
`-noattach`	Do not register as the system proxy on startup, even if otherwise configured to do so. You can manually register Fiddler as the proxy for an individual application or set it as the system proxy using the option on the File menu.
`-noversioncheck`	Do not send a web service request to check for updates on startup.
`-extoff`	Do not load Fiddler Inspectors or Extensions. This flag is used to troubleshoot problems related to buggy extensions.
`-noscript`	Do not load FiddlerScript. This flag is used to determine whether your Fiddler-Script is causing some problem.
`-port:####`	Specify the port that Fiddler should listen on, overriding the default setting configured in the Fiddler Options window.

Examples

Launch Fiddler without attaching:

```
"C:\program files (x86)\Fiddler2\fiddler.exe" -noattach
```

Launch Fiddler with no UI, running on port 1234:

```
fiddler -port:1234 -quiet
```

Open a SAZ file in a new Fiddler Viewer instance:

```
fiddler -viewer "C:\users\joe\desktop\Sample.saz"
```

APPENDIX C: SESSION FLAGS

A `StringDictionary` field in each Session object contains flags that control the processing or display of the Session.

Some flags are set by Fiddler itself, but most are set script or extensions. The list of supported flags grows with each update to Fiddler, and extensions may use their own flags (which have no meaning to Fiddler) to add state information to a given Session.

The flags can be accessed by `oSession.oFlags["flagname"]` or by using the default indexer on the Session object: `oSession["flagname"]`. If the named flag does not exist, it will return `null`.

Flag names are case-insensitive strings, and most flag values are interpreted case-insensitively. Most of Fiddler's flags are simply checked for their *existence*, such that setting *any* value (even misleading strings like `0`, `false`, and `heck no!`) enables the named behavior. To disable a flag, remove the flag from the Session like so:

```
oSession.oFlags.Remove("flagname");
```

Because most flags are simply tested for existence, a best practice is to use the flag's value to store a terse explanation of *why* the flag was set. For instance:

```
oSession["ui-hide"] = "Rules>Hide Images";
```

You can view a Session's flags by using the Properties item on the Web Sessions list's context menu.

Session Display Flags

The following flags control how a session appears within the Web Sessions list.

Flag Name	`ui-hide`
Explanation	The Session will not appear within the Web Sessions list. One of the most commonly used flags, `ui-hide` is used by script or extensions to avoid cluttering the Web Sessions list with uninteresting traffic.
Supported Values	Any value will hide the Session. Typically, you should provide a terse explanation of *why* the Session was hidden, so that if the user activates the **Troubleshoot...** feature on the Help menu, the UI will explain why the Session was hidden. By default, Fiddler will not hide requests that it itself generated (e.g. using the Composer). However, if the `ui-hide` flag's value contains the word `stealth`, the Session will be hidden unconditionally.

Flag Name	`ui-bold`
Explanation	The Session's list item in the Web Sessions list is rendered using **bold** text.
Supported Values	Any value triggers the font formatting.

Flag Name	`ui-indent`
Explanation	The icon of the Session is indented in the Web Sessions list.
Supported Values	1

Flag Name	`ui-italic`
Explanation	The Session is rendered using *italicized* text.
Supported Values	Any value triggers the font formatting.

Flag Name	`ui-strikeout`
Explanation	The Session is rendered in ~~struck~~ text.
Supported Values	Any value triggers the font formatting.

Flag Name	`ui-color`
Explanation	The Session is rendered in text of the specified color.
Supported Values	The color string value may be a .NET Color constant like red, or may be a HTML-formatted color code, like #ff0000.

Flag Name	`ui-backcolor`
Explanation	The Session's background is rendered in specified color.
Supported Values	The color string value may be a .NET Color constant, like red, or may be a HTML-formatted color code, like #ff0000.

Flag Name	`ui-comments`
Explanation	This string, set by FiddlerScript, extensions, or the Comment button on the toolbar, is shown in the **Comments** column in the Web Sessions list.
Supported Values	The string that you'd like to display in the column.

Flag Name	`ui-customcolumn`
Explanation	This string, set by FiddlerScript or extensions is shown in the **Custom** column in the Web Session's list.
Supported Values	The string that you'd like to display in the column.

Breakpoint and Editing Flags

Breakpointing and editing features are triggered by setting flags during the processing of the Session.

Flag Name	x-BreakRequest
Explanation	When this flag is set on a Session before the request is sent to the server, Fiddler will pause the Session to allow you to use Inspectors to modify the request.
Supported Values	Any value will enable a request breakpoint. It is customary to set this string to a terse explanation about why this request was chosen to be breakpointed.

Flag Name	x-BreakResponse
Explanation	When this flag is set on a Session before the response is sent to the client, Fiddler will pause the Session to allow you to use Inspectors to modify the response. Response tampering is incompatible with streaming. The response breakpoint is only checked after a streamed response has been returned to the client.
Supported Values	Any value will enable a response breakpoint. It is customary to set this string to a terse explanation about why this response was breakpointed.

Flag Name	x-Unlocked
Explanation	This flag, set by Fiddler's **Unlock for Editing** option, allows you to use Inspectors to modify a completed Session as if it were paused at a breakpoint.
Supported Values	Any value will unlock the Session.

Networking Flags

The following flags control and log Fiddler's use of the network:

Flag Name	x-overrideHost
Explanation	Controls the hostname used for DNS resolution (and optionally the target port) when deciding what address this request should be sent to. This flag will not change any of the Headers in the request itself.
Supported Values	Specify either an alternative hostname or an IP Address (and optionally a Port) to which this request should be targeted. Setting this flag may have no effect if the request is sent to an upstream gateway, because the upstream gateway will perform its own DNS resolution.

Flag Name	x-overrideHostName
Explanation	Controls the hostname used for DNS resolution when deciding what address this request should be sent to. This flag will not change any of the Headers in the request itself.
Supported Values	Specify either an alternative hostname or an IP Address to which this request should be targeted. Setting this flag may have no effect if the request is sent to an upstream gateway, because the upstream gateway will perform its own DNS resolution.

Flag Name	x-OverrideGateway
Explanation	Controls which upstream gateway proxy, if any, this request is sent to.
Supported Values	Provide a string that specifies the target gateway proxy in the format `ProxyHost:Port`, for example, `myproxy:8080`. The provided address information will be used instead of any default gateway proxy. If you prefix the string with `socks=` the provided gateway will be used as a SOCKS proxy. For instance, the string `socks=127.0.0.1:9150` can be used to send traffic to a locally running instance of the Tor SOCKS proxy. A value of `DIRECT` means that the request will be sent directly to the server, bypassing any gateway. This value is equivalent to setting the Session's `bypassGateway` boolean to `true`.

Flag Name	x-ReplyWithTunnel
Explanation	When set on a `CONNECT` tunnel's Session, this flag causes Fiddler to automatically respond with a `200 OK` response without contacting the server or gateway. This flag is set by the AutoResponder to enable capture of HTTPS requests from a client even when the system is offline. Otherwise, the `CONNECT`'s failure would prevent subsequent HTTPS requests from being sent by the client.
Supported Values	Any value will result in returning a `200 OK` response to the `CONNECT`.

Flag Name	FTP-UseASCII
Explanation	When this flag is present, Fiddler will use ASCII mode rather than Binary mode when acting as a FTP gateway.
Supported Values	Any value will result in using ASCII mode when talking to the server.

Flag Name	x-HostIP
Explanation	Set by Fiddler, this flag contains the IP address of the server to which this request was sent.

Flag Name	x-OriginalURL
Explanation	Set by the AutoResponder, this flag contains the original request URL in the event that the URL was changed by an AutoResponder rule.

Flag Name	X-EgressPort
Explanation	Set by Fiddler, this flag contains the local port number used to establish the connection to the server or gateway proxy.

Flag Name	X-ServerSocket

Explanation	Set by Fiddler, this flag contains diagnostic information about the connection to the server or gateway proxy, including information about whether the connection was reused.

Flag Name	X-SecurePipe
Explanation	Set by Fiddler, this flag contains diagnostic information about the HTTPS connection to the server or gateway proxy, including information about whether the connection was reused.

Authentication Flags

The following flags control Fiddler's automatic authentication behavior:

Flag Name	x-AutoAuth
Explanation	If this flag is set, Fiddler will attempt to automatically respond to HTTP/401 challenges sent by servers and HTTP/407 challenges sent by upstream proxies. This flag supports the Digest, NTLM, and Negotiate protocols.
Supported Values	When set to (default), the current logon user's credentials will be used. To use different credentials, set the flag to a string in the format username:password. **Warning**: If Fiddler is configured to accept requests from other devices or user-accounts, use of (default) introduces a security vulnerability. That's because those requests will be authenticated using the credentials of the account in which Fiddler is running.

Flag Name	X-AutoAuth-Retries
Explanation	When the x-AutoAuth is set, this flag specifies the maximum number of attempts Fiddler will make to supply the credentials in response to HTTP/401 authentication challenges.
Supported Values	Any positive integer; the default value is 5.

Flag Name	X-AutoAuth-SPN
Explanation	This flag enables you to specify the Service Principal Name (SPN) that should be used when requesting a Kerberos ticket to automatically authenticate to this site.
Supported Values	The desired SPN string.

Flag Name	X-AutoAuth-Failed
Explanation	This flag is set if Fiddler fails to successfully authenticate to the server because the X-AutoAuth-Retries limit was reached.

Client Information Flags

The following flags track information about the source of the request:

Flag Name	x-ProcessInfo
Explanation	Set by Fiddler, this flag contains the name and ID of the local process which issued the

	request to Fiddler. Generally, you should prefer the oSession.LocalProcess property, which returns String.Empty if the x-ProcessInfo flag does not exist.

Flag Name	x-ClientIP
Explanation	Set by Fiddler, this flag contains the IP address of the client that issued the request. Typically, this will be the current PC's IP address, unless remote connections have been permitted using the option in the **Fiddler Options** > **Connections** tab.

Flag Name	x-ClientPort
Explanation	Set by Fiddler, this flag contains the port number of the connection from the client that issued the request.

Performance Simulation Flags

Fiddler offers simple flags that allow you to roughly simulate limited-bandwidth connections like modems, DSL, or Satellite connections.

Flag Name	request-trickle-delay
Explanation	Set this flag to control the rate at which Fiddler writes the request headers and body to the server. Fiddler will ensure that every 1kb of data written to the server is delayed by the amount specified.
Supported Values	Specify this flag's value as an integer number of milliseconds. For instance, the value 300 will result in Fiddler sending the request to the server in 1kb chunks, with a 150ms delay before the chunk and a 150ms delay after the chunk.

Flag Name	response-trickle-delay
Explanation	Set this flag to control the rate at which Fiddler writes the response headers and body to the client. Fiddler will ensure that every 1kb of data written to the client is delayed by the amount specified.
Supported Values	Specify this flag's value as an integer number of milliseconds. For instance, the value 300 will result in Fiddler sending the response to the client in 1kb chunks, with a 150ms delay before the chunk and a 150ms delay after the chunk.

HTTPS Flags

The following flags are related to HTTPS handling in Fiddler. Several of the flags are set automatically by Fiddler to reflect information about the HTTPS connection, while others can be set by script or extensions to influence the connection.

Flag Name	x-no-decrypt
Explanation	When set on a CONNECT tunnel, this flag instructs Fiddler not to attempt to decrypt the HTTPS traffic that flows through the tunnel.
Supported Values	Any value will disable decryption for the CONNECT tunnel. Typically, you should provide a terse explanation of why the CONNECT's traffic will not be decrypted so that a user examining the CONNECT Session's properties can understand why its traffic is not being

	decrypted.

Flag Name	x-OverrideCertCN
Explanation	When HTTPS decryption is enabled, this value controls the hostname that is used for the self-signed certificate generated by Fiddler to send to the client when a CONNECT tunnel is created. This flag is most useful when you've used other flags to reroute HTTPS traffic to a different server and do not want the client to encounter an unexpected certificate error.
Supported Values	Specify the hostname to be sent to the client. For instance www.example.com.

Flag Name	x-IgnoreCertCNMismatch
Explanation	This value controls whether Fiddler validates that the server's certificate's Subject Common Name (CN) field matches the hostname expected for the target server. This flag is meaningful only for CONNECT tunnels and only when HTTPS decryption is enabled. Set this flag when you have rerouted HTTPS traffic to a different server and do not want Fiddler to complain that the server's certificate is invalid. Fiddler's Host Remapping tool sets this flag on CONNECT tunnels that it has rerouted.
Supported Values	Any value will disable Certificate Subject CN validation. Typically, you should provide a terse explanation of why Subject CN validation was disabled, so that a user examining the CONNECT Session's properties will understand why the flag was present.

Flag Name	x-IgnoreCertErrors
Explanation	When HTTPS decryption is enabled, this value controls whether Fiddler validates that the server's certificate is unexpired, chains to a trusted root, and is valid for the target hostname. This flag is meaningful only for CONNECT tunnels and only when HTTPS decryption is enabled. Set this flag when interacting with Test or Development servers which are using self-signed or otherwise invalid certificates. To enable this behavior globally (unsafe), tick the **Ignore server certificate errors** checkbox inside **Tools > Fiddler Options > HTTPS**.
Supported Values	Any value will disable warnings about Certificate Errors on the CONNECT tunnel. Typically, you should provide a terse explanation of why certificate errors are being ignored, so that a user examining the CONNECT Session's properties will understand why the flag was present.

Flag Name	x-OverrideSslProtocols
Explanation	Controls what SSL and TLS versions are advertised when talking to the server
Supported Values	Provide a semi-colon delimited string containing one or more of the following tokens: ssl2; ssl3; tls1.0; tls1.1; tls1.2

The specified versions are used instead of the default versions shown on the Tools > Fiddler Options > HTTPS tab. tls1.1 and tls1.2 are only supported when running Fiddler 4. |

Flag Name	https-Client-Certificate

Explanation	Set this flag on a CONNECT tunnel to provide the location of a certificate file that Fiddler should use if the server prompts for HTTPS Client Authentication. The .CER file must have a matching private key in the Windows Certificate store. If this flag is not present, Fiddler will look for the file %USERPROFILE%\Documents\Fiddler2 \ClientCertificate.cer and attach any certificate it finds.
Supported Values	Specify a fully-qualified path to the file. If you're setting this property from script or C#, remember to escape backslashes by doubling them up. E.g. oS["https-Client-Certificate"] = "C:\\test\\someCert.cer";

Flag Name	https-Client-SessionID
Explanation	Set by Fiddler on a CONNECT tunnel, this flag reports the HTTPS Session ID sent by the client in the HTTPS handshake.

Flag Name	https-Server-SessionID
Explanation	Set by Fiddler on a CONNECT tunnel, this flag reports the HTTPS Session ID sent by the server in the HTTPS handshake.

Flag Name	https-Client-SNIHostname
Explanation	Set by Fiddler on a CONNECT tunnel, this flag contains the hostname sent by the client in a TLS Handshake's Server Name Indication TLS extension, if any.

Flag Name	https-DropSNIAlerts
Explanation	Set this flag on a CONNECT tunnel to ignore any unrecognized_name TLS alerts sent by the server before the HTTPS handshake. These alerts, sent by some servers against the advice of the TLS standard, cause .NET and Java clients to hang or fail the handshake.
Supported Values	Any value activates this workaround.

Flag Name	X-Client-Cert
Explanation	Set by Fiddler when a given connection is secured by a client certificate, this string contains the client certificate's Subject Field and Serial number.

Flag Name	X-HTTPS-Decryption-Error
Explanation	This flag is set by Fiddler when it is unable to find or generate a self-signed HTTPS interception certificate.

Request Composer Flags

While these flags were designed for use by the Composer, your script or extensions may use them as well.

Flag Name	X-Builder-Inspect
Explanation	When this flag is present (set by the Composer when the **Inspect Session** option is enabled) the Session will be automatically inspected when added to the Web Sessions list.
Supported	Any value will trigger the inspection.

Values	

Flag Name	X-Builder-MaxRedir
Explanation	Controls the number of HTTP/3xx redirections Fiddler is willing to follow before giving up.
Supported Values	Any positive integer value. The default is 0.

Flag Name	X-From-Builder
Explanation	This flag is set if the request was built and issued by the Request Composer.

Other Flags

Flag Name	x-no-parse
Explanation	When this flag is set, Fiddler will skip parsing WebSocket messages for this connection.
Supported Values	Any value will disable WebSocket message parsing.

Flag Name	log-drop-request-body
Explanation	When this flag is set, Fiddler "forgets" the request body to save memory when Session processing completes.
Supported Values	Any value will cause the request body to be dropped after Session processing completes.

Flag Name	log-drop-response-body
Explanation	When this flag is set, Fiddler "forgets" the response body to save memory when Session processing completes.
Supported Values	Any value will cause the response body to be dropped after Session processing completes.

Flag Name	X-Fiddler-Stream1xx
Explanation	When the fiddler.network.leakhttp1xx preference is set to true (its default), Fiddler will stream any HTTP/1xx intermediate responses from the server to the client. This flag's value, if present, indicates which HTTP/1xx codes were returned.

Flag Name	X-Fiddler-Streaming
Explanation	When the fiddler.network.leakhttp1xx preference is set to false, Fiddler will "swallow" any HTTP/1xx intermediate responses from the server. This flag's value, if present, indicates which HTTP/1xx codes were swallowed.

Flag Name	X-Divorced-ServerPipe
Explanation	When set, this flag indicates that Fiddler was forced to use a different connection to the server than expected. This might occur, for instance, if FiddlerScript or an extension changed the target URL of a Session that had been designated to reuse an existing

connection from a prior Session.	

Flag Name	X-CreatedTunnel
Explanation	When set, this flag indicates that Fiddler was forced to generate a CONNECT tunnel to the server in order to process a Session. This might occur, for instance, if FiddlerScript or an extension changed a HTTP request to a HTTPS request, or an existing secure connection cannot be reused because it has been closed.

Flag Name	X-Fiddler-Generated
Explanation	Set by Fiddler, this flag is present if Fiddler itself generated the response with the utilCreateResponseAndBypassServer method.

Flag Name	X-DNS-Failover
Explanation	If present, this flag contains a string indicating the number of times that Fiddler failed over to another DNS record when attempting to contact the host. A +1 is added to the string each time this occurs, up to the maximum number of DNS failover attempts.

Flag Name	x-Original-Host
Explanation	This flag is set if the inbound request violated the HTTP protocol by specifying a different hostname in the request URL and the Host request header. This flag contains the original Host header value. The request's Host header will be overwritten with the host parsed from the request URL.

Flag Name	x-URI-Host
Explanation	This flag is set if the inbound request violated the HTTP protocol by specifying a different hostname in the request URL and the Host request header. This flag contains the host value parsed from the URL.

Flag Name	x-UsedVirtualHost
Explanation	This flag is set to the virtual hostname value that was parsed from an inbound request; e.g. ipv4.fiddler or localhost.fiddler.

Flag Name	X-Fiddler-Aborted
Explanation	This flag is set when the Session is aborted by calling its Abort method. From the Fiddler UI, right-clicking an in-progress Session and choosing **Abort Session** from the context menu will call Abort.

Flag Name	X-TTFB
Explanation	Legacy flag reports the number of milliseconds until the first byte was read from the server.

Flag Name	X-TTLB
Explanation	Legacy flag reports the number of milliseconds until the last byte was read from the

	server.

Flag Name	X-ReplyWithFile
Explanation	Set this flag to instruct Fiddler to load the specified file and use it to respond to the request instead of sending the request to the server.
Supported Values	Supply either a fully-qualified filepath to the file to load. If only a bare filename is supplied without a path, Fiddler will look for the specified filename in the \ResponseTemplates\ or \Captures\Responses\ folders.

Flag Name	X-RepliedWithFile
Explanation	When Fiddler reacts to X-ReplyWithFile by loading the specified file, the X-ReplyWithFile flag is copied to the X-RepliedWithFile flag.

Flag Name	X-ResponseBodyTransferLength
Explanation	This flag stores the response body byte count computed immediately after the response is read from the network, prior to any unchunking, decompression, or manipulation of the response from script or extensions.

Flag Name	x-RequestBodyLength
Explanation	If the log-drop-request-body flag is set, Fiddler "forgets" the request body to save memory when Session processing finishes. The X-RequestBodyLength flag records the request body byte count at the point that the body is dropped.

Flag Name	X-ResponseBodyFinalLength
Explanation	If the log-drop-response-body flag is set, Fiddler "forgets" the response body to save memory when Session processing finishes. The X-ResponseBodyFinalLength flag records the response body byte count at the point that the body is dropped.

Flag Name	X-Format-JS
Explanation	This flag controls the automatic reformatting of JavaScript performed by the JavaScript Formatter extension.
Supported Values	When this flag is set to a value of 0, the JavaScript Formatter extension will not format the response body, even if the **Make JavaScript Pretty** option is enabled on the Rules menu. Any other value will cause the JavaScript response body to be formatted, even if the **Make JavaScript Pretty** option is not enabled on the Rules menu.

APPENDIX D: PREFERENCES

Fiddler's Preferences system allows you to control myriad aspects of Fiddler's behavior. This appendix contains a list of the Preferences that affect Fiddler and its default set of extensions.

Network Preferences

The following preferences control Fiddler's network behavior:

Name	`fiddler.network.timeouts.dnscache`
Default	150000 (2.5 minutes)
Explanation	Number of milliseconds for which Fiddler should cache DNS lookup results.

Name	`fiddler.network.timeouts.serverpipe.reuse`
Default	115000 (115 seconds)
Explanation	Number of milliseconds for which Fiddler is willing to leave a server connection idle. A connection which has been idle for this time without being reused will be closed. The Firefox team has found that values over 115 seconds can cause problems with buggy servers.

Name	`fiddler.network.timeouts.clientpipe.receive.initial`
Default	60000 (1 minute)
Explanation	Number of milliseconds for which Fiddler is willing to wait for a client to begin sending a request on a newly established connection. After this timeout expires, Fiddler will send a HTTP/408 timeout and close the connection from the client.

Name	`fiddler.network.timeouts.clientpipe.receive.reuse`
Default	60000 (30 seconds)
Explanation	Number of milliseconds for which Fiddler is willing to wait for a client to begin sending a request on a previously used connection. After this timeout expires, Fiddler will close the connection from the client.

Name	`fiddler.network.timeouts.serverpipe.send.initial`
Default	-1 ("infinite")
Explanation	Number of milliseconds for which Fiddler is willing to wait when sending to a newly established server connection. After this timeout expires, Fiddler will close the connection to the server.

Name	`fiddler.network.timeouts.serverpipe.send.reuse`
Default	-1 ("infinite")

Explanation	Number of milliseconds for which Fiddler is willing to wait when sending to a server on a previously used connection. After this timeout expires, Fiddler will close the connection to the server.

Name	`fiddler.network.timeouts.serverpipe.receive.initial`
Default	-1 ("infinite")
Explanation	Number of milliseconds for which Fiddler is willing to wait for a server to begin sending a response on a newly established connection. After this timeout expires, Fiddler will close the connection to the server.

Name	`fiddler.network.timeouts.serverpipe.receive.reuse`
Default	-1 ("infinite")
Explanation	Number of milliseconds for which Fiddler is willing to wait for a server to begin sending a response on a previously used connection. After this timeout expires, Fiddler will close the connection to the server.

Name	`fiddler.network.egress.IP`
Default	
Explanation	Set this preference if your computer has multiple outbound connections and you need requests to be sent on a particular outbound connection. This preference is rarely used, but is sometimes needed if you have particular routing needs. For instance, if you have tethered a 3G phone to your PC, you may want Fiddler to send outbound requests from its IP address so that traffic is sent from the 3G connection. Warning: If you set this preference to an IP address that is not currently bound to one of your network connections, all outbound requests will fail.

Name	`fiddler.network.auth.ReuseMode`
Default	0
Explanation	This preference controls how Fiddler is willing to reuse server connections upon which an authentication (HTTP header authentication or HTTPS client certificate authentication) has taken place. The default value of 0 requires "Process Affinity." Fiddler will only reuse the authenticated connection to service requests that originated from the same process that authenticated the connection originally. The value 1 requires "Client Connection Marriage." Fiddler will only reuse the authenticated connection to service requests that originated from the same client connection that authenticated the connection originally. The value 2 allows "Arbitrary reuse." Fiddler will reuse the authenticated connection to service any request from any client. **Warning**: This value will yield better performance but unexpected and insecure behavior.

Name	`fiddler.auth.SPNIncludesPort`
Default	`false`
Explanation	This preference controls how Fiddler calculates the Service Principal Name (SPN) when requesting a Kerberos Ticket for automatic authentication. When set to `true`, the SPN will include the port of the target service (if it's not 80 or 443).

Name	`fiddler.auth.SPNMode`
Default	`3`
Explanation	This preference controls how Fiddler calculates the Service Principal Name (SPN) when requesting a Kerberos Ticket for automatic authentication. The following values are supported: • `0` - Disable setting of SPN • `1` - Use hostname from the URL as the SPN target • `2` - Use the target server's canonical name as the SPN target, if the hostname is dot-less; otherwise use the hostname from the URL • `3` - Use the target server's canonical name as the SPN target Option #2 matches the .NET Framework's default behavior, while Option #3 matches Firefox and Chrome behavior. Internet Explorer's behavior is controlled by several registry keys and downloadable hotfixes.

Name	`fiddler.ftp.UseBinary`
Default	`true`
Explanation	When set to `true`, Fiddler (acting as a FTP gateway) will use `BINARY` mode for file transfers. When set to `false`, Fiddler will use ASCII mode instead. To control this option on a per-request basis, set the `FTP-UseASCII` flag on the Session object.

Name	`fiddler.ftp.UsePassive`
Default	`true`
Explanation	When set to `true`, Fiddler will use the `PASV` option when acting as a FTP gateway. When set to `false`, Fiddler will make active FTP connections, which are not compatible with most firewalls.

Name	`fiddler.ftp.AlwaysDemandCredentials`
Default	`False`
Explanation	When set to `true`, Fiddler returns a `HTTP/401` on FTP-targeted requests lacking an `Authorization` header in order to collect a username and password before attempting a FTP download.

Name	fiddler.network.sockets.ClientReadBufferSize
Default	8192
Explanation	This preference controls the size, in bytes, of the buffer used to read from client connections.

Name	fiddler.network.sockets.ServerReadBufferSize
Default	32768
Explanation	This preference controls the size, in bytes, of the buffer used to read from server connections.

Name	fiddler.network.proxy.RegistrationHostName
Default	127.0.0.1
Explanation	This preference controls the hostname used to register as the system proxy. There are some cases where you will need to register as the system proxy using a different hostname. For instance, the Windows Phone Emulator requires that the hostname be set to the machine name of the current machine.

Name	fiddler.network.dns.fallback
Default	true
Explanation	A DNS server may return multiple addresses for a single hostname resolution. This allows "failing over" if one or more servers is offline. When this preference is set to false, Fiddler will fail a connection if the first IP address cannot be reached. When this preference is set to true, Fiddler will try up to MaxAddressCount addresses before giving up.

Name	fiddler.network.dns.MaxAddressCount
Default	5
Explanation	A DNS server may return multiple addresses for a single hostname resolution. This preference allows you to control the maximum number of addresses returned, which in turn limits the number of DNS fallbacks that are permitted when fiddler.network.dns.fallback is true.

Name	fiddler.network.leakhttp1xx
Default	true
Explanation	This preference controls whether Fiddler will automatically pass HTTP/1xx messages through to the client connection as they are read from the server. HTTP/1xx responses are "non-final" headers-only responses and they are not shown in Fiddler's UI. HTTP/100 Continue responses are sent by a server in response to a client sending an Expect: Continue header on POST requests.

Name	fiddler.network.streaming.AbortIfClientAborts

Default	false
Explanation	This preference controls whether Fiddler will close the server connection if the client connection closes while a response is being streamed from the server to the client. The default value of false ensures that Fiddler will attempt to read the entire response from the server even if the client that originally requested the data closes its connection. Set this preference to true if you would like Fiddler to close the server connection when the client connection closes during streaming. This configuration can significantly reduce the amount of memory used by Fiddler by aborting downloads that the client application has cancelled.

Name	fiddler.network.streaming.ForgetStreamedData
Default	false
Explanation	When set to true, Fiddler will "forget" response data from the server as soon as that data is sent to the client. This precludes you from using Fiddler to examine streamed responses, but significantly decreases memory usage when streaming video or other large responses through Fiddler.

Name	fiddler.network.gateway.DetermineInProcess
Default	false
Explanation	Fiddler uses the WinHTTP library for proxy auto-configuration support (either via WPAD or a manually-specified PAC script). When this preference is set to true, Fiddler will direct WinHTTP to perform proxy determination in-process rather than calling out to the WinHTTP service.

Name	fiddler.network.gateway.UseFailedAutoProxy
Default	false
Explanation	By default, Fiddler will begin to ignore an automatically-detected upstream proxy script if it returns errors; requests will instead be sent directly to the target. Set this preference to true to disable that optimization and always attempt to use a proxy script even if it is non-responsive.

Name	fiddler.network.limit.maxrequestheaders
Default	1048576
Explanation	To help mitigate accidental or intentional denial-of-service conditions (especially when acting as a reverse proxy), Fiddler can abort processing of a request if the end of the request headers is not found within a reasonable number of bytes.

Name	fiddler.proxy.pacfile.UseFileProtocol
Default	true
Explanation	When the **Use PAC Script** option is enabled on the **Fiddler Options** > **Connections** tab, Fiddler will register as the system proxy by providing a proxy auto-configuration script

URL. By default, the URL points to the `BrowserPAC.js` file in your `Documents` folder.

When this preference is set to `false`, Fiddler will instead register using a HTTP URL, in the format http://127.0.0.1:8888/proxy.pac. You must then respond to inbound requests for the script using the AutoResponder or FiddlerScript.

Name	`fiddler.proxy.pacfile.text`
Default	`return 'PROXY 127.0.0.1:8888';`
Explanation	This preference controls the body of the `FindProxyForURL` function stored in the `%UserProfile%\Documents\Fiddler2\Scripts\BrowserPAC.js` file.

HTTPS Preferences

The following preferences control Fiddler's behavior when interacting with HTTPS requests.

Name	`fiddler.network.https.StoreServerCertChain`
Default	`false`
Explanation	When set to `true`, Fiddler will walk the entire certificate chain provided by the server and add information about each certificate in the chain to the text shown in the Response Inspector for the `CONNECT` tunnel.

Name	`fiddler.network.https.CheckCertificateRevocation`
Default	`false`
Explanation	When set to `true`, Fiddler will perform a revocation check to determine whether the server's certificate has been revoked by the issuer. While validation enhances security, it will slow down HTTPS connection establishment.

Name	`fiddler.network.https.SetCNFromSNI`
Default	`false`
Explanation	When set to `true`, Fiddler will use the Server Name Indication TLS extension from the client's HTTPS handshake to set the CN field of the certificate used in the HTTPS handshake with the client. When set to `false`, the CN field will be set using the request's `Host` header. This preference can be handy if you have a client which sends a `Host` header that contains a literal IP address rather than the hostname of the target server. This may occur, for instance, if you're using `iptables` to send traffic to Fiddler from an Android device that does not accept a proxy setting.

Name	`fiddler.network.https.NoDecryptionHosts`
Default	
Explanation	A semi-colon delimited list of hostnames for which HTTPS decryption should not take place. This preference is exposed by the textbox on the **Fiddler Options** > **HTTPS** tab.

Name	`fiddler.network.https.BlindTunnelIfCertUnobtainable`
Default	`true`
Explanation	If Fiddler is configured to decrypt HTTPS traffic, but a certificate could not be generated to secure a connection, Fiddler will treat the connection as a blind tunnel if this preference is set to `true`. When set to `false`, Fiddler will fail the HTTPS connection if the certificate cannot be obtained.

Name	`fiddler.CertMaker.CleanupServerCertsOnExit`
Default	`false`
Explanation	If HTTPS-decryption is enabled, Fiddler's default certificate maker will add certificates to the user's certificate store. When this preference is set to `true`, all such certificates will be removed when Fiddler shuts down. This preference is not used by FiddlerCore; instead call `CertMaker.removeFiddlerGeneratedCerts(false);` before your application exits.

Name	`fiddler.CertMaker.Assembly`
Default	`CertMaker.dll`
Explanation	When this preference is set, Fiddler will attempt to load specified assembly when a certificate is needed to secure a HTTPS connection. If the specified assembly cannot be found or does not contain a `public class` that implements the `ICertificateProvider2` interface, Fiddler's default certificate provider will be used instead.

Name	`fiddler.CertMaker.Root.ExtraParams`
Default	
Explanation	Specifies any extra parameters that should be passed to `makecert.exe` when the Fiddler root certificate is generated.

Name	`fiddler.CertMaker.EE.ExtraParams`
Default	
Explanation	Specifies any extra parameters that should be passed to `makecert.exe` when generating end-entity certificates for HTTPS servers.

Name	`fiddler.CertMaker.OfferMachineTrust`
Default	`false` except on Windows 8 and later.
Explanation	Set this preference to `true` to configure Fiddler to offer to use an elevated process to add the root certificate to the per-Machine Trusted Root certificate store. By default, Fiddler prompts you to add its Root Certificate to the per-*User* Trusted Root certificate store. If you plan to use Fiddler across multiple user-accounts, or need Windows 8-style Metro applications to trust Fiddler's root certificate, the Root must instead be stored in the per-*Machine* Trusted Root certificate store.

Name	`fiddler.network.https.cacheclientcert`
Default	`true`

Explanation	Controls whether Fiddler will cache, for the lifetime of the Fiddler process, the default client certificate upon its first use. Caching ensures that you will not be prompted with a PIN request if your certificate requires one. However, caching also means that you cannot use a different certificate without restarting Fiddler or using script to `null` the property `FiddlerApplication.oDefaultClientCertificate`.

Name	`fiddler.config.path.defaultclientcert`
Default	`%USERPROFILE%\Documents\Fiddler2\ClientCertificate.cer`
Explanation	If a HTTPS server demands a client certificate, Fiddler will look for a client certificate file in this location.

Name	`fiddler.network.https.clientcertificate.ephemeral.prompt-for-missing`
Default	`true`
Explanation	This preference controls whether Fiddler will prompt the user if a server demands a client certificate but no certificate location was specified in the Session's flags and no certificate is present in the default location.

Name	`fiddler.network.https.RequestClientCertificate`
Default	`false`
Explanation	When this preference is set to `true`, Fiddler will request a client certificate every time a client attempts to establish a HTTPS connection. Set this preference to test client software to see how it handles client certificate demands.

Fiddler UI Preferences

Preferences under the `Fiddler.UI` branch track the state of options and settings that are shown within the Fiddler user interface, including the toolbar.

Name	`fiddler.ui.toolbar.visible`
Default	`true`
Explanation	This preference controls whether the toolbar is displayed.

Name	`fiddler.ui.toolbar.ShowLabels`
Default	`true`
Explanation	Controls whether optional text labels are shown on toolbar's buttons.

Name	`fiddler.ui.toolbar.BrowserList`
Default	
Explanation	Adds one or more additional entries to the toolbar's Browse dropdown. For instance, the value `IE (Private)=IExplore.exe*-private %U|Firefox=Firefox.exe` adds Firefox and Internet Explorer (Private) to the menu. The Selected Session's URL is passed in the `%U` parameter, if present.

Name	`fiddler.ui.StayOnTop`

Default	false
Explanation	Controls the **View > Stay on Top** menu checkbox. When set to true, Fiddler will remain on top of all other windows on the system.

Name	fiddler.ui.font.size
Default	8.25
Explanation	Controls the default font size for text in Fiddler. It can be adjusted using the **Tools > Fiddler Options > Appearance > Font Size** dropdown.

Name	fiddler.ui.LastView
Default	Statistics
Explanation	Stores the last active View tab when Fiddler is shutdown. That tab is subsequently reactivated the next time Fiddler is started.

Name	fiddler.inspectors.HideList
Default	
Explanation	Stores the list of Inspectors which should be hidden. You can hide an Inspector by right-clicking on it and choosing **Hide Inspector** from the menu. Unhiding an Inspector by editing this preference requires that you restart Fiddler.

Name	fiddler.filters.ResetOnRestart
Default	false
Explanation	When set to true, Fiddler will reset all filters each time the debugger is launched. This option is helpful if you're in the habit of applying filters, using them for a while, closing Fiddler, restarting it days later, forgetting you've applied filters, and then spending frustrated hours trying to figure out why Fiddler isn't showing you traffic.

Name	fiddler.ui.rules.KeepOnly
Default	0
Explanation	When set to a non-zero value, Fiddler will automatically trim the Web Sessions list to the specified number of Sessions. This preference backs the **Keep** dropdown on the toolbar.

Name	fiddler.ui.rules.HideImages
Default	false
Explanation	Stores the **Rules > Hide Images** menu option.

Name	fiddler.ui.rules.HideConnects
Default	false
Explanation	Stores the **Rules > Hide CONNECTs** menu option.

Name	fiddler.ui.rules.RemoveEncoding
Default	false
Explanation	Stores the **Rules > Remove all Encodings** menu option and the **Decode** toolbar toggle.

Name	`fiddler.ui.rules.ForceGZIP`
Default	`false`
Explanation	Stores the **Rules** > **Apply GZIP Encoding** menu option.

Name	`fiddler.ui.rules.BufferResponses`
Default	`true`
Explanation	Stores the **Stream** toolbar toggle.

Name	`fiddler.ui.ephemeral.rules.RequireProxyAuth`
Default	`false`
Explanation	Stores the **Rules** > **Require Proxy Authentication** menu option.

Name	`fiddler.ui.inspectors.request.AlwaysUse`
Default	
Explanation	Use this preference to always choose a particular Request Inspector when activating a Session. Set the preference to the Inspector tab's title text, e.g. `Raw`.

Name	`fiddler.ui.inspectors.response.AlwaysUse`
Default	
Explanation	Use this preference to always choose a particular Response Inspector when activating a Session. Set the preference to the Inspector tab's title text, e.g. `WebView`.

Name	`fiddler.reissue.AutoAuth`
Default	`false`
Explanation	When set to `true`, Fiddler will attempt to automatically respond to authentication challenges when you reissue a request from the Web Sessions list.

Name	`fiddler.reissue.AutoRedirCount`
Default	`0`
Explanation	Specifies the maximum number of redirections Fiddler will perform if a `HTTP/3xx` redirect response is returned when a Session is reissued using the context menu or toolbar. When the redirection limit is exceeded, Fiddler will ignore the `Location` header specified on the final redirect.

Name	`fiddler.differ.UltraDiff`
Default	`true`
Explanation	The UltraDiff option is used when comparing two Sessions. When set to `true`, Fiddler reorders the headers of both Sessions such that headers that exactly match in both Sessions are listed first, then headers with different values are listed, then headers that are entirely different are listed last. When set to `false`, this reordering does not occur.

Name	`fiddler.differ.Params`

Default	"{0} {1}"
Explanation	Specifies the command line arguments to supply to the file comparison tool when the Compare command is invoked. {0} is replaced with the first filename and {1} is replaced with the second filename.

Name	fiddler.differ.ParamsAlt
Default	"{0} {1} -p"
Explanation	Specifies the command line arguments to supply to the file comparison tool when the Compare command is invoked while holding the SHIFT key. The default value adds the -p parameter to instruct WinDiff to use its "break on punctuation" mode.

Name	fiddler.filters.ephemeral.DebugMode
Default	false
Explanation	Stores the **Help > Troubleshoot...** menu state. When set to true, Sessions that would normally be hidden are instead shown in the Web Sessions list using a strikethrough font.

Name	fiddler.ui.ephemeral.rules.BreakOnRequest
Default	false
Explanation	When set to true, Fiddler will automatically break on each request.

Name	fiddler.ui.ephemeral.rules.BreakOnResponse
Default	false
Explanation	When set to true, Fiddler will automatically break on each response.

Name	fiddler.ui.SessionList.UpdateInterval
Default	80
Explanation	This preference contains the number of milliseconds for which Fiddler should accumulate new Web Sessions before showing them in the Web Sessions list. **Warning**: Setting a lower value will force Fiddler to repaint the Web Sessions list more often, and can dramatically slow down Fiddler. You may wish to increase the value from the default when running on a slow PC or through a Remote Desktop connection.

Name	fiddler.ui.CtrlX.PromptIfMoreThan
Default	0
Explanation	When set to a positive integer, you will be prompted when pressing CTRL+X before clearing more than the specified number of Sessions from the Web Sessions list.

Name	fiddler.ui.Colors.LoadedFromSAZ fiddler.ui.Colors.AutoResponded fiddler.ui.Colors.ColumnDuplicate fiddler.ui.Colors.ImageBloat fiddler.ui.Colors.ImageBloatMortar fiddler.ui.Colors.QuickExec

	fiddler.ui.Colors.QuickExecText
Default	*various*
Explanation	Each of these Preferences controls a color used by Fiddler in the UI. Set the preference to either a hexadecimal color string (e.g. `#FF0000` equals Red) or a .NET color string.

Name	fiddler.sounds.ScriptCompile fiddler.sounds.ScriptError fiddler.sounds.Screenshot fiddler.sounds.Countdown fiddler.sounds.Gallery.SlideShowAdvance
Default	*Various*
Explanation	Each of these Preferences controls a sound played by Fiddler. Specify the full path to a WAV file to use that sound instead of the default sound.

Name	fiddler.Screenshot.DelayMS
Default	5000
Explanation	Number of milliseconds the Toolbar's Screenshot button should wait before capturing.

Name	fiddler.ui.MaskPasswords
Default	false
Explanation	When set to true, the Password prompt shown when saving or opening an encrypted SAZ file will show dots instead of the password's characters. Note: You can manually toggle this behavior on a one-off basis by double-clicking on the prompt's key icon.

Name	fiddler.ui.CtrlX.KeepMarked
Default	false
Explanation	When set to true, hitting CTRL+X to clear the Web Sessions list will leave behind any Sessions which are marked. The same behavior can be triggered by clicking the **Remove** > **Complete and Unmarked** item in the toolbar.

Name	fiddler.QuickExec.autocomplete
Default	true
Explanation	When set to true, the QuickExec box will autocomplete as you type.

Name	fiddler.QuickExec.KeepHistory
Default	true
Explanation	When set to true, the QuickExec box will keep a history of executed commands.

Name	fiddler.session.prependIDToSuggestedFilename
Default	false
Explanation	This preference controls whether the Session's ID number is prepended to the automatically generated filename used to save Sessions, Requests, and Responses to disk. For instance, when saving Session #4's response to disk, the default filename of download.exe becomes 4_download.exe when this preference is set to true.

Name	`fiddler.log.DropMessagesUnlessActive`
Default	`false`
Explanation	When set to `true`, the Log tab will not collect logged strings unless it is the active tab. This saves memory but obviously could lead to lost messages.

Name	`fiddler.find.ephemeral.LastSearch`
Default	
Explanation	Stores the last search term supplied to Fiddler's **Edit** > **Find Sessions** prompt. An extension *might* choose to use this value to pre-fill its own inline search box for convenience.

FiddlerScript Preferences

Name	`fiddler.script.AutoRef`
Default	`true`
Explanation	When this Preference is set to `true`, Fiddler will automatically determine which assemblies to reference based on the `import` statements at the top of the FiddlerScript file. When set to `false`, library references must be manually provided in the **Fiddler Options** > **Extensions** tab.

Name	`fiddler.script.LibPath`
Default	
Explanation	Specify a fully-qualified path that contains assemblies your FiddlerScript will use. For instance, set the value to `C:\src\library dlls\` and when your FiddlerScript is next compiled, Fiddler will look for referenced assemblies in the `Library DLLs` folder.

Name	`fiddler.script.CompileToFilename`
Default	
Explanation	Set this preference to a fully-qualified `.DLL` filename and upon next compilation, your FiddlerScript will generate an assembly of the provided name. Use this option to create an assembly that you can load into Reflector or another code-inspection tool to inspect the compiled output. **Warning:** When you use this preference, your FiddlerScript will not execute until the preference is removed and you recompile your script.

TextWizard Preferences

Name	`fiddler.textwizard.InputEncoding`
Default	`UTF-8`
Explanation	Specify a character set from which %-encoded characters will be decoded by the TextWizard. The string value provided must be an `Encoding` name recognized by the .NET Framework; valid values can be found at `http://fiddler2.com/r/?EncodingNames`.

Name	`fiddler.textwizard.OutputEncoding`

Default	UTF-8
Explanation	Specify a character set to which characters will be %-encoded by the TextWizard. The string value provided must be an Encoding name recognized by the .NET Framework; valid values can be found at http://fiddler2.com/r/?EncodingNames.

Request Composer Preferences

Name	fiddler.composer.FollowRedirects
Default	true
Explanation	Controls whether the Composer will automatically follow a redirect when the server returns one for a request sent by the Composer. Set this preference using the Composer's **Options** tab.

Name	fiddler.composer.FollowRedirects.Max
Default	10
Explanation	Controls the number of redirects that the Composer is willing to follow before giving up. This preference sets the x-Builder-MaxRedir flag on the new Session.
Name	fiddler.composer.AutoAuth
Default	true
Explanation	Controls whether the Composer will automatically attempt to respond to Authentication challenges sent by servers. Set this preference using the Composer's **Options** tab.

Name	fiddler.composer.AutoAuthCreds
Default	(default)
Explanation	Controls which credentials are used when the Composer attempts to respond to Authentication challenges sent by servers. This preference sets the x-AutoAuth flag on the new Session. When set to (default), the current logon user's credentials will be used. To use different credentials, set the preference to a string in the format username:password.

Name	fiddler.composer.InspectSession
Default	true
Explanation	Controls whether the Inspectors will be automatically activated when you send a request using the Composer. Set this preference on the Composer's **Options** tab. This preference sets the x-Builder-Inspect flag on the new Session.

Path Configuration

Fiddler and FiddlerCore use a variety of paths on the filesystem when loading and storing content or invoking utilities. Some paths may be configured using the user-interface, but some can only be controlled using preferences.

Name	fiddler.config.path.captures
Default	%USERPROFILE%\Documents\Fiddler2\Captures\

Explanation	Path under which captured requests and responses will be stored.

Name	`fiddler.config.path.differ`
Default	`Windiff.exe`
Explanation	Path to the file comparison tool used when comparing two Sessions.

Name	`fiddler.config.path.defaultclientcert`
Default	`%USERPROFILE%\Documents\Fiddler2\ClientCertificate.cer`
Explanation	Path to the client certificate which will be used to respond to any certificate demands during HTTPS handshaking.

Name	`fiddler.config.path.requests`
Default	`%USERPROFILE%\Documents\Fiddler2\Captures\Requests`
Explanation	Path under which captured requests will be stored.

Name	`fiddler.config.path.responses`
Default	`%USERPROFILE%\Documents\Fiddler2\Captures\Responses`
Explanation	Path under which captured responses will be stored.

Name	`fiddler.config.path.templateresponses`
Default	`%ProgramFiles%\Fiddler2\ResponseTemplates\`
Explanation	Path under which Template Responses used by the AutoResponder are stored.

Miscellaneous

Name	`fiddler.updater.CheckFreshness`
Default	`true`
Explanation	When set to `true`, you will be prompted for permission to check for a new version each time you launch a version of Fiddler built over 200 days ago. When set to `false`, this prompt will not be shown.

Name	`fiddler.websocket.ParseMessages`
Default	`true`
Explanation	When set to `true`, Fiddler will attempt to parse bytes transmitted over WebSocket connections into WebSocket messages; otherwise, bytes will be transferred without interpretation. You can disable parsing on a single WebSocket by setting the `x-no-parse` flag on its Session.

Name	`fiddler.echoservice.enabled`
Default	`true`
Explanation	By default, Fiddler will display a HTML "Echo Service" page if the user navigates the browser directly to Fiddler's listening URL (e.g. http://localhost:8888/). When `false`, this page is not displayed and Fiddler will return a TCP/IP RST if this URL is requested.

Name	`fiddler.debug.extensions.ShowErrors`
Default	`false`
Explanation	When set to `true`, any exceptions raised when Fiddler calls into extensions will be shown in a notification window. When set to `false`, exceptions raised when calling into extensions will be silently discarded.

Name	`fiddler.debug.extensions.verbose`
Default	`false`
Explanation	When set to `true`, all extension-related messages will be logged on Fiddler's Log tab and any exceptions raised when Fiddler calls into extensions will be shown in a notification window. Set this preference to `true` when developing and debugging Fiddler extensions.

Name	`fiddler.SAZ.AES.Use256Bit`
Default	`false`
Explanation	When set to `true`, Fiddler will store password-protected SAZ files using 256-bit encryption instead of the default of 128-bit encryption. The higher level of encryption is much slower and is probably unnecessary if your adversary is not a government intelligence agency.

Name	`fiddler.script.delaycreate`
Default	`true`
Explanation	When set to `true`, Fiddler will create the `CustomRules.js` file from the default `SampleRules.js` file only when you attempt to edit the script using **Rules** > **Customize Rules**. This ensures that if you never edit the script, you always have the latest script when you perform build-to-build upgrades.

Extension Preferences

Many Fiddler Inspectors and extensions offer Preferences that control their behavior. The following is a list of commonly used Preferences for these modules.

Raw Inspector

Name	`fiddler.inspectors.request.raw.TruncateBinaryAt`
Default	128
Explanation	When the AutoTruncate feature is enabled, the Raw Inspector will display at most the specified number of bytes of a Request body that is believed to be binary in nature.

Name	`fiddler.inspectors.request.raw.TruncateTextAt`
Default	262144
Explanation	When the AutoTruncate feature is enabled, the Raw Inspector will display at most the specified number of bytes of a Request body that is believed to be textual in nature.

Name	`fiddler.inspectors.response.raw.TruncateBinaryAt`
Default	128
Explanation	When the AutoTruncate feature is enabled, the Raw Inspector will display at most the

| | specified number of bytes of a Response body that is believed to be binary in nature. |

Name	`fiddler.inspectors.response.raw.TruncateTextAt`
Default	`262144`
Explanation	When the AutoTruncate feature is enabled, the Raw Inspector will display at most the specified number of bytes of a Response body that is believed to be textual in nature.

JavaScript Formatter

Name	`fiddler.extensions.JSFormat.AutoFormat`
Default	`false`
Explanation	When set to `true`, the JavaScript Formatting extension will attempt to automatically auto-format all script files before they are returned to the client application. When set to `false`, you must manually format JavaScript files using the **Make JavaScript Pretty** context menu item in the Web Sessions list.

Certificate Maker Add-on

The Certificate Maker add-on (`http://fiddler2.com/r/?FiddlerCertMaker`) offers many flags that enable it to generate certificates which are compatible with a wide variety of platform, including iOS and Android devices. In its default configuration, iOS-compatible certificates are generated.

Name	`fiddler.CertMaker.BC.Debug`
Default	`false`
Explanation	When set to `true`, the Certificate Maker plugin will emit logging information to the Log tab.

Name	`fiddler.CertMaker.BC.ReusePrivateKeys`
Default	`true`
Explanation	When set to `true`, the Certificate Maker plugin will use the same private key for each certificate it generates. This is obviously insecure remotely, but harmless and improves when debugging locally.

Name	`fiddler.CertMaker.BC.LogPrivateKeys`
Default	`false`
Explanation	When set to `true`, the Certificate Maker plugin will emit Private keys to the Log tab.

Name	`fiddler.certmaker.bc.KeyLength`
Default	`1024`
Explanation	Specifies the RSA key length used in the server and end-entity certificates.

Name	`fiddler.CertMaker.BC.AddCRL`
Default	`false`
Explanation	When set to `true`, the Certificate Maker plugin will add a Certificate Revocation List URL to the certificates it generates. The CRL added is hardcoded to point to `http://www.fiddler2.com/revocationlist.crl`, a nonexistent URL that you can

	intercept in Fiddler or FiddlerCore.

Name	`fiddler.CertMaker.BC.EE.CriticalAKID`
Default	`true`
Explanation	When set to `true`, the end-entity certificates generated by the Certificate Maker plugin will have the `AuthorityKeyID` extension marked as `Critical`.

Name	`fiddler.CertMaker.BC.EE.CriticalBasicConstraints`
Default	`true`
Explanation	When set to `true`, the end-entity certificates generated by the Certificate Maker plugin will have the `BasicConstraints` extension marked as `Critical`.

Name	`fiddler.CertMaker.BC.EE.CriticalEKU`
Default	`true`
Explanation	When set to `true`, the end-entity certificates generated by the Certificate Maker plugin will have the `ExtendedKeyUsage` extension marked as `Critical`.

Name	`fiddler.CertMaker.BC.EE.CreatedDaysAgo`
Default	`-7`
Explanation	Specifies the number of days prior to the current date that the end-entity certificates' Validity period begins. This value is one week by default to account for clock skew between the PC running Fiddler and any connecting device which may have a different clock.

Name	`fiddler.CertMaker.BC.EE.YearsValid`
Default	2
Explanation	Specifies the number of years (relative to today's date) before the end-entity certificate should be treated as expired.

Name	`fiddler.CertMaker.BC.EE.SigAlg`
Default	SHA1withRSA on Windows XP SHA256WITHRSA otherwise.
Explanation	Specifies the signature algorithm used for the end-entity certificate. Specify `MD5WithRSAEncryption` to use MD5 as the hash algorithm, or to use SHA-256.

Name	`fiddler.CertMaker.BC.Root.SetAKID`
Default	`false`
Explanation	When set to `true`, the Certificate Maker plugin will add an `AuthorityKeyID` to the root certificate which points at itself.

Name	`fiddler.CertMaker.BC.Root.CriticalBasicConstraints`
Default	`true`
Explanation	When set to `true`, the root certificate generated by the Certificate Maker plugin will have the `BasicConstraints` extension marked as `Critical`.

Name	fiddler.CertMaker.BC.Root.CriticalKeyUsage
Default	true
Explanation	When set to true, the root certificate generated by the Certificate Maker plugin will have the KeyUsage extension marked as Critical.

Name	fiddler.CertMaker.BC.Root.CriticalAKID
Default	false
Explanation	When set to true, the Certificate Maker plugin will mark the root certificate's AuthorityKeyID as Critical.

Index

A

Android
  HTTPS Decryption, 126
AppContainers, 103
Apple
  HTTPS Decryption, 126
  iOS, 107
  Mac OS X, 103
audio and video
  previewing, 163
  streaming, 115
authentication
  Auth Inspector, 141
  automatic, 133
  channel-binding, 134
  client certificates, 135
  loopback, 102, 135
  methods, 132
  problems, 134
  WinHTTP, 134
AutoResponder
  action text, 56
  drag-and-drop, 59
  FARX files, 59
  match condition, 53
  playback mode, 60
  regular expressions, 57

B

bindpref, 212
breakpoints
  Breakpoint bar, 84
  Filters tab, 45
  overview, 82
  resuming, 84
  using QuickExec, 83

C

caching
  Inspector, 143
capturing
  .NET Framework, 99
  browsers, 96
  devices, 106
  DirectAccess, 112
  FTP, 131
  Java, 100
  loopback, 100
  Mac OS X, 103
  other PCs, 105
  PHP/cURL, 100
  reverse proxy, 108
  VPNs/Modems, 111
  Win8 apps, 102
  Windows Phone, 107
  Windows RT, 107
  WinHTTP, 98
certificates
  CertMgr.msc, 123
  troubleshooting, 308
  trusted root, 121
  Windows 8, 122
clipboard
  pasting from, 26
  pasting to, 18
Clone Response, 22
code samples
  extension example, 270
  general scripts, 227
  implementing OnValidateServerCertificate, 292
  RegisterCustomHotkey, 227
  scripts to manipulate requests, 224
  scripts to manipulate responses, 226
  transcoder example, 280
  trusting a root certificate, 300

columns, 15
  adding from code, 216
  Customization UI, 22
  SetColumnOrderAndWidth function, 219
COMETPeek, 21
  overview, 116
Composer
  automatic breakpoints, 68
  history list, 64
  options, 63
  overview, 63
  parsed, 64
  raw requests, 64
  scratchpad, 63
  sequential requests, 65
  uploading files, 66
cookies
  Inspector, 144
CPU architecture and bitness, 113
cURL
  capturing from, 100
  export script, 191
  mimic with Composer, 64
  paste as Sessions, 26

E

EnableLoopback.exe, 102
encoding
  decoding from Transformer, 160
  decoding programmatically, 265
  decoding using UI, 161
  headers, 94
  HTTP Chunking, 159
  HTTP Compression, 159
  text encoding overview, 94
  TextWizard, 61
execaction
  driving FiddlerScript, 205
export
  cURL Script, 191
  HTML5 AppCache, 191
  HTTPArchive format, 193
  MeddlerScript, 194

  Raw Files, 194
  Visual Studio WebTest, 195
  WCAT Script, 195
extensions
  AnyWHERE, 179
  assemblies, 275
  best practices, 236
  building in .NET, 235
  Content Blocker, 174
  debugging, 235
  delay-loading, 236
  Developing, 268
  directory, 167, 168
  example code, 270
  FiddlerScript tab, 176
  for Performance analysis, 167
  for Security analysis, 167
  Gallery tab, 170
  installing, 256
  JavaScript Formatter, 169
  options, 93
  overview, 167
  Show Image Bloat, 172
  third-party, 167
  Traffic Differ, 175

F

FiddlerApplication overview, 292
FiddlerCap, 185
FiddlerCore
  common tasks, 299
  get started, 288
  overview, 287
  StartupFlags, 291
FiddlerScript
  adding new tabs, 215
  automation, 205
  ClassView sidebar, 177
  cross-process messaging, 206
  Editing, 176
  engine, 252
  examples, 224
  extending menus, 208

FiddlerObject, 220
general functions, 203
JScript.NET, 199
new top-level menus, 213
overview, 199
referencing assemblies, 223
resetting, 201
session-handling functions, 202
standalone editor, 177
filtering
Filters tab, 43
Find, 70
fonts
previewing, 163
FTP
capturing, 131

H

headers
create from script, 228
Inspector, 145
RemoveRange method, 230
HTTPS
Certificate Maker plugin, 126
certificate pinning, 129
certificate validation, 128
client certificates, 135
configuring devices, 126
configuring other clients, 125
configuring remote computers, 125
CONNECT tunnels, 120
decryption, 120
handshake failures, 128
limiting decryption, 123
options, 88
overview, 120
protocol versions, 128
use existing certificate, 129

I

IFiddlerExtension, 268
import and export

export formats, 191
import formats, 190
overview, 190
Transcoders, 276
Inspectors
assemblies, 267
Auth, 141
Caching, 143
Cookies, 144
develop, 259
Headers, 145
HexView, 148
ImageView, 150
JSON, 153
PDFView, 155
Raw, 154
SyntaxView, 156
TextView, 158
Transformer, 159
WebForms, 162
XML, 164
installation, 12

J

JavaScript
formatting, 169

K

keyboard shortcuts
general, 14
hotkeys, 40
Web Sessions list, 17

L

Log
macro commands, 251
writing to, 251
loopback
authentication, 102
bypass, 101
capturing, 100

Windows 8, 102

M

memory
  conserving, 113
  overview, 113
  usage, 31
Menus
  Copy submenu, 18
  Edit menu, 25
  extending with extensions, 270
  extending with FiddlerScript, 208
  File menu, 25
  Filter submenu, 20
  Help menu, 30
  Mark submenu, 20, 26
  Performance submenu, 28
  Replay submenu, 20
  Rules menu, 27
  Save submenu, 19
  Select submenu, 21
  Tools menu, 28
  View menu, 29
  Web Sessions context menu, 18

N

NetMon, 1
NSIS installer, 256

O

object model
  BitFlags, 246
  FiddlerApplication events, 292
  FiddlerApplication methods, 295
  FiddlerApplication properties and fields, 297
  FiddlerScript engine, 252
  HostList objects, 249
  Log, 251
  Preferences, 253
  Session objects, 242
  SessionStates, 246

TextWizard, 250
Timers, 248
Web Sessions list, 240
WebSocketMessage objects, 119

P

P3P, 144
Parallels, 104
performance
  add-ons, 167
  Caching Inspector, 143
  image optimization, 172
  simulation, 28
  Timers object, 248
PNGDistill, 152
preferences
  binding script fields to, 212
Preferences
  about:config, 95
  IFiddlerPreferences, 253
  observe changes, 255
  overview, 95
  programming with, 253
  Reference List, 324
protocols
  references, 4
  support, 7
proxy server, 5
  client applications, 96
  SOCKS, 110
  upstream chaining, 109

Q

QuickExec
  commands, 35
  default FiddlerScript commands, 38
  extension integration, 269
  general commands, 36
  overview, 35
  selecting Sessions, 35

R

request object, 242
response object, 243
reverse proxy, 108

S

SAZ Files
    encrypting with password, 184
    overview, 183
    save automatically, 73
    saving with FiddlerCap, 185
searching
    Find Sessions window, 70
security
    add-ons, 167
Sessions
    aborting, 21
    adding mock Sessions, 228
    combining partial responses, 229
    compare, 80
    comparing multiple, 175
    hashing responses, 228
    inspecting in a new window, 22
    properties, 22
    rerouting, 77
    Selecting with QuickExec, 35
    Session Clipboards, 72
    unlocking, 22, 26
settings
    Appearance tab, 92
    command-line, 312
    Connections tab, 90
    Extensions tab, 93
    Fiddler Options, 87
    FTP, 131
    gateway tab, 91
    General tab, 87
    HeaderEncoding, 94
    HTTPS tab, 88
    Preferences, 95
    tools tab, 93
status bar

overview, 33
streaming
    COMET, 116
    minimizing memory usage, 114
    requests, 115
    responses, 115
    Timeline, 49
    vs. buffering, 115
System Requirements, 11

T

Tabs
    adding from extensions, 275
    Composer, 63
    FiddlerScript, 176
    Filters, 43
    Gallery, 170
    Inspectors, 139
    Log, 69
    Statistics, 41
TextWizard
    invoking from code, 250
    overview, 61
threading
    IAutoTamper, 269
    Transcoders, 280
Timeline
    client pipe map, 50
    server pipe map, 50
    timeline mode, 48
timing
    Session Timers, 248
    Statistics tab, 41
    timer resolution, 249
toolbar
    hiding text, 33
tools
    PNGDistill, 152
Tools
    Configure AutoSave, 73
    HOSTS..., 74
    New Session Clipboard, 72
Tor

chain to, 110

Transcoders, 276
   example code, 280
   progress events, 279
   supporting options, 278

troubleshooting
   IPsec, 107
   out-of-memory, 113
   WiFi isolation, 107
   Windows Phone tethering, 112

U

upstream gateway
   user-interface, 91

V

viewer mode, 189

W

Web Sessions list
   colors, 16

columns, 15
icons, 16
overview, 15

WebSockets
   message objects, 119
   overview, 117

windows
   About box, 31
   Fiddler Options, 87
   Find Sessions, 70
   HOSTS, 74
   Session Clipboards, 72

Windows 8 Metro
   capturing, 102

Windows Phone
   HTTPS Decryption, 126

Windows RT, 107

Z

Zopfli
   Transformer option, 161
   used by PNGDistill, 152

26294515R00205

Made in the USA
Middletown, DE
23 November 2015